BABY
NAMES
2024

Eleanor Turner

white
LADDER

First published in Great Britain in 2023 by White Ladder
An imprint of Hodder & Stoughton
An Hachette UK company

1

Copyright © Eleanor Turner 2023

The right of Eleanor Turner to be identified as the Author
of the Work has been asserted by her in accordance with
the Copyright, Designs and Patents Act 1988.

A CIP catalogue record for this title is available from the British Library

Trade Paperback ISBN 978 139970 257 7

Typeset in Zapf Humanist BT by Hewer Text UK Ltd, Edinburgh
Printed and bound in Great Britain by Clays Ltd, Elocraf S.p.A.

Hodder & Stoughton policy is to use papers that are natural, renewable
and recyclable products and made from wood grown in sustainable
forests. The logging and manufacturing processes are expected to
conform to the environmental regulations of the country of origin.

Hodder & Stoughton Ltd
Carmelite House
50 Victoria Embankment
London EC4Y 0DZ

www.hodder.co.uk

Contents

Author's note

Baby names vary widely in spelling and pronunciation. To keep things simple, this book usually lists each name only once: under the most common initial and spelling.

If a name has an alternative spelling with a different initial, it may also be listed under that letter.

Information relating to statistics and trends in baby names is based on the most recent data at the time of writing.

Acknowledgements

Many thanks to Sophie Lazar at White Ladder Press: once again, your patience and editorial insights have helped this series endure to its fourteenth year. Thank you!

To my husband Mike, who brings me snacks and blankets when I'm typing late into the night, and tolerates my obsession with names as only a long-suffering partner can. I can't do any of it without you.

And finally, the greatest thanks of all go to my children, who are the inspiration for this book series and the reason I keep going. I was expecting my oldest, Owen Henri, when I wrote the original *Baby Names* book back in 2009, and, although he departed this world in 2021, I will continue to love him (and his name) forever. To my younger children Jasper Hugh, Josie May and Felix Brian: you are incredible, wonderful, hilarious, and brave, and I hope that never changes. Love you, Mama.

Introduction

I have a party trick. With a fair degree of accuracy, I can tell certain things about a person just from their name. I can tell where they were born, how old they are, how successful they were at school, the political leanings of their parents, and the education level of their parents. No, I'm not psychic – I'm just fascinated by baby names and all the wonderful, weird, and obscure insights they can provide us with. You can learn a lot about a person from their name.

Welcome to *Baby Names 2024*, where I'll take a deep dive into everything you've ever wanted to know about the monikers we give our little monkeys.

Inside this book you'll find out:

- How to impress your friends with my party trick

- The most popular names for babies from around the world

- The wackiest names people have given their kids

- Where to register your baby's name

- . . . and what to do if you change your mind!

All the data and statistics used in this book come from official sources, and have been collected from many different countries. I've also scoured thousands of news reports, pop culture articles, and social media posts to bring you the weirdest and most delightful titbits about baby names that I can find. Everything you need to know (and probably a lot of stuff you don't *need* to know but is fun anyway) is right here, so let's get going.

Your new favourite baby name is in here – somewhere.

Eleanor Turner

Part one

Naming your baby

1 The Best, The Bad, and The Bonkers

Look, I'm going to level with you. I know you've picked up this book because of the cute babies on the front and have cracked the spine because you're looking for inspiration on what to name your own bundle of joy, and we'll get there, I promise. But before we start down the road of genuine advice and what the research says about baby names, we have a few things to cross off the list first.

We need to talk about the other side of naming babies .

You know what I'm talking about.

It's the side where the ridiculous people live. It's where we snigger at news articles because some D-list celebrity just admitted the inspiration for their son's name came from a box of condoms, and where we gossip about your second cousin's poor spelling choices. It's the side where we speak in hushed tones about that poor child in your daughter's nursery class whose name sounds awfully like a swear word, and where midwives across the country draw a sharp intake of breath after asking "So, do we have a name yet?!"

This, my friends, is where we're starting our journey.

Let's go.

Trendy or tacky?

I want to make something clear upfront. I'm not here to poke fun at names that are culturally significant or meaningful, and I don't for a second believe the many baby-name urban legends out there that are often just a thinly veiled excuse to be racist or classist. (Looking at you, "my neighbour's-brother's-girlfriend's-aunt had twins called Lemonjello and Oranjello".) No, that's not what this is about.

This is about those glorious gems hidden at the very end of national Top Names lists that look as though someone threw a bag of Scrabble letters into the air and tried to pronounce whatever fell face up, and about the glorious oddballs who've legally changed their names as adults – but we'll get to those in a bit.

For now, let's start with the names at the very top of the charts around the world and those at the very bottom. Who are the winners and who are the losers, and why?

On the next page are the current Top 5 names for both boys and girls from around the world.

What I find fascinating about all these lists is how common some of the names are, no matter which country you're looking at. Olivia and Charlotte appear all over the place on the girls' lists, along with a staggering number of similar-sounding names such as Isla, Amelia, Emilia, Emma, Amaia, Maja, Mila, Mia, Alma, Julia, Ella, Fiadh, Aarya, Amahle, and Aria. Sophia, Sofia, and Sophie are also grouped up there, as are Ivy, Ava, and Vera.

For boys, Jack, Noah, and Oliver are tip top for parents all over the globe, and there are also similar-sounding names we can group together here too: William, Liam, Leo, and Leon, alongside Lucas, Lukas, and Luca, and then Mateo, Martin, and Matías.

My point here is that name trends wax and wane, but we'd be naïve to think that those trends only strike individual countries. While there are certainly more marked differences between countries that primarily speak English and those that don't, it's fascinating to see how similar the sounds of the most popular names are – no matter what language is being spoken.

Top 5 Boys' Names in 2024

Country	Rank 1	Rank 2	Rank 3	Rank 4	Rank 5
England	Noah	George	Oliver	Muhammad	Arthur
Wales	Noah	Oliver	Arthur	Theo	Leo
Scotland	Jack	Noah	Leo	Oliver	Harris
Northern Ireland	Jack	Noah	James	Charlie	Oliver
Republic of Ireland	Jack	Noah	James	Conor	Rian
Netherlands	Noah	Liam	Luca	Lucas	Mees
Germany	Noah	Matteo	Leon	Finn	Paul
Sweden	Noah	William	Liam	Hugo	Lucas
Norway	Noah/Noa	Oskar/Oscar	Oliver	Lukas/Lucas	Isak/Isac/Isaac
Iceland	Jón	Sigurður	Guðmundur	Gunnar	Ólafur/Olav
Portugal	Francisco	João	Duarte	Afonso	Tomás
Spain	Hugo	Mateo	Martin	Lucas	Leo
South Africa	Enzokuhle	Lethabo	Melokuhle	Lubanzi	Amogelang
India	Mohammad	Shivansh	Dhruv	Kabir	Vedant
Australia	Oliver	Noah	Jack	Henry	William
New Zealand	Oliver	Noah	Leo	Jack	Luca
NZ Maori	Nikau	Ari	Niko	Koa	Mateo
Canada	Liam	Noah	Oliver	Jack	William
USA	Liam	Noah	Oliver	Elijah	James
Mexico	Santiago	Mateo	Leonardo	Matías	Sebastián

Top 5 Girls' Names in 2024

Country	Rank 1	Rank 2	Rank 3	Rank 4	Rank 5
England	Olivia	Amelia	Isla	Ava	Ivy
Wales	Olivia	Amelia	Isla	Freya	Ivy/Rosie
Scotland	Olivia	Emily	Isla	Freya	Ella
Northern Ireland	Grace	Emily	Fiadh	Olivia	Isla
Republic of Ireland	Fiadh	Grace	Emily	Sophie	Éabha
Netherlands	Emma	Julia	Mila	Sophie	Olivia
Germany	Emilia	Hanna	Sofia/Sophia	Emma	Mia
Sweden	Alice	Maja	Vera	Alma	Selma
Norway	Nora/Norah	Emma	Sofie/Sophie	Olivia	Ella
Iceland	Guðrún	Anna	Kristín	Sigríður	Margrét/Margrjet
Portugal	Maria	Leonor	Matilde	Alice	Carolina
Spain	Lucia	Sofia	Martina	Maria	Julia
South Africa	Enzokuhle	Melokuhle	Amahle	Lethabo	Amogelang
India	Aditi	Inaya	Aarya	Kiara	Aadhya
Australia	Isla	Charlotte	Olivia	Amelia	Ava
New Zealand	Isla	Amelia	Charlotte	Mila	Lily
NZ Maori	Mia	Aria	Maia	Aurora	Amaia
Canada	Olivia	Emma	Charlotte	Sophia	Amelia/Emilia
USA	Olivia	Emma	Charlotte	Amelia	Ava
Mexico	Sofia	Regina	Valentina	Victoria	Isabella

2024's Movers and Shakers

Let's turn our attention now to a different but related topic: the names that are up and coming, and those that are tumbling down the charts.

In the UK's Top 100, two names stand out as up-and-comers. For boys, Brody jumped up 36 places to arrive in the charts for the first time, and for girls, Olive moved up 25 positions into 74th place. Brody's leap could be down to the influence of the Kardashian-Jenner family, with Brody Jenner continuing to make headlines along with his siblings; and Olive is such a close sister to Olivia that it makes sense she's storming up the charts as well.

The USA provides an even more impressive breakdown of changes in popularity, publishing lists of the highest climbers among all names – not just the Top 100. In here we find Raya (jumped 441 places), Wrenley (up 397 places), and Angelique (moved 306 spots) for girls; and Amiri (up 534 places), Eliam (jumped 442 spots), and Colter (moved 344 places) for boys. Other big movers include Ozzy and Loyal on the boys' list, and Vida and Emberlynn on the girls'.

The names at the bottom of the list (my personal guilty favourites) are a bit harder to gather, because not all countries publish a complete list of baby names rankings every year. However, of the countries that do provide that information, we can find some truly eye-popping data. Let's start with names that are falling out of fashion when compared to previous years.

A surprising turnup in the UK is that the names Molly and Holly are on the way down. For years they've bounced around the Top 100, and a decade ago both were in the Top 50. It's too soon to say whether this is the start of a new trend away from the names ending in -y/-ie that we've loved for years, but it's certainly interesting! However, both the UK and

Australia agree that even with the added influence of 2019's live-action version of *Aladdin* and a sequel in the works, the name Jasmine doesn't have the same spark that it used to.

In the USA, both Denisse and Denise are losing steam, and fast. Joining them on the unpopular list is also Karen, which shouldn't surprise anyone with an active social media account. Poor Karen – back in the mid-20th century it used to be one of the most popular names in the English-speaking world, but thanks to the unfortunate stereotype assigned to it, it's become deeply unpopular.

	UK	US	Australia
Highest Climbers (Girls)	Olive	Raya	Willow
	Margot	Wrenley	Florence
	Lyla	Angelique	Violet
	Maeve	Vida	Ivy
	Delilah/Lyra	Emberlynn	Audrey
Highest Climbers (Boys)	Brody	Amiri	Theodore
	Blake	Eliam	Leo
	Luca	Colter	Hudson
	Oakley	Ozzy	Hugo
	Otis	Loyal	Arlo
Fastest Fallers (Girls)	Molly	Denisse	Jasmine
	Lucy	Denise	Lara
	Hannah	Karen	Summer
	Jasmine	Keily	Emma
	Holly	Nathalie	Claire
Fastest Fallers (Boys)	Logan	Jaxtyn	Connor
	Gabriel	Karsyn	Luke
	Adam	Xzavier	Nicholas
	Samuel	Willie	Matthew
	Mohammad	Tristen	Jayden

Now then – on to the really good stuff. Let's poke around at the very bottom of the lists and see what we can dig up!

For privacy reasons, the UK doesn't publish names with fewer than three registrations and the USA ignores those with fewer than five. So, while there are definitely even more obscure names floating around out there each year, we're going to have to focus on only those we know about.

Each of the following is a genuine name that can be found at the very bottom of the charts in either the UK or USA.

Bizarre Names from 2024

	UK	USA
Girls	Barley	Bunny
	Binkie	Diary
	Bunny	Dreamy
	Bunty	Fairy
	Fable	Feather
	Fizzy	Fizza
	Harbor	Hawkins
	Jazz	Lyfe
	Lake	Riggin
	North	Shelsea
	Petal	Sthefany
	Pixie	Symphanie
	Pslam	Syrinity
	Story	Vignette
	Tulip	Yunique
	Winslet	Zamantha

	UK	USA
Boys	Bam	Albino
	Banksy	Angelgabriel
	Christ	Boomer
	Cruise	Chambers
	Echo	Cub
	Euros	Early
	Future	Flex
	Bodstime	Furious
	Gracious	Galaxy
	Halo	Infinite
	Koven	Kamp
	Lucky	Keeper
	Lyrc	Khance
	Marvellous	Kurrency
	Million	Money
	Nature	Patch
	Silver	Science
	Wealth	Wealth

I promised you some spectacular names, didn't I? Looking through those lists of – and let's never forget this – genuine names given to genuine babies, it's so hard to pick a favourite. The idea of picking up your fresh, sweet little baby that you've waited so long for, and deciding to name him Furious, will never not be funny to me. Or imagining your darling daughter's cherubic face as your rub your pregnancy bump, and determining that the only name you could possibly give her is Sthefany?

Other standouts in this crowd include Euros, Binkie, Early (I'm assuming for a premature baby, which is a bit of a cruel jibe), Boomer (BOOMER?! In this era of generational conflict??), plus a veritable charcuterie board of interesting spellings: Khance, Koven, Kurrency, Shelsea, Syrinity, Yunique and Zamantha. And even if *Carnival Row* and *Friday Night Lights* are your favourite TV shows, I'm really not convinced names like Vignette and Riggin will age well.

Granted, some of the names in these lists aren't as bad as the others. Naming your child something aspirational such as Wealth, Gracious, or Money might not be the most traditional of choices, but I do understand why parents go for them. The parental desire to want your babies to lead successful lives is universal, so giving them names like Science and Future in hopes that they go on to do incredible things is at least somewhat logical. There is data that suggests that the names we give our children can have a real impact on their lives, so maybe these parents are on to something here. For more on how names influence our lives see page 37.

What was wrong with the old one?

If you change your mind about your kiddo's name after you've already registered their birth, there are ways to change it (more on that on page 51). But what do you do if you're an adult who fancies altering it? Of course there are legitimate reasons to do so, such as gender reassignment or getting rid of a bothersome name that's always caused you issues, but those won't get you in the pages of a best-selling baby names book. No, what I'm here to discuss is those bonkers examples of people who decided – probably on a drunken bet – that the name Sam or Jennifer simply will not do anymore, and that they needed to spend money on changing it. Don't believe me? Well, here are some real-life examples of people who decided to announce to the world publicly that they have more money than sense.

Bacon Double Cheeseburger (formerly Simon Smith)
Beezow Doo-Doo Zopittybop-bop-bop (formerly Jeffrey Drew Wilschke)
Captain Fantastic Faster Than Superman Spiderman Batman Wolverine
Hulk And The Flash Combined (formerly George Garratt)
Darren QX Bean! (exclamation included – formerly Darren Lloyd Bean)
Fire Exit (Deano Wilson)
Happy Adjustable Spanners (formerly Daniel Westfallen)
Henry Lizardlover (formerly Henry Schiff)
King Arthur Uther Pendragon (formerly John Rothwell)
Mark I Love Spam (formerly Mark Benson)
Sexy Crabtree (formerly Sheila Ranea Crabtree)
Ynot Bubba (formerly Justin Brady)

And introducing pop-mad twin sisters: Lianne Madonna Vogue On
The Cover Of A Magazine McHale Dawson and Emma Madonna
Confessions On A Dance Floor Dawson.

At the start of this chapter I promised you some truly oddball names, and I hope I delivered. But you might be asking yourself why we haven't delved into the oddest names of all yet – those of celebrity children – and I'm here to reassure you that I haven't forgotten. The wonderful celebrity missteps we've seen over the years are coming up next.

On to Chapter Two!

2 The World of Celebrity Baby Names

This book wouldn't be complete without a look at what the world's influencers are naming their kids. Firstly because if you spend any time online at all it's difficult to avoid, and secondly because celebrity baby names are a treasure trove of wonder and hilarity.

Let's take a look at the past year's most memorable superstar baby names.

Celebrity Babies

Abram (Shay Mooney and Hannah Billingsley)
Baker Weston (Lauren Bushnell and Chris Lane)
Bambi (Tommy Fury and Molly-Mae Hague)
Esti Maxine (Chrissy Teigen and John Legend)
Iceland (Keyshia Ka'Oir and Gucci Mane)
Ilaria Catalina Irena (Alec Baldwin and Hilaria Baldwin)
Jackson Joanne (Billie Lourd and Austen Rydell)
Jupiter (Ed Sheeran and Cherry Seaborn)
Love Sean (Diddy Combs)
Malibu Barbie (Trisha Paytas and Moses Hacmon)
Mia Bella Elizabeth (Mike "The Situation" Sorrentino and Lauren Sorrentino)
Oscar Bennett (Mandy Moore and Taylor Goldsmith)
Patrick Lavon III "Bronze" (Patrick Mahomes and Brittany Mahomes)
Pixie Rose (Christina Perri and Paul Costabile)
Rome Valentin (Jenna Johnson and Val Chmerkovskiy)
Royce Lillian Elizabeth (Rebel Wilson and Ramona Agruma)
Sullivan Louis (Jesse Tyler Ferguson and Justin Mikita)

For a couple of years now we've had pretty normal names emerge from the pages of glossy magazines, and disappointingly few truly bizarre ones. It's therefore refreshing to see some total bangers in that list, such as Love Sean, the name Sean/Diddy/Puff Daddy/Combs gave to his newborn daughter. Putting aside for a moment the fact Mr Combs can't seem to make up his mind about his own name, I do understand the urge to pass on family forenames down generational lines – but using an instruction for a name seems a little odd, no? Love your father Sean, or else? Or how about Malibu Barbie, the name YouTuber Trisha Paytas chose for her daughter. She should probably check whether she's infringing copyright law there.

Several of the celebrity couples here are also parents to older children. Probably the most impressive sibling duo are Ice and Iceland, son and daughter respectively of rapper Gucci Mane and wife Keyshia Ka'Oir. What will they do if they have a third child – name it Freezer? Meanwhile, country singer Shay Mooney and his wife Hannah Billingsley have a theme going of A names with their kids, which is actually kind of adorable: Asher, Ames, and little Abram. Power couple Chrissy Teigen and John Legend, both masters of Instagram and beyond, have been very open about their growing family over the last few years, and for some reason have received judgement for their perfectly normal choices of baby names: Luna, Miles, Jack, and now Esti. Compared to other celebrity choices of Baker, Bambi, and Jupiter, I'd say Tiegen and Legend are playing things extremely safe!

> Did you know Kylie Jenner and Travis Scott originally named their son Wolf? Also parents to Stormi, they changed Wolf's name to Aire after a month because they "just really didn't feel it was him". If you're having second thoughts about your own choices and want to take a deep breath of Aire, see page 51 for how to change your baby's name too.

A list like this, however, isn't complete without a couple of honourable mentions. Presenter and actor Nick Cannon has been . . . shall we say . . . busy over the last couple of years expanding his family. At the time of writing, Cannon has had 12 children with six women, and several of his children were born mere weeks apart. In the interests of high-quality journalism I'll break it down for you:

April 2011: Twins Monroe and Moroccan Scott, with mother Mariah Carey (yes, that Mariah Carey)
February 2017: Golden Sagon, with mother Brittany Bell
December 2020: Powerful Queen, with mother Brittany Bell
June 2021: Twins Zion Mixolydian and Zillion Heir, with mother Abby De La Rosa
June 2021: Zen, with mother Alyssa Scott
June 2022: Legendary Love, with mother Bre Tiesi
September 2022: Onyx Ice, with mother LaNisha Cole
September 2022: Rise Messiah, with mother Brittany Bell
November 2022: Beautiful Zeppelin, with mother Abby De La Rosa
December 2022: Halo Marie, with mother Alyssa Scott

No shade to Mr Cannon or any of his children's mothers for how they've chosen to live their lives: you do you, boo. But can we talk about the impressive array of names here please? I remember when Monroe and Moroccan Scott were born and how the world's collective eyebrows went up, but since 2011 things have only gotten wilder. Zillion? Legendary? Beautiful Zeppelin?? Somebody please take away this man's dictionary and tell him that random words do not necessarily great baby names make.

Longest Name Ever

According to the Guinness Book of World Records, the world's longest name belongs to Hubert Blaine Wolfeschlegelsteinhausenbergderorff, Sr. Hubert was born in 1914 and his full name (without the Sr. because that's going just too far) was Adolph Blaine Charles David Earl Frederick Gerald Hubert Irvin John Kenneth Lloyd Martin Nero Oliver Paul Quincy Randolph Sherman Thomas Uncas Victor William Xerxes Yancy Zues Wolfeschlegelsteinhausenbergerdorffwelchevoralternwarengewissen haftschaferswessenschafewarenwohlgepflegeundsorgfaltigkeit wohlgepflegeundsorgfaltigkeitbeschutzenvonangreifendurchihrraub gierigfeindewelchevoralternzwolftausendjahresvorandieerscheinen vanderersteerdemenschderraumschiffgebrauchlichtalsseinursprung vonkraftgestartseinlangefahrthinzwischensternartigraumaufdersuch enachdiesternwelchegehabtbewohnbarplanetenkreisedrehen sichundwohinderneurassevonverstandigmenschlichkeitkon ntefortpflanzenundsicherfreuenanlebenslanglichfreudeundruhemit nichteinfurchtvorangreifenvonandererintelligentgeschopfsvonhin zwischensternartigraum. The full name can apparently be translated into a story about shepherds, electricity, and space travel (of course), and he became a minor celebrity when he refused to pay his utility bill unless the company spelled his name correctly. And if that isn't a reason to love feisty ol' Hubert I don't know what is.

Our second honourable mention goes to Alec Baldwin and his wife Hilaria Baldwin, who have also chosen to have a large family. The Baldwins are parents to eight children: Carmen Gabriela, Rafael Thomas, Leonardo Ángel Charles, Romeo Alejandro David, Eduardo Pau Lucas, María Lucía Victoria, Ilaria Catalina Irina, and Ireland Eliesse – the last of whom Alec Baldwin shares with former wife Kim Basinger. Personally I am loving their Spanish-influenced names, but they don't come without controversy. Hilaria Baldwin has spent much of her adult life passing herself off as European, but tabloids were overjoyed in 2020 to reveal that despite her Spanish-sounding accent, she was actually born in Massachusetts, raised speaking American English, and her birth name wasn't Hilaria but Hillary.

For someone accused of cultural appropriation, it does seem a little bizarre to keep choosing these specific names for your kids, doesn't it?

Whatever happened to Apple?

Ever thought about those mad celebrity baby names from yesteryear and wondered what happened to those kids as they become adults? Unsurprisingly, most of them are following in their parents' footsteps and doing something creative, where having a bonkers first name is probably more of an asset than a hindrance. You don't find many accountants called Banjo, anyway.

Apple Blythe Alison Martin, daughter of Gwyneth Paltrow and Chris Martin, is an up-and-coming model.
Audio Science Clayton, son of Shannyn Sossaman and Dallas Clayton, is making a name for himself in music production, which seems rather apt!
Banjo Patrick Taylor, son of Rachel Griffiths and Andrew Taylor, is now a regular student who stays out of the spotlight.
Jermajesty Jackson, the son of Jermaine Jackson and Genevieve Oaziaza, performs music with his dad and brother Jaafar.
Rocco Ritchie, the son of Madonna and Guy Ritchie, is forging a career in art and goes by the name Rhed.

Tu Simone Morrow (say it without the middle name), the daughter of Rob Morrow and Debbon Morrow, is pursuing a career in acting like her parents.

> When magician Penn Jillette announced his new daughter's name in 2005 was going to be Moxie CrimeFighter Jillette, he justified the choice by saying, "Moxie is a name that was created by an American for the first national soft drink and then went on to mean chutzpah, and that's nice. It's only losers named Dave that think having an unusual name is bad, and who cares what they think. They're named Dave". Yes Penn, we get that . . . but really our question was about her middle name. CrimeFighter??

Problematic Pronunciation

As much as we (okay, I) like to poke fun of them, celebrities have also found ways to use their powers for good when it comes to names. Stars have begun speaking up when their names are mispronounced, drawing particular attention to those times when it's used as a tool for micro-aggression and even blatant racism. The #MyNameIs social media campaign attracted attention when actors such as Kumail Nanjiani, Uzo Aduba, and Lupita Nyong'o pointed out that their names are no harder to pronounce than anyone else's if you take the time to just learn, and actor Hasan Minhaj was quoted as saying, "If you can pronounce Ansel Elgort, you can pronounce Hasan Minhaj". Too damn right.

This doesn't just impact actors, either. When US Vice President Kamala Harris was running her campaign in the lead-up to the 2020 election, news pundits openly pronounced her name wrong and some even rebuffed on-air corrections with "So what?". A fellow politician, who had been on Senate committees with Harris previously, even made an ongoing joke about how to mispronounce her name during a rally for the opposition. Kamala Harris, to her credit, has never been shy about swiftly correcting folks who get her name wrong, and, while most people appreciate the correction and make an effort to get it right next time, it's sad to see how many others use it as a weapon against her.

For the record, let's hear from Vice President Harris herself on how to say her name properly: "First, my name is pronounced 'comma-la', like the punctuation mark. It means 'lotus flower', which is a symbol of significance in Indian culture". Now that doesn't seem so hard, does it?

> Did you know the royal family thinks the name John is unlucky and that's why they never use it? Apparently the name is associated with two unlucky Johns: King John, who was on the throne from 1199 to 1216, lost the Crown Jewels and half

of France, died of dysentery after eating too many spoiled peaches, and is more commonly known as one of Robin Hood's enemies; and Prince John, who was King George V's youngest son, and who died from epilepsy-related causes in 1919 at the young age of 14. Don't worry if you're thinking of picking John for your own baby's name though: apparently the bad luck only extends to those with royal blood.

Influencer Inspiration

Celebrities aren't just known for coming up with the oddest baby names around – their own names are also a rich source of inspiration. Everything to do with entertainment, sports, politics, and more, has the potential to catch a soon-to-be parent's eye and become the next trend in names.

Take Disney/Pixar's fantastical seashore adventure *Luca*, released in 2021. Since its release the name Luca has become the 15th most popular name for little boys in Australia, 28th in the UK, the 42nd most popular in both the USA and Spain, and it just keeps climbing. *Raya and the Last Dragon*, another Disney pandemic-era hit released in 2021, has had a similar impact on names for little girls. Raya jumped an astonishing 441 places last year in the USA and 190 places in the UK, and is one of the fastest-growing names worldwide.

> Kim Kardashian named her son Saint in 2015, and since his birth the name has seen an impressive rise in popularity. There were more than 1,000 baby boys called that last year, with more and more added every year.

On the small screen, Netflix has a great deal to answer for. The fourth season of *Stranger Things* glued us all to the TV in 2022, and with it came the popularity of names of not only the characters but also the cast. Perhaps the most surprising (although these days I'm not sure much surprises me about names anymore) is that parents are picking Eleven for their daughters. I get it: I love Elle as much as the next person, but giving your baby what was effectively a tracking number for a really bizarre experiment seems a little weird. Just me? There were 19 babies called Eleven in the USA last year and a sprinkling in the UK, so we'll see what 2024 brings when the final season is released (and Elle kicks some ass again).

Eleven is played by actor Millie Bobby Brown, who is herself no stranger (see what I did there?) to influencing baby names. Since her first on-screen nosebleed in 2016, the name Millie has rushed up the charts all over the world. It's now in 27th place in the UK, 61st place in Australia, and leaped 150 places in the USA to position 174 last year.

Big (and Little) Screen Inspo

Eleven
(Elle)
Ezra
Luca
Maeve
Millie
Otis
Raya
Saint

Netflix also brought us the spicy world of teenage antics with *Sex Education*. Otis and Maeve, the names of two of the cast's central characters, have spiked in popularity since the first season launched in 2019, and they're only ranking better and better with season four looming. Otis is now in 81st place in the UK, and Maeve is not only in 77th there but also in 70th place in Australia. Both names are also climbing the charts in the USA, and last year Maeve swung up another 50 places.

Elsewhere, the world of pop music has left its mark in recent years. Musician George Ezra's melodic baritone has clearly impressed us, as the name Ezra is now in 37th place in the USA, 51st place in the UK, and 64th in Australia. Considering this name was languishing in the 780s thirty years ago this is quite the leap in popularity, but it's especially impressive that the bulk of the jump in all three countries came after 2015 when George Ezra's breakthrough album was released.

The Original Influencers?

Naming babies after celebrities isn't a new thing, you know. Broadway and early silent movie stars of the 1910s and 1920s were also trendsetters, with the following names appearing on the baby-name charts for the first time thanks to their celebrity namesakes:

Allyn (after dancer Allyn King)
Avonne (after dancer Avonne Taylor)
Francelia (after silent movie star Francelia Billington)
Ormi (after silent movie star Ormetta "Ormi" Hawley)
Seena (after silent movie star Seena Owen)

3   The Nitty Gritty

Okay, okay, we've had our fun. It's time to put our minds to the real reason you've picked up this book: you want to know what you should name your baby and you've turned to the experts to help you make the decision. I got you.

There are several unspoken rules about baby names that I think we should get out of the way first. Keep in mind these aren't hard and fast and you're welcome to ignore as many of them as you like, but as general guidelines they really do make sense.

- Fall in love with the name(s) you've chosen. You'll be yelling this name out for the rest of your life, so it might as well be something you truly adore.

- This is supposed to be fun! Laugh at the ones you'd never dream of using and write down all the ones you like in a sparkly pen if it makes it more entertaining.

- Try it out. While you're pregnant, talk to your baby using their name and see if they respond. Granted, it's hard to tell whether that kick was because they loved it or hated it, but at least it provoked a reaction.

- Don't listen to other people. Even though I'm literally here telling you what and what not to do with names, I cannot stress this one enough. Grandparents and friends will offer you so much well-intended advice, but it may not always be welcome. If you've got your heart set on a specific name already, keep it a secret until after the birth to avoid any unnecessary criticism.

- Don't steal ideas. One survey found that friends stealing each other's baby names was a legitimate reason for the breakdown of adult friendships. A name is really not worth losing a friend over.

- Find a name with meaning. Choosing a name that is rooted in history or folklore might just inspire your little one to be as great as their namesake. There's research to suggest this inspirational rub-off effect has real legs so, even if you pick a name clean out of the air, consider making something up to tell them later . . .

- Expand your mind. Be brave and bold if that's what you want (although from the bottom of my heart, please don't pick one of the disasters from Chapter One), but just in case you get it massively wrong – definitely a possibility, let's face it – you might want to give them a simpler middle name so they can jump ship to that instead.

- What if you can't agree with your partner? This is probably the trickiest problem to solve in the baby names world. My suggestion is to research a handful of names that you and your partner each like, and make a point of discussing each one long before the baby is due. The delivery room is not the place for these discussions.

- Compromise is key. Pick two middle names so that you each have one in there you love, or you could each have five names that you're allowed to veto but no more. Whichever way you go about it, it's crucial that you eventually agree on the final name you're giving your baby – even if it means losing out on the one you've had your heart set on for a while.

- Finally, keep reading and re-reading this book! The answer is in here somewhere.

> A study by the University of Hertfordshire in the UK asked members of the opposite sex to rate names according to attractiveness, luck, and success. The top names were James and Elizabeth, which authors concluded was a result of them being traditionally royal names, and therefore aspirational and associated with intelligence and success. However, the lowest-ranked name for sexiness was George, which is also traditionally royal . . . and I'm fairly sure fans of George Clooney would dispute those results anyway.

Statistical stuff

I don't know about you, but I find the data and statistics behind baby name trends really interesting. There's something so fascinating about learning how similarly (or not) parents think, and if you look at last year's trends it's clear that there are a lot of parents who think the same way.

In both the UK and the USA (the two countries with this level of detailed data available) there was a greater variety of names for girls than for boys. This stands in contrast to the actual numbers of registered births, where there were more boys than girls. You would expect the variety to match the registrations, but it's apparent that parents pick from a smaller pool of names for their baby boys than they do for their baby girls.

	UK		USA	
	Boys	**Girls**	**Boys**	**Girls**
Individual names registered	6,201	7,329	13,993	17,544
Total registrations	295,057	274,046	1,734,277	1,627,098
Top names	Noah (4,525 registrations)	Olivia (3,649 registrations)	Liam (20,272 registrations)	Olivia (17,728 registrations)
Babies with names in Top 10	35,786	25,101	134,924	124,772
Top 10 names as percentage	12.13%	9.16%	7.78%	7.67%
Highest climbers	Brody	Olive	Amiri	Raya
Fastest fallers	Logan	Molly	Jaxtyn	Denisse

You can see a similar pattern with the percentage of names from each group that appear in the Top 10, which is higher for boys in both countries. We can interpret this as saying that parents of little boys are more likely to stick with a smaller selection of familiar and popular names than parents of little girls.

Why is this, though? Well, it may be that it is socially acceptable to get creative with girl names, whereas messing around too much with spellings for boy names or inventing brand-new ones is more frowned upon. There's also the possibility that more traditional names are preferred for boys, especially when it comes to names with a religious influence.

Divine Deities

Religion has long played a role in the names we give our children, and the most recent chart-toppers are no exception. In the UK, the name Muhammad is now the fifth most popular name in the country, with the spelling Mohammed in 35th place and Mohammad in 83rd. In fact, combining the spellings of the first five versions of the name tells us there were over 6,600 baby boys named after the Islamic Prophet last year, which puts it in first place. Amazing.

Judeo-Christian influences are strong all over the world, and there are a staggering number of names for both boys and girls that can be traced back to the Bible. At the top of course is the UK's favourite name, Noah, which also occupies second place in the USA and Australia. Then there are other traditional picks such as Benjamin, James, Thomas, Luke, Daniel, David Michael, and Levi – all of which have appeared in the charts for hundreds of years.

For girls, while Mary has been slipping down the ranks in English-speaking countries since its heyday in the 1950s, it remains the name given to the greatest number of girls in history. Elsewhere in the world, Maria is the top pick in Portugal and the fourth-highest name in Spain and still an incredibly common name elsewhere. Other Biblical options for girls include Rebecca, Rachel, Sarah, Ruth, and Abigail.

Hindu families have a wonderful naming tradition for their babies, culminating in a naamkaran ceremony where the name is finally given to the baby and the family celebrates its birth. Babies are often named after Hindu gods and goddesses, or the names of characters from mythological stories. Popular names in the Hindu faith include Meera, Aditi, and Lakshmi for girls, and Krishna, Ishaan, and Bhavesh for boys.

Religious (Naming) Icons

Boys	Girls
Amir	Abigail
Benjamin	Aditi
Ishaan	Fatima
Krishna	Layla
Michael	Mary
Muhammad	Meera
Peter	Rebecca
Paul	Ruth
Samuel	Sarah

Bending Gender Norms

How do we define what makes a name masculine or feminine? Well, it may be connected to the sounds that the letters create when spoken. Harder-sounding combinations (-ter, -it, -ld, -id) tend to be found in masculine names, whereas softer-sounding combinations (-ie, -ay, -la) are generally associated with feminine names. You therefore end up with Sophie, Joanie, and Bella, versus Harold, Walter, and David.

A trend we've been seeing for the last couple of years has been the increase in unisex names, and names traditionally given to one gender that are now being given to both. The stalwarts such as Alex, Robin, Max, and Jude are always reasonably popular, but now we're also seeing traditional boy names such as James given to girls (a celebrity example of this is the daughter of Ryan Reynolds and Blake Lively), and vice versa. The following is a list of names that have appeared in the UK and USA charts over the last year, and, while some might surprise you, watch out for the real-life examples appearing in a classroom near you soon.

One explanation for this increase in unisex and opposite-sex names is the increased awareness and acceptance of there being a spectrum of gender identities. For parents who are acutely aware that the gender their child is assigned at birth may not be the one they stay, picking a name that is acceptable for both boys and girls is an elegant way to avoid issues with dead names and paperwork down the road. And hey, who knows – maybe one day we will all have unisex names and avoid the whole issue entirely. Now there's a thought.

	UK	USA
Girls	Brody	Anthony
	Cooper	Casper
	Dan	Henri
	Elliot	Idris
	Hudson	Jimi
	Kingsley	Larson
	Max	Lucas
	Spencer	Marshall
	Theo	Monty
	Toby	Santiago
	Tyler	Thomas
	Wilder	Tyson
Boys	Ada	Claire
	Camille	Denise
	Honor	Eleanor
	Jade	Elizabeth
	Joan	Hannah
	Jocelyn	Honour
	Joy	Hope
	Mina	Josie
	Patsy	Lacey
	Sandy	Louise

Interestingly, a study by the University of Illinois found that boys with androgynous names (the example given in the study was Ashley) tend to act up and do worse in high school exams than their counterparts with harder-sounding names. The theory was that they get teased in school and compared to girls with the same name, so their academic progress stalls. There was a different study done in the UK that found that girls who were given very feminine-sounding names, such as Tiana and Isabella, were much more likely to misbehave in school and to choose to study subjects like science and mathematics than their sisters with more masculine-sounding names such as Morgan and Alexis. Equally fascinating and terrifying, and it would be interesting to replicate these studies in other countries, particularly non-English speaking ones, to see if the theories remain true.

A final thought here about sex and gender: what about your own? A study by British company Bounty found that mothers tend to win arguments over who gets to pick the name of a newborn, with 40 per cent of new mothers simply ignoring the choices selected by fathers, and 10 per cent of dads just simply backing down. However, a further 40 per cent of couples don't make the final decision until after the baby is born, and a third will argue about it before settling. Now, I'm not saying that the person who grows the baby and goes through the process of removing said baby from her own body should get final say, but . . . actually, that's exactly what I'm saying . . .

Nicknames

> "Nicknames are fond names. We do not give them to people we dislike."
> Edna Ferber

Nicknames are unavoidable. They can range from the common – such as Mike from Michael or Sam from Samantha – to the trendy, funny, or downright insulting (although the latter is probably more common in university dorm rooms than maternity floors). If you're planning to give your baby a long name that can be shortened intentionally, make sure you'll be happy with any of the potential nicknames that emerge.

You can pre-empt problem nicknames to some extent by saying the name you've chosen out loud and trying to find rhymes and short versions of it. This is a simple way to try and avoid playground chants and nursery-rhyme insults, such as Mickey Mouse or Winnie the Pooh, but it isn't fool proof! It's inevitable that children will find a way to poke fun at literally anything, however carefully you plan, so new mums out there should probably worry less about their children's classmates, and more about what to do when their child discovers their name rhymes with "bum".

Another way to head off awful nicknames is by picking them yourself. If your daughter is Josephine and you hate Joey, what about JoJo or Josie? If your son is Santiago and you hate San, what about Iago or even Santi? There are no rules here, so get creative!

For more on how nicknames are now uber-trendy, see page 41.

Celebrities who go by nicknames

Bob Marley (Nesta Robert Marley)
Brad Pitt (William Bradley Pitt)
Keke Palmer (Lauren Keyana Palmer)
Lucy Hale (Karen Lucille Hale)
Tina Fey (Elizabeth Stamatina Fey)
Tom Cruise (Thomas Cruise Mapother IV)
Tom Hardy (Edward Thomas Hardy)

Middle Names

Giving your child a middle name or several names is pretty standard practice in many places in the world. In fact, it's becoming fairly uncommon not to do so, so let's have a wee history lesson about what these names are for and the history behind their usage.

The use of second and third names only became popular around the start of the twentieth century. Prior to that point, giving a child a middle name was seen as a status symbol; it was really only used when a man married a higher-class woman and they wanted to keep the woman's maiden name as a reminder of their child's heritage. Since this time, middle names have become pretty much the norm for everyone. A study by website Netmums found that three-quarters of parents chose a single middle name for their baby, and one in six parents chose two or more.

In Spanish and Latin cultures, middle names are often the mother's surname or other name, to preserve the matriarchal lineage. Similarly, parents who have chosen not to take their spouse's surname or aren't married can choose to give their child one surname as a middle name and the other as the actual surname so that both parents are represented. However, be aware that doing either of those options can create some strange combinations – as Richard Tiffany Gere and Courtney Bass Cox can testify.

> Britain's royal family has a penchant for loading up its members with multiple middle names. King Charles's full name is Charles Philip Arthur George Mountbatten-Windsor, and Prince William is William Arthur Philip Louis Mountbatten-Windsor. The newest member of the royal family is of course Lilibet Diana Mountbatten-Windsor, who was named after two giants of royal history: Queen Elizabeth and Princess Diana. Lilibet was Queen Elizabeth's nickname as a child, so it's a rather sweet way to link the tiniest royal to her heritage

Other traditions use an old family name, passed down to each first-born son or daughter, to encourage a sense of family pride and history, and some families will use a pattern for middle names for each of their children. In addition, many people choose to go by their middle name instead of their first name, so it could be a good safety net if you're worried your child won't like their name.

If you're struggling to choose a middle name, here are some trends to help you narrow it down.

- Names from the family tree. Parents frequently look back to their own lineage for interesting, unusual or influential names, and it is becoming increasingly popular to use one partner's surname as a middle name.

- Opposite-length names. Generally, if the first name has only one or two syllables (Owen, Steven, Yasmin, Zoe) then the middle name could have two, three, or even four syllables (Owen Jonathan, Steven Michael, Yasmin Samantha, Zoe Jessica). And vice versa, so if the first name is three or four syllables long (Anthony, Jennifer, Nicholas, Rosemary) the middle name may be only one or two (Anthony Kevin, Jennifer Ruth, Nicholas John, Rosemary Dawn). This technique helps keep the pacing of the name nicely flowing when spoken aloud.

- Unusual names. Parents are typically able to get away with more unusual middle names than forenames, which makes sense if you're sticking to something traditional for the first name. There's a little more wiggle room here for using the middle name to show some individuality and creativity, so you could go with Elizabeth Bronte, Katherine Keilyn or Thomas Titan, and few people would bat an eye.

Some famous examples of people with multiple middle names are British musician Brian Eno, whose full name is a bit of a mouthful: Brian Peter St John le Baptiste de la Salle Eno, and Canadian actor Kiefer Sutherland, who has shortened his name considerably from Kiefer William Frederick Dempsey George Rufus Sutherland. Imagine trying to fit all that on to a job application form.

Celebrities who go by middle names

Antonio Banderas (Jose Antonio Dominguez Banderas)
Ashton Kutcher (Christopher Ashton Kutcher)
Bruce Willis (Walter Bruce Willis)
Brooke Shields (Christa Brooke Camille Shields)
Dakota Fanning (Hannah Dakota Fanning)
Drake (Aubrey Drake Graham)
Evangeline Lilly (Nicole Evangeline Lilly)
Hugh Laurie (James Hugh Calum Laurie)
Jason Momoa (Joseph Jason Namakaeha Momoa)
Jude Law (David Jude Heyworth Law)
Kelsey Grammer (Allen Kelsey Grammer)
Mindy Kaling (Vera Mindy Chokalingam)
Paul McCartney (James Paul McCartney)
Reese Witherspoon (Laura Jean Reese Witherspoon)
Rihanna (Robyn Rihanna Fenty)
Will Ferrell (John William Ferrell)

Surnames

Tied to your child's potential new initials is their new surname. Whether they are receiving their name from their mother, father, or a hyphenated combination of both, matching their first name to their surname is key. Try writing down all the names you like alongside your child's surname and have someone else read them out loud. This second pair of eyes and ears might just spot something that you didn't.

The age of the internet has given parents a wonderful new weapon in their baby-naming arsenal: the search engine. Before you settle on anything final, try searching for any examples of the complete first name, middle name and surname of your new baby. You may find out that your baby has an axe-murderer namesake or, like one of my former colleagues, the same name as a well-known porn star.

There is also the possibility of your child having a spoonerism made out of their name, where the first letters or syllables get swapped around to form words. Named after the Reverend Dr William Archibald Spooner (1844-1930), a spoonerism can be created out of almost anything to make clever, amusing or downright inappropriate phrases instead.

An unfortunate example of this would be the daughter of Angelina Jolie and Brad Pitt, Shiloh. Thankfully they named her Shiloh Jolie-Pitt, thus avoiding the inevitable Shiloh Pitt spoonerism.

Initials

Here are some things to consider when figuring out initials for your baby's name. What surname will they have? Does its first letter already lend itself to amusing acronyms or initialisms? And would choosing certain first names only exacerbate the problem? There's a bit of family lore on my husband's side that says when his brother was born he was going to be called Andrew Steven Schmitt – until my in-laws realised at the last minute what his initials would spell...

All this is to say, it's worth taking the time to think about the acronyms your baby's initials might spell out, and whether this could lead to disaster (or sniggering). Picture how those initials might look on a credit card or written out on a form. Nobody should have to go through life as S. Lugg or A. Bottom just because their parents didn't think that far ahead.

Unfortunate name combinations

Barry	Cade
Duane	Pipe
Grace	Land
Hazel	Nutt
Jenny	Taylor
Oliver	Sutton
Paige	Turner
Stan	Still
Teresa	Green

Nominative Determinism

Anthroponomastics is the term used for the study of personal names, and nominative determinism is the theory that people will naturally gravitate towards careers that fit their names. First identified in 1994 in *New Scientist* magazine, the term was originally a humorous observation about the authors of some scientific studies, whose names were spookily similar to the fields they were studying. It included Daniel Snowman's book on polar explorations, Richard Trench's work on subterranean London tunnels, and a urology article by A.J. Splatt and D. Weedon (snigger).

Sounds too odd to be true? How about the fastest man on Earth, sprinter Usain Bolt? Or Igor Judge, the former Lord Chief Justice of England and Wales? Maybe there's truth to it after all. If you fancy your child as a future career talent, consider giving them a name that directs them towards that field. I mean, if it didn't hurt dentist Dennis Smiler and academic researcher Richard Wiseman, then it won't hurt your little one either!

Future career names

Cooper

Deacon

Hunter

Marshall

Mason

Paige

Ryder

Sawyer

Scout

Taylor

Naming Laws

The last thing to mention in this chapter is a warning: whatever name you're leaning towards, make sure you're not breaking the law!

Most countries have laws in place to prevent parents from seriously messing up their kids' names. The regulations are varied and wide-ranging, and the penalties for breaking them can be anything from being forced to choose a different name, to monetary fines, or even jail time. Yikes. To be sure you don't run afoul of the long arm of the law, here are a few of my personal favourites from around the world:

China: Names may not use Latin characters or numerals, or Chinese characters that cannot be inputted on a computer. Aside from this, however, naming laws in China are pretty easygoing – which comes with its own problems. Children can be named after celebrities, companies, and even products, because Chinese copyright and trademark laws do not extend to personal names, so there have been legal issues with intellectual property rights and public mixups. Banned names include religious names such as Jihad and Quran, and the use of the character @ as a name.

Denmark: According to Danish law, names must be chosen from a list of 18,000 female names and 15,000 male names. They cannot be surnames or offensive, and must follow Danish writing conventions. If parents want to use a name that goes against the rules then they have to apply for an exception – including for names that are otherwise commonly used in other countries. Banned names include Anus, Pluto, and Monkey.

Germany: German law states the right of a parent to choose their child's name is protected – with a couple of exceptions. If the chosen name adversely affects the welfare of the child or is considered offensive, the state has a right to intervene; and the state also says that boys must be given male names and girls must be given female names. For this reason, the name Matti was rejected for a baby boy because it was too gender neutral.

Iceland: Iceland maintains a strict list of approved names, maintained by the official-sounding Iceland Naming Committee. Parents may only choose names that include letters from the Icelandic alphabet and that fit grammatically with the language. Names must also not cause offence or embarrassment, and children cannot be given more than three first names. Banned names include Harriet and Duncan, because neither can be pronounced or written in Icelandic, and while Blær was originally rejected for a baby girl the parents eventually won the appeal.

Japan: First names in Japan must be comprised of the 843 'name kanji' characters and 2,136 commonly-used other characters. This is to ensure names can always be written down and read easily. Banned names include the kanji used for 'weak' and 'failure'; and Akuma, which translates to Devil.

New Zealand: Kiwi law states that parents aren't allowed to name their children anything that might cause offence, is longer than 100 characters, includes numbers or symbols, or resembles an official title or rank (like Royal, Saint, or Lord). Some incredible names that have broken this law include Yeah Detroit, Fish and Chips, Twisty Poi, Keenan Got Lucy, Sex Fruit, and Satan. However, officials in New Zealand felt that Benson and Hedges (a set of twins), Midnight Chardonnay, Violence, and Number 16 Bus Shelter (before the law about numbers was in place) were all acceptable. Oookay then.

Norway: In Norway, you cannot use a surname as a first name, or pick a name that causes offence or becomes a major inconvenience for the child, and you must use gender-appropriate names. A Norwegian mother was jailed in the mid-90s for refusing to change her child's name after her first choice of Gesher (translated to 'bridge') was rejected by the courts.

Portugal: Portugal maintains a list of names that are approved, most of which are very traditional and have the goal of preserving Portuguese culture. It even specifies the spellings of names and rejects shortened versions – so Tomás is fine, but Thomas, Thomaz, or Tom are all out.

Names must also be gender-specific, and cannot be confused for a surname. Banned names include Thor and Nirvana.

Sweden: Parents must register their child's name within three months of the birth, and the name must not be offensive or cause discomfort for the person using it. Rejected names in Sweden include Allah and Brfxxccxxmnpcccclllmmnprxvclmnckssqlbb11116 (supposedly pronounced 'Albin'), but approved ones include Metallica and Google.

United Kingdom: The UK is pretty laissez-faire when it comes to name laws and the only hard and fast rule is that names for babies must not contain obscenities, numerals or titles, or be impossible to pronounce. However, as we saw in Chapter One, if you're an adult you can choose pretty much anything you like – and the loonier, the better.

United States: Naming laws in the USA vary according to state. You cannot use numerals in some states, pictograms in others, and names over a certain character limit are banned in others. California has a rule that names cannot contain diacritical marks, such as umlauts and tildes, which can cause issues for the large Hispanic populations there as well as other cultures (think of names like José, Noël, Rosalía, or Siân). However, the US Constitution – specifically the First and Fourteenth Amendments – generally supports parents' rights to name their children whatever they like. Banned names include Nutella, F!nn, and Harry 3.

4 Trends, Twins, and Tips

Whether you're a fashionista or a homebody, everybody – and I do mean everybody – plays a role in creating baby name trends. Each of us impacts trends the moment we sign the birth registration form, and, even though you might have picked the most obscure or unique name you could think of, it can quickly become apparent that you weren't the only one . . .

Some of the trends we've spotted over the last year include nicknames-as-names, strong names, 100-year-rule names, nature names and x-rated names. Let's take a quick look at each one and see why they've become so popular.

Nicknames-as-Names

As a rule, most pop culture trends move west to east, with the American music and entertainment industries heavily influencing those of European and other Western countries. However, when it comes to baby names it's actually the Europeans who tend to lead the charge. This is no more apparent than when it comes to the trend for giving babies shortened versions of traditional names, or using nicknames as full names. The Brits, for example, have spent the last decade opting for names such as Theo over Theodore and Rosie over Rosemary, and the Americans and Aussies caught up with those trends about five years ago.

What's really fascinating about this trend is that it appears to be dependent on the age of the mother. Generally speaking, younger mothers are more likely to pick nicknames-as-names than older mothers, leaving older mothers to pick more traditional names. As an example, the most recent statistics to come out of the UK show that for mothers under the age of 25, half of the Top 10 names for boys were nicknames or shortened versions of traditional names. For comparison, for mothers over the age of 35, their list of Top 10 names for boys only included one nickname/shortened name. A similar pattern (although not quite as distinct) emerges in the baby girl lists as well, where more modern names appear frequently in the under-25s category and more classic names appear in the over-35s.

Confused? I hear you. Here's a breakdown:

UK baby names by age of mother

	Under 25	25 to 29	30 to 34	35 and Over
Top 10 Boy Names	Noah	Noah	George	George
	Archie	Oliver	Oliver	Oliver
	Leo	Muhammad	Noah	Jack
	Tommy	Arthur	Arthur	Muhammad
	Freddie	George	Jack	Noah
	Arthur	Freddie	Henry	Leo
	Theo	Harry	Leo	Alexander
	Elijah	Archie	Harry	Henry
	Muhammad	Leo	Oscar	Thomas
	Arlo	Oscar	Muhammad	William

	Under 25	25 to 29	30 to 34	35 and Over
Top 10 Girl Names	Amelia	Olivia	Olivia	Olivia
	Olivia	Amelia	Amelia	Isla
	Ava	Isla	Isla	Charlotte
	Isla	Ava	Ava	Emily
	Ivy	Ivy	Florence	Amelia
	Willow	Elsie	Lily	Sophia
	Isabella	Freya	Freya	Ava
	Harper	Rosie	Ivy	Sophie
	Delilah	Lily	Rosie	Grace
	Freya	Mia	Mia	Florence

100-Year Rule

If you've ever picked up a baby name book in the past, you'll have heard of this trend before. Essentially, the 100-year rule refers to the idea that names that popular a century ago will fall out of fashion and then come back around a hundred years later. The reason for this is pretty simple: the original generation to have these names are passing on, so they're not heard as frequently anymore. This means that parents searching for unique or uncommon names are more likely to rediscover ones from their grandparents' and great-grandparents' generations, pushing them back into style. So, if you're seeking inspiration in 2024, look back and see what parents were picking in 1924! You'd be surprised how modern some of these older names seem now.

The flip side of this trend is of course that mid-cycle names are seen as deeply, deeply unpopular and even – dare I say – embarrassing? Older millennials will be horrified to learn that mid-cycle is now 1974, which frankly seems unreasonable as it means my own birth year is inching ever closer to being considered 'mid-cycle', but here we are. Popular names in 1974 include Jason, Brian, Simon, Joanne, Lisa and Karen.

Karen was the 10th most popular name for baby girls in the UK in 1974, but only 7 kiddos were given it last year, and, while Lisa appears in the Top 10 for both the UK and the USA, it's now slid way way waay down to position 1,029 in the States and 755 in the UK. Shoutout to all my high school mates called Lisa – sorry you're not cool anymore.

	1924 Top 10 (UK)	1924 Top 10 (USA)	1974 Top 10 (UK)	1974 Top 10 (USA)
Boys	John	Robert	Paul	Michael
	William	John	Mark	Jason
	George	William	David	Christopher
	James	James	Andrew	David
	Thomas	Charles	Richard	James
	Ronald	George	Christopher	John
	Kenneth	Joseph	James	Robert
	Robert	Richard	Simon	Brian
	Arthur	Edward	Michael	Matthew
	Frederick	Donald	Matthew	William
Girls	Margaret	Mary	Saah	Jennifer
	Mary	Dorothy	Claire	Amy
	Joan	Helen	Nicola	Michelle
	Joyce	Betty	Emma	Heather
	Dorothy	Margaret	Lisa	Anglea
	Kathleen	Ruth	Joanne	Kimberly
	Doris	Virginia	Michelle	Melissa
	Irene	Mildred	Helen	Lisa
	Elizabeth	Doris	Samantha	Stephanie
	Eileen	Frances	Karen	Rebecca

Strong Names

One trend I am enjoying at the moment is the emphasis on names tha mean strength or tenacity. A lot of parents choose names that have special meaning to them, but I have a theory that this recent trend fo picking strong names has emerged out of the pandemic. The pandemic was a lonely and often frightening time for new families, who weren't guaranteed to have friends and family close by when welcoming their little ones into the world. It makes sense, then, that parents over the last few years would give their kids names that provide hope, inspiration and strength. Here are some names on the up and up from last year's lists, as well as some other more traditional choices that mean strong:

	UK Newcomers	USA Newcomers	Traditional Choices
Girls	Blaze	Epic	Aila
	Destiny	King	Audrey
	Flourish	Kourage	Brianna
	Jet	Major	Bridget
	Mars	Myricle	Everette
	Onyx	Mystique	Gabriella
	Queen	Power	Matilda
	Royal	Rocket	Philomena
	Royalty	Titan	Valentina
Boys	Blade	Action	Aaron
	Excel	Axe	Angus
	Haze	Butch	Bernard
	Jet	Clever	Ethan
	Legacy	Destined	Everett
	Maximum	Fate	Griffin
	Rocket	God	Kwan
	Steele	Grit	Liam
	Talon	Life	Maximus
	Titan	Majestci	Oscar

Nature Names

Similarly to the strong names trend, names inspired by nature are on a bit of a roll. Is it that the pandemic helped us to appreciate the simpler things in life such as long walks and the smell of freshly-cut grass? Or that we can now satisfy our long-denied lust for travel once more? Whatever the cause, nature names are super trendy at the moment and likely to stay that way. See if your favourite appears on the lists below.

Boys	Girls	Neutral
Beckett	Clementine	Arden
Callum	Dahlia	Aspen
Caspian	Daphne	August
Finn	Ivy	Jay
Jonas	Laurel	Koko
Kai	Luna	Phoenix
Leo	Olive	River
Oliver	Violet	Robin
Ronan	Willow	Sage
Rowan	Wren	Sky

X-Rated Names

Okay, you got me: this category doesn't mean quite what you think it does. No, there aren't hordes of parents running around giving their children explicit names (which is definitely a good thing as this practice is banned in several countries and can result in fines or even jail time for parents), although this does sound like a hilarious episode of *Call the Midwife*. What we're actually talking about here are names that include the letter X, which have suddenly become massively popular all over the world. For boys this means names such as Alexander, Felix, Paxton and Xavier; and for girls it includes Alexandra, Lexie, Trixie and Xanthe. But there are so many more on the rise! Take a look at our favourite x-rated names below and see if one piques your interest:

Boys	Girls	Neutral
Alexander	Alexandra	Alex
Baxter	Beatrix	Axel/Axelle
Dexter	Dixie	Beaux
Felix	Lexie	Dax
Huxley	Margaux	Jax
Maddox	Maxine	Lex
Macmillan	Roxanne	Loxley
Paxton	Roxy	Max
Xander	Trixie	Nix/Nyx
Xavier	Xanthe	Phoenix

Multiples and More

Ah, multiples. One of those beautiful little gifts of nature and science that strikes a unique combination of simultaneous terror and infatuation into the heart of any parent. If you have discovered you are expecting multiples, congratulations! When it comes to baby names, naming multiples needn't be any different from naming one child – unless you want it to be. You could stick to the same process as everyone else by picking a unique name for each child. Or . . . you could be awesome.

Some parents do like to use a pattern, such as going down the alphabet (think Alastair, Benjamin, Christopher and David) or doing what the famous Phoenix acting clan did and give each child a name to do with nature: River, Rain, Leaf (now Joaquin), Liberty and Summer.

Celebrity twins

Alexander and Ella (George Clooney and Amal Clooney)
Boo and Walt (Chris Evans and Natasha Shishmanian)
Estere and Stella (Madonna)
Eva and Mateo (Cristiano Ronaldo and Georgina Rodriguez)
Nicholas and Lucy (Enrique Iglesias and Anna Kournikova)
Ottilie and Delilah (Clemmie Hooper and Simon Hooper)
Roman and Malachi (Ashley Graham and Justin Ervin)
Rumi and Sir (Beyoncé and Jay Z)
Saint Leo and Thunder (Usain Bolt and Kasi Bennett)
Shiloh and Luna (Kristen Wiig and Avi Rothman)
Zeppelin and Arrow (Jensen Ackles and Danneel Harris)
Zion and Zillion (Nick Cannon and Abby De La Rosa)

Others choose matching initials (Cash and Cainen; Stella and Sophia), or names that mean the same – such as Bernard and Brian, both of which mean strong; or Lucy and Helen, which both mean light. You could use two Roman deities, such as Jupiter and Juno; or monarchs of England, such as Elizabeth and Victoria, or Henry and Charles.

The possibilities for triplets go even further – think of the fun you could have! You could have a row of beautiful flowers for your triple threats, such as Daisy, Violet and Lily; or a collection of Shakespearean heroes such as Beatrice, Helena and Antonio. Be bold with a set of House of Stark kids from *Game of Thrones* (Brandon, Robb and Arya), or be fabulous with some baby girls from *Clueless* (Cher, Tai and Dionne) – as if!

> ## Twin names with matching meanings
> Bernard and Brian (strong)
> Daphne and Laura (laurel)
> Deborah and Melissa (bee)
> Dorcas and Tabitha (gazelle)
> Elijah and Joel (god)
> Eve and Zoe (life)
> Irene and Salome (peace)
> Lucius and Uri (light)
> Lucy and Helen (light)
> Sarah and Amira (princess)

Big families, big opportunities

The record for the highest number of babies born during a single birth was broken in 2021 when the first ever surviving nonuplets were announced! Halima Cissé and Kader Arby named their four boys and five girls as Mohammed, Bah, El Hadji, Oumar, Hawa, Adama, Fatouma, Oumou and Kadidia, and they joined big sister Souda. The babies were born at 30 weeks and have all turned into healthy (and probably very loud) toddlers.

The official Guinness World Record for the most siblings baptised with the same initial is held by the LeBlanc family from Canada, who had ten sons and six daughters all given names beginning with the letter E. However, unofficial challenger to this would be the notorious Duggar family from the USA, whose 19 children all have names starting with J: Joshua, Jana, John-David, Jill, Jessa, Jinger, Joseph, Josiah, Joy-Anna, Jedidiah, Jeremiah, Jason, James, Justin, Jackson, Johannah, Jennifer, Jordyn-Grace and Josie.

The UK's biggest family belongs to Sue and Noel Radford, who have 22 children. (Twenty-two!) While each child has their own unique name, there are a couple of themes going: all the girls have names ending in an -ie sound (Sophie, Millie, Katie, Ellie, Aimee, Tillie, Hallie, Phoebe, Bonnie and Heidie). The boys, however, have short punchy names: Chris, Jack, Daniel, Luke, James, Josh, Max, Oscar, Casper, Archie and Alfie. Meanwhile in Australia, the biggest family crown goes to the Bonell family. The names of Ray and Jeni Bonell's 16 children don't seem to have a running theme, but see if you can spot one even if I can't: Jesse, Brooke, Claire, Natalie, Karl, Samuel, Cameron, Sabrina, Tim, Brandon, Eve, Nate, Rachel, Eric, Damian and Katelyn.

Now, there are a few simple things to keep in mind when naming twins or multiples.

- Avoid using very long names. There's nothing worse than trying to yell at your children to come down for dinner using their full names, and it taking 20 minutes because you gave them all 11-letter first names and 8-letter middle names.
- Don't get too complicated. Stick with traditional spellings when possible, such as Cameron instead of Kamrynn and Riley instead of Rhyleigh (both real spellings for real children on last year's baby name charts . . . sigh).
- Remember individuality. Your babies are still individuals, even if they'll be spending their entire lives answering the question 'what's it like being a twin??' If you use names that sound so familiar you'll often mix them up, your children may express frustration as they get older and other people confuse them. Hell, I already do this with my singlet children, and throwing similar spellings on top of that sounds like a nightmare. Instead, keep those nearly identical names you love for middle names and use this opportunity to explore more individual first names to match your little ones' unique personalities.

Names for triplets

Aidan, Diana and Nadia (anagrams)
Amber, Jade and Ruby (jewels)
Amy, May and Mya (anagrams)
Atlas, Damon and Adonis (mythological)
Ava, Eva and Iva (similar)
Kaia, Keanu and Kailani (Hawaiian)
Daisy, Lily and Rose (flowers)
Ginger, Saffron and Rosemary (herbs)
Jay, Robin and Wren (birds)
Olive, Violet and Sage (colours)
River, Rain and Summer (nature)

Changing your mind

So, you've made up your mind and awarded your sweet-smelling new baby the best name you can possibly imagine. It took you hours of research and pondering, but you've done it. Perfect.

But what if . . . you suddenly realise that you actually hate that name after all? Or that the spelling you chose makes it look as though you've invented a new language?

It's okay – never fret. You're not alone. A survey by baby website Channelmum found that one in seven parents regrets at least one part of their child's name. A staggering twenty-eight per cent of respondents admitted to telling their child they regret the choice they went with, and more than one in ten said their child confessed that they hated their own name. Two of the most common reasons given were that the name suddenly became extremely popular, or that a celebrity chose the same one, and sadly nearly in one in five members said they had felt pressured into using the name by a relative or other person. Which just underscores my first and most important rule about naming your own baby: you HAVE to love it! (See page 24 for more on the rules.) Love it and you won't regret it; feel apathetic about it, and you'll almost certainly look back with remorse.

Anyway! If you later decide that you want to change details on a birth certificate there are procedures in place, depending on where you live, although this can be a time-consuming process. In fact, even if the name was copied down incorrectly and is now misspelled, the burden is on the parents to prove it wasn't intentional. Documents showing the correct spelling at the time of the birth must be produced – and those can be tricky to find.

If you've simply changed your mind about your baby's name, you only have about 12 months to act before it becomes an even bigger headache. Visit the website of your country's national records agency for instructions on what to do, and remember that it can only be done once. The original name will still appear on the new birth certificate, with the new name listed underneath.

> One family in the USA changed their daughter's name when she was three months old, from Ottilie to Margot. Their reason? Ottilie is a German name, and when it's pronounced in Europe it comes with hard T sounds (Ot-ti-lee). But due to the slacker T sounds of many regional accents in the USA, their poor daughter's name ended up sounding like Oddly . . . oddly enough.

In addition, in most of the world changing the surname of your baby is only possible in two cases: either if the spelling is incorrect or if the details of the parents are being changed (such as the inclusion of the father or the parents now being married). A fee is usually incurred if a new certificate is required.

If you are in any way unsure about the choice you're about to make, keep in mind how difficult it may be for you to change your child's birth certificate at a later stage. On the bright side, though, bear in mind that if something unexpected happens and you need to make the change, it will be possible.

Once the 32nd most popular name in the US, Alexa has dramatically fallen out of fashion since Amazon's introduction of its robot assistant. The name now languishes in position 442 in the US and 1,866 in the UK.

Part two

Boys' names
A–Z

Baby names vary widely in spelling and pronunciation. To simplify
things, this book usually lists each name only once: under the most
common initial and spelling. If a name has an alternative spelling
with a different initial, it may be listed under that letter also.

Boys' names

Aaron

Hebrew, meaning 'mountain of strength'. In the Bible, Aaron was the older brother of Moses and the first high priest of Israel.

Abasi

Egyptian Arabic, meaning 'male'; Swahili, meaning 'stern'.

Abdiel

Hebrew, meaning 'servant of God'. Also the name of an important seraph in Milton's *Paradise Lost*.

Abdul

Arabic, meaning 'servant'. Often followed by a suffix indicating who Abdul is the servant of (e.g. Abdul-Basit, 'servant of the creator').

Abdullah

(alt. Abd-Allah, Abdallah, Abdollah)
Arabic, meaning 'servant of God'.

Abdur Rahman

Arabic, meaning 'one who serves a merciful man'.

Abel

Hebrew, meaning 'breath' or 'breathing spirit'. Associated with the biblical son of Adam and Eve, who was killed by his brother Cain.

Abelard

German, meaning 'resolute'.

Aberforth

Gaelic, meaning 'mouth of the river Forth'. The name of Dumbledore's younger brother in J.K. Rowling's *Harry Potter* books.

Abhik

(alt. Abheek)
Sanskrit, meaning 'fearless'. Popular name for boys in India.

Abhishek

Sanskrit, meaning 'bath for a deity' or 'anointing'. Abhishek Bachchan is currently one of Bollywood's highest-paid and most popular actors.

A Baby Names 2024

Abner

Hebrew, meaning 'father of light'. Abner was the commander of Saul's army in the Bible.

Abraham
(alt. Abram; abbrev. Abe)

Hebrew, meaning 'father of the multitude'. Famous Abrahams include President Abraham Lincoln and Abraham Van Helsing – the vampire hunter and doctor in Bram Stoker's *Dracula*.

Absalom
(alt. Absalon)

Hebrew, meaning 'father/leader of peace'. The name of King David's favourite son in the Bible, and one of Chaucer's curly-haired characters in *The Canterbury Tales*.

Acacio

Greek, meaning 'thorny tree' or 'honourable'. Now widely used in Spain.

Ace

Latin, meaning 'unit'. Also used in English to mean 'number one' or 'the best'.

Achilles

Greek, mythological hero of the Trojan war, whose heel was his only weak spot.

Achim

Hebrew, meaning 'God will establish'; Polish, meaning 'the Lord exalts'. Also, in Germany, a shortened version of the name 'Joachim'.

Ackerley

Old English, meaning 'oak meadow'.

Adam
(alt. Adão (Portuguese))

Hebrew, meaning 'man' or 'Earth'. In the Bible the Creation story names Adam as the first man on Earth.

Addison

Old English, meaning 'son of Adam'. Also used as a female name in the USA.

Ade

Yoruba, meaning 'peak' or 'royal'; a common name in Nigeria.

Adelard

French or German, meaning 'brave' or 'noble'.

Adelbert
(alt. Adalberto)

Old German form of Albert. Popularity decreased in the 19th century, when Albert became more commonly used.

Adetokunbo

Yoruba, meaning 'the crown came from over the sea'.

Adin

Hebrew, meaning 'slender' or 'voluptuous'. Also Swahili, meaning 'ornamental'.

Aditya

Sanskrit, meaning 'belonging to the sun'. In Hindi, Aditya means 'sun god'. Aditya refers to the offspring of Aditi, the mother of the Gods.

Adlai

Hebrew, meaning 'God is just', or sometimes 'ornamental'.

Adler

Old German, meaning 'eagle'.

Adley

English, meaning 'son of Adam'.

Admon

Hebrew, variant of Adam meaning 'Earth'. Also the name of a red peony.

Adolph
(alt. Adolf)

Old German, meaning 'noble majestic wolf'. Once popular before World War II, this name has now become deeply unpopular due to its association with Adolf Hitler, and several European nations have actually banned its use.

Adonis

Phoenician, meaning 'Lord'. Adonis was the god of beauty and desire in Greek mythology.

Adrian

Latin, meaning 'from Hadria', a town in northern Italy.

Adriel

Hebrew, meaning 'of God's flock'. Adriel was one of Saul's sons-in-law in the Bible.

Adyn
(alt. Ade)

Irish, meaning 'manly'. Also the name of a UK men's streetwear company.

Aeneas

Greek/Latin, meaning 'to praise'. Name of the hero who founded Rome in Virgil's *Aeneid*.

Aero

Greek, meaning 'air'.

Aeson
(alt. Aesion)

Greek, father of Jason in ancient Greek mythology.

Afonso

Portuguese, meaning 'eager noble warrior'.

Agamemnon

Greek, meaning 'leader of the assembly'. Figure in mythology, commanded the Greeks at the siege of Troy.

Agathon

Greek, meaning 'good' or 'superior'. The name of a tragic poet in ancient Greece.

Agustin

Latin/Spanish, meaning 'venerated'.

Ahab

Hebrew, meaning 'father's brother'. Name of the obsessed captain in *Moby-Dick*.

Ahijah

Hebrew, meaning 'brother of God' or 'friend of God'.

Ahmad
(alt. Ahmed)
Arabic/Turkish, meaning 'worthy of praise'. Ahmad is also one of the prophet Muhammad's many given names.

Aidan
(alt. Aiden, Aodhán)
Gaelic, meaning 'little fire'. Derives from Aodh, which is the name of a Celtic sun god.

Aidric
Old English, meaning 'oaken'. St Aidric was a bishop and court diplomat in the ninth century.

Ainsley
Old English, meaning 'meadow' or 'clearing'. Also a girls' name. Ainsley Harriott is a well-known TV chef.

Airyck
Old Norse, from Eric, meaning 'eternal ruler'.

Ajani
Swahili, meaning 'he fights for what he is'; Sanskrit, meaning 'of noble birth'.

Ajax
Greek, meaning 'mourner of the Earth'. A Greek hero from the siege of Troy.

Ajay
Hindi, meaning 'unconquerable'. One of the most popular names in India.

Ajit
Sanskrit, meaning 'invincible'. Alternative name for both Shiva and Vishnu in Hindu mythology.

Akeem
Arabic, meaning 'wise or insightful'. Popular name throughout Africa, particularly in Nigeria.

Akio
Japanese, meaning 'bright man'. Akio Morita was one of the co-founders of the electronics company Sony.

Akira
Japanese, meaning 'intelligent'. Name of a hugely influential animated Japanese film.

Akiva
Hebrew, meaning 'to protect' or 'to shelter'.

Akon
American, meaning 'flower'. Made popular by the rapper.

Aladdin
Arabic, meaning 'servant of Allah'. From the medieval story in *1001 Arabian Nights*.

Alan
(alt. Allan, Allen, Allyn, Alun)
Gaelic or old French, meaning 'rock'. Alan is one of the oldest names still in popular use in the UK, and its roots can be traced back to the Norman invasion in the 11th century.

Alaric
(alt. Aleric)

Old German, meaning 'noble regal ruler'. King Alaric I of the Visigoths played a key role in the downfall of the Roman Empire.

Alastair
(alt. Alasdair, Alastor, Alistair, Allister; abbrev. Ali, Allie)

Greek/Gaelic, meaning 'defending men'. Famous Alastairs include comedian and TV presenter Alistair McGowan, English cricketer Alastair Cook and Ali G, whose 'real name' is Alistair.

Alban

Latin, meaning 'from Alba'. Also the name of St Alban, the first British Christian martyr.

Alberic

Germanic, meaning 'Elfin king'.

Albert
(abbrev. Albie, Bert, Bertie)

Old German, meaning 'noble, bright, famous'. Probably most commonly associated with Prince Albert, Queen Victoria's husband, who died in 1861.

Albin

Latin, variant of Albus, meaning 'white'. Popular in some areas including Scandinavia, Slovenia, Germany and Poland.

Less common three-syllable names

Alastair	Elijah
Barnaby	Lancelot
Dominic	Roberto
Dorian	Theodore

Albus ·

Latin, meaning 'white'. Made famous by Albus Dumbledore, the headmaster of Hogwarts in J.K. Rowling's *Harry Potter* books.

Alcaeus

Greek, meaning 'strength'. Alcaeus of Mytilene was an influential ancient Greek poet.

Alden

Old English, meaning 'old friend'. More commonly used as a given name in the USA.

Aldis

English, meaning 'battle-seasoned'.

Aldo
(alt. Aldous)

Latin, meaning 'the tall one'. Aldo is the main gorilla character in the *Planet of the Apes* movie series.

Aldric

English, meaning 'old king'.

Aled

Welsh, meaning 'child' or 'offspring'. Aled Jones is a Welsh singer and TV presenter, who shot to fame as a choirboy with *Walking in the Air*.

Aleph
(*alt. Alef*)

Hebrew, meaning 'first letter of the alphabet', or 'leader'.

Aleron
(*alt. Aileron, Alerun, Ailerun, Alejandro*)

Latin, meaning 'child with wings'.

Alessio
(*alt. Alejo*)

Italian, meaning 'defender'.

Alexander
(*alt. Alexandro, Alessandro, Alejandro; abbrev. Alec, Alex, Alexei, Sandy, Xander*)

Greek, meaning 'defender of mankind'. Alexander the Great was an undefeated fourth-century king whose empire stretched from Greece to modern Pakistan.

Alfonso
(*alt. Alonso, Alonzo*)

Germanic/Spanish, meaning 'noble and prompt, ready to struggle'. Associated with *Gravity* director Alfonso Cuarón Orozco, and actor Alfonso Ribeiro.

Alford

Old English, meaning 'old river/ford'.

Alfred
(*abbrev. Alf, Alfie*)

English, meaning 'elf' or 'magical counsel'. Alfred the Great was a ninth-century king of England who defended the Anglo-Saxons against Viking invasion. *Alfie* is the name of a successful 1966 film starring Michael Caine.

Algernon

French, meaning 'with a moustache'. A popular name among the nobility in 18th- and 19th-century England.

Alois

German, meaning 'famous warrior'.

Alok

Sanskrit, meaning 'cry of triumph'. Also the name of a style of singing in Javanese gamelan.

Alon

Hebrew, meaning 'oak tree'.

Aloysius

Old German, meaning 'fame and war'. Also the name of an Italian saint.

Alpha

First letter of the Greek alphabet.

Alphaeus

Hebrew, meaning 'changing'. Alphaeus is mentioned in the Bible as being the father of two of the twelve Apostles, Matthew and James.

Alpin

Gaelic, meaning 'related to the Alps'. The House of Alpin refers to a dynasty of Scottish kings.

Altair

Arabic, meaning 'flying' or 'bird'. Altair is one of the brightest stars seen in the night sky from Earth.

Alter
(alt. Altar)

Yiddish, meaning 'old man'.

Alton

Old English, meaning 'old town'.

Alva

Latin, meaning 'white'. Used more commonly for girls than boys.

Alvin
(alt. Alvie)

English, meaning 'friend of elves'. Alvin and the Chipmunks are a cartoon singing group, first created in 1958 and still featuring in films today.

Alwyn

Welsh, meaning 'wise friend'. May also come from the River Alwen in Wales.

Amachi

Swahili, meaning 'who knows what God has brought us through this child'.

Amadeus

Latin, meaning 'God's love'. One of the given names of the composer Wolfgang Amadeus Mozart.

Amadi

Igbo, meaning 'appeared destined to die at birth'. Often given to babies who unexpectedly survive against the odds.

Amado

Spanish, meaning 'God's love'.

Amador

Spanish, meaning 'one who loves'.

Amari

Hebrew, meaning 'given by God'. Can be a boys' or girls' name.

Amarion

Arabic, meaning 'populous, flushing'.

Amasa

Hebrew, meaning 'burden'.

Ambrose

Greek, meaning 'undying, immortal'.

Americo

Germanic, meaning 'ever powerful in battle'. Popular in the 19th century, this is now an infrequently used baby name.

Amias
(alt. Amyas)

Latin, meaning 'loved'.

Amil

Sanskrit, meaning 'unavailable'. Popular name for boys in India.

Amir
(alt. Emir)

Arabic, meaning 'chieftain' or 'commander'. Emir or Amir is a title for a high-ranking sheikh, used in many Muslim communities.

Amit

Hindi, meaning 'infinite'. One of the 108 names for the Hindu God Shri Ganesha.

Ammon

Hebrew, meaning 'the hidden one'. The Ammonites were an ancient tribe of people mentioned in the Bible.

Amory

German/English, meaning 'work' and 'power'. Its popularity has waned since the 19th century, when it was a common name.

Amos

Hebrew, meaning 'encumbered' or 'burdened'. St Amos wrote the Book of Amos in the eighth century, which is part of the Hebrew Bible.

Anacletus

Latin, meaning 'called back' or 'invoked'. Pope Anacletus was the third pope in history, and served during the first century.

Anakin

American, meaning 'warrior'. Made famous by Anakin Skywalker in the *Star Wars* films.

Ananias

Greek/Italian, meaning 'answered by the Lord'. Ananias Dare was the first baby born to English parents in North America, making him the first-ever 'modern' American.

Anastasius
(alt. Anastasios)

Greek, meaning 'resurrection'. Popular name for popes, emperors, and saints – there are nearly 20 St Anastasiuses on record.

Anatole
(alt. Anatolius)

French, meaning 'sunrise'. Monsieur Anatole was an influential 19th-century French composer, ballet dancer and ballet master.

Anders

Scandinavian, meaning 'lion man'. A popular name for boys in Sweden.

Anderson

English, meaning 'male'.

Andrew
(alt. Andreas)

Greek, meaning 'man' or 'warrior'. One of the Top 10 names for baby boys during the 1980s and '90s.

Androcles

Greek, meaning 'glory of a warrior'. *Androcles and the Lion* was a well-known folktale of the second century, made famous in the 20th century by George Bernard Shaw's play of the same title.

Angel
(alt. Angelo)

Greek, meaning 'messenger'. Angels appear throughout the Bible and modern culture, and the name Angel is often used in Spanish-speaking cultures as a name for both boys and girls.

Angus

Gaelic, meaning 'one choice'. An ancient name especially popular in Scotland.

Anil

Sanskrit, meaning 'air' or 'wind'. Anil Gupta is the producer (and for some the creator) of many leading television comedies, including *Goodness Gracious Me*, *The Kumars at No. 42* and *The Office*.

Anselm

German, meaning 'helmet of God'. St Anselm was an archbishop of Canterbury and influential figure in the Christian religion.

Anson

English, meaning 'son of Agnes'. Most commonly used in the USA.

Anthony
(alt. Antony; abbrev. Ant, Tony)

English, meaning 'invaluable grace'. *Antony and Cleopatra* is a Shakespearean play depicting the romance between the Roman general Mark Antony and Queen Cleopatra of Egypt.

Antipas

Latin, meaning 'for all or against all'. Herod Antipas was the leader mentioned in the Bible as being responsible for the executions of John the Baptist and Jesus.

Antwan
(alt. Antoine)

Old English, meaning 'flower'. Older and more unusual spelling of Antoine.

Apollo

Greek, meaning 'to destroy'. Greek god of poetry, music and the sun.

Apostolos

Greek, meaning 'apostle'. The Apostolos book is a text believed to have been written by one of the twelve disciples of Jesus.

Ara

Arabic, meaning 'brings rain'.

Aragorn

Literary, a character in J.R.R. Tolkien's *The Lord of the Rings* trilogy.

Aram

Hebrew, meaning 'royal highness'. Aram is an ancient region in modern-day Syria, mentioned in the Bible.

Aramis

Latin, meaning 'swordsman'. Aramis is one of the three musketeers in Alexandre Dumas's eponymous novel.

Arcadio

Greek/Spanish, from a place in ancient Greece. The word 'Arcadia' (meaning paradise) comes from this.

Archibald
(abbrev. Archie)

Old German, meaning 'genuine, bold, brave'. A popular name in Scotland. Archie is the son of Prince Harry and Meghan Markle.

Ardell

Latin, meaning 'eager, burning with enthusiasm'.

Arden

Celtic, meaning 'high'. A very early English motor car.

Ares

Greek, meaning 'ruin'. Son of Zeus and Hera, and the Greek god of war.

Ari

Hebrew, meaning 'lion' or 'eagle'. Can also be used in Hebrew to refer to an important or honourable man.

Arias

Germanic, meaning 'lion'.

Aric

English, meaning 'merciful ruler'. Alternative spelling of Eric.

Ariel

Hebrew, meaning 'lion of God'. One of the archangels, the angel of healing and new beginnings.

Arild

Old Norse, meaning 'battle commander'. Arild Andersen is an internationally popular Norwegian jazz musician.

Aris

Greek, meaning 'best figure'. Popular name in both ancient and modern Greece.

Ariston

Greek, meaning 'the best'. Ariston of Athens was the philosopher Plato's father.

Aristotle

Greek, meaning 'best'. Also an ancient Greek philosopher.

Arjun

Sanskrit, meaning 'bright and shining'. Name is derived from Arjuna, an ancient and legendary archer.

Arkady

Greek, a region of central Greece. Popular name for boys throughout Eastern Europe.

Arlan

Gaelic, meaning 'pledge' or 'oath'.

Arlie

Old English place name, meaning 'eagle wood'. Sometimes used as a shortened form of Arlan.

Arliss
(alt. Arlis)

Hebrew, meaning 'pledge'.

Arlo

Spanish, meaning 'barberry tree'. Can also be linked back to the Old Norse word for 'army of troops'.

Armand
(alt. Armani)

Old German, meaning 'soldier'. Armand van Helden is a top American DJ and producer of electronic house music. Armani is the name of an Italian fashion house after designer Georgio Armani.

Arnaldo

Spanish, meaning 'eagle power'.

Arnav

Hindi, meaning 'the sea'. Can be pronounced as 'Arnav' or 'Arnaf'.

Arnold
(abbrev. Arnie)

Old German, meaning 'eagle ruler'. Also the name of actor, former bodybuilder and US politician Arnold Schwarzenegger.

Arrow

English, from the common word denoting weaponry.

Art

Irish, name of a warrior in Irish mythology, Art Oenfer (Art the Lonely). Also a shortened form of Arthur.

Arthur
(alt. Art, Arte, Artie, Artis)

Celtic, probably from 'artos', meaning 'bear'. Made famous by the tales of King Arthur and the Knights of the Round Table.

Arvel

From the Welsh 'Arwel', meaning 'wept over'. Used in literature for mythical characters – for example, Arvel Crynyd in *Star Wars*, and Arvel the Swift in *The Elder Scrolls V: Skyrim*.

Arvid

Old Norse, meaning 'eagle in the woods'. Commonly used in Scandinavia.

Arvind
(alt. Aravind)

Sanskrit, meaning 'red lotus'. May also be derived from the word for 'white lotus', upon which the Hindu goddess Lakshmi sits.

Arvo

Finnish, meaning 'value' or 'worth'.

Asa

Hebrew, meaning 'doctor' or 'healer'.

Asante

Asante, meaning 'thank you'. Also refers to the language of the Ashanti people.

Asher

Hebrew, meaning 'fortunate' or 'lucky'. One of the 12 sons of Jacob in the Bible, and one of the brothers who sells Joseph into slavery in the story of Joseph and his multi-coloured coat.

Ashley

Old English, meaning 'ash meadow'. The name of several football players, including Ashley Cole and Ashley Young.

Ashok

Sanskrit, meaning 'not causing sorrow'. Popular in India and Sri Lanka.

Ashton

English, meaning 'settlement in the ash-tree grove'. Name has been popularised due to the American actor Ashton Kutcher.

Aslan

Turkish, meaning 'lion'. Strongly associated with the lion Aslan in C.S. Lewis's *The Lion, the Witch and the Wardrobe*.

Asriel

Hebrew, meaning 'help of God'. Lord Asriel is an important character in Philip Pullman's *His Dark Materials* trilogy.

Astrophel

Latin, meaning 'star lover'. *Astrophel and Stella* is the name of a group of sonnets by Philip Sidney, written in the 1590s, and the first time the name is recorded as being used.

Athanasios
(abbrev. Thanasis, Thanos)

Greek, meaning 'eternal life'.

Atílio

Portuguese, meaning 'father'. Can also be lengthened to Attilius.

Atlas

Greek, meaning 'to carry'. In Greek mythology Atlas was a Titan forced to carry the weight of the heavens.

Atlee

Hebrew, meaning 'God is just'.

Atticus

Latin, meaning 'from Athens'. Atticus Finch is one of the main characters in Harper Lee's influential novels *To Kill A Mockingbird* and *Go Set a Watchman*.

Auberon

Old German, meaning 'royal bear'. Also the name for a fairy king. It is the French spelling for Oberon.

Aubrey

French, meaning 'elf ruler'. Popular for boys during the Middle Ages; now more usually given to girls.

Auden

Old English, meaning 'old friend'. W.H. Auden is considered one of the most influential 20th-century poets.

Audie

Old English, meaning 'noble strength'. Audie L. Murphy was one of the most decorated and honoured American soldiers of World War II.

Augustus
(alt. Augastas)

Latin, meaning 'venerated'. The first Roman emperor. Also a character in Roald Dahl's *Charlie and the Chocolate Factory*.

Aurelien

French, meaning 'golden'. Also the name of a Roman emperor.

Austin

Latin, meaning 'venerated'. Austin Healey played rugby union for England. Also the name of a classic car.

Avery

(alt. Avrie, Averey, Averie)

English, meaning 'wise ruler'. Can also be derived from the name Alfred, or the ancient English word for elf.

Avi

Hebrew, meaning 'father of a multitude of nations'. Name of an author of popular children's and teens' fiction.

Awnan

Irish, meaning 'little Adam'.

Axel

(alt. Aksel, Axl)

German and Scandinavian, a form of the Hebrew Absalom, meaning 'father of peace'. Its name day is 23 March, and babies with this name are sometimes celebrated in Nordic countries on this day. Made famous by Guns 'n' Roses front man Axl Rose.

Ayers

(alt. Ayer, Aires, Aire)

English, meaning 'heir to a fortune'.

Azarel

(alt. Azaryah)

Hebrew, meaning 'helped by God'. Also the name of an evil spirit in the Bible.

Azriel

Hebrew, meaning 'God is my help'. Name is often used to describe the angel of death in many religions, including Christianity and Judaism.

Azuko

Igbo, meaning 'past glory'. Most commonly found in Japan.

B Boys' names

Baden

German, meaning 'battle'. Also the name of a city in Switzerland known for its hot springs.

Bailey

English, meaning 'bailiff'.

Baird

Scottish, meaning 'poet' or 'one who sings ballads'. John Logie Baird was a Scottish engineer credited with inventing the world's first working television.

Bakari

Swahili, meaning 'hope' or 'promise'.

Baker

English, from the word 'baker'.

Baldwin

Old French, meaning 'bold, brave friend'. The Baldwin family is a well-known acting dynasty in Hollywood, with brothers Alec, Stephen, William, and Daniel.

Balin

Old English. Balin was one of the Knights of the Round Table.

Balthazar

Babylonian, meaning 'protect the King'. A name commonly attributed to one of the Three Wise Men in the Christian Nativity story.

Balwinder
(alt. Balvinder)

Hindi, meaning 'merciful, compassionate'. Balwinder Singh Sandhu is a well-known former Indian Test cricketer.

Bannon

Irish, meaning 'descendant of O'Banain'. Also a river in Wales.

Barack

Contraction of the Swahili name Baruch and the Hebrew name Mubarak. Made popular by the 44th US President, Barack Obama.

Barclay

Old English, meaning 'birch tree meadow'.

Barker

Old English, meaning 'shepherd'.

Barnaby
(abbrev. Barney)

Greek, meaning 'son of consolation'. *Barnaby Rudge* is a novel by Charles Dickens.

Barnard

English, meaning 'strong as a bear'.

Baron
(alt.. Barron)

Old English, meaning 'young warrior'. Baron is a title given to men of nobility.

Barrett

English, meaning 'strong as a bear'.

Barry
(abbrev. Baz)

Irish Gaelic, meaning 'fair haired'. Famous Barrys include Barry Humphries, best known as the comedian behind Dame Edna Everage. Also Baz Luhrmann, the Australian film director.

Bartholomew
(abbrev. Bart)

Hebrew, meaning 'son of the farmer'. The name of one of Jesus' apostles. Bart is the name of the eldest child of the cartoon family the Simpsons.

Barton

Old English, meaning 'barley settlement'. One of the more popular names of towns in England, with at least 25 on record.

Baruch

Hebrew, meaning 'blessed'. Also a term for a Jewish blessing.

Barzillai

Hebrew, meaning 'made of iron'. Found in the Bible, Barzillai supposedly teaches youngsters not to be afraid of old age.

Bashir

Arabic, meaning 'well educated' and 'wise'.

Basil

Greek, meaning 'royal, kingly'. Basil is the lead character in the TV comedy *Fawlty Towers*. Also the name of a herb.

Basim

Arabic, meaning 'smile'.

Bastien

Greek, meaning 'revered'. Bastien Pagez was one of the most important servants to Mary, Queen of Scots.

Baxter

Old English, meaning 'baker'.

Bay

From the bay tree or the indentation in the coastline. Also a girls' name.

Bayard

French, meaning 'auburn haired'. Bayard Rustin was one of Martin Luther King Jr's mentors and advisors during the American Civil Rights movement.

Bayo
(alt. Baio)

Swahili, meaning 'to find joy'.

Bayre

American, meaning 'beautiful'.

Beau

French, meaning 'handsome'. Beau Bridges is an American actor. Beau Brummell was a fashionable figure in Regency England and friend of the future King George IV. Beau was not the given name of either man, but an adopted name.

Beck

Old Norse, meaning 'stream'.

Beckett

Old English, meaning 'beehive' or 'bee cottage'. Associated with the Irish writer Samuel Beckett.

Beckham

English, meaning 'homestead by the stream'. Made famous by David and Victoria Beckham.

Béla

Hungarian, meaning 'within'. Famously associated with the actor Bela Lugosi.

Belarius

Shakespearean, meaning 'a banished lord'. From Shakespeare's play *Cymbeline*.

Benedict
(abbrev. Ben)

Latin, meaning 'blessed'. Benedict Cumberbatch is a succsssful actor and the star of the TV series *Sherlock*. Ben Ainslie is the most successful Olympic sailor ever.

Benicio

Spanish, meaning 'benevolent'. Benicio del Toro is an Oscar-winning actor from Puerto Rico.

Benjamin
(abbrev. Ben, Benjie, Bennie, Benny)

Hebrew, meaning 'son of the south'. Benjamin Franklin, American inventor and discoverer of electricity was one of the Founding Fathers of the United States. Ben Affleck, actor, and Ben Fogle, adventurer and TV personality, are both Benjamins.

Bennett

French/Latin vernacular form of Benedict, meaning 'blessed'.

Benoit

French form of Benedict, meaning 'blessed'.

Benson

English, meaning 'son of Ben'. Also linked to the village of Benson in Oxfordshire.

Bentley

Old English, meaning 'bent grass meadow'. Usually associated with the British luxury car company.

Benton

Old English, meaning 'town in the bent grass'. Derived from the towns of Long Benton and Little Benton in Northumberland.

Beriah

Hebrew, meaning 'in fellowship' or 'in envy'. Beriah was a son of Asher in the Bible.

Bernard

(abbrev. Bernie)

Germanic, meaning 'strong, brave bear'.

Berry

Old English, meaning 'berry'.

Berton

Old English, meaning 'bright settlement'. Guitartist Berton Averre was part of the band The Knack, known for its hit 'My Sharona'.

Bertrand

(alt. Bertram; abbrev. Bert, Bertie)

Old English, meaning 'illustrious'. Bertrand Russell was a British philosopher and social critic. Bertram (Bertie) Wooster was one of P.G. Wodehouse's most beloved characters.

Bevan

Welsh, meaning 'son of Evan'.

Bilal

Arabic, meaning 'wetting, refreshing'. Popular in many Muslim communities.

Bill

(alt. Billy)

English, from William, meaning 'strong protector'.

Birch

Old English, meaning 'bright' or 'shining'. Also a type of tree.

Birger

Norwegian, meaning 'rescue'.

Bishop

Old English, meaning 'bishop'.

Bjorn

Old Norse, meaning 'bear'. Bjorn Ulvaeus was one of the founding members of Swedish pop supergroup ABBA, and is still a prolific songwriter with partner Benny Andersson.

Blaine

Irish Gaelic, meaning 'yellow'.

Blair

Scottish Gaelic, meaning 'plain'. Can be used as a boys' or a girls' name.

Blaise

French, meaning 'lisp' or 'stutter'. St Blaise was an Armenian bishop who was beaten and beheaded for his faith. Also commonly used as a girls' name.

Blake

Old English, meaning 'dark, black'.

Blas
(alt. Blaze)

German, meaning 'firebrand'. Also a mountain in the Alps.

Bo

Scandinavian, short form of Robert, meaning 'bright fame'. Rock and roll pioneer and musician Ellas Otha Bates was known by his stage name Bo Diddly.

Boaz

Hebrew, meaning 'swiftness' or 'strength'. Found in the Bible, in the Book of Ruth.

Bob
(alt. Bobby)

Old German, from Robert, meaning 'bright fame'.

Boden
(alt. Bodie)

Scandinavian, meaning 'shelter'. In some translations Boden also means 'messenger'.

Bogumil

Slavic, meaning 'God's favour'. Usually associated with Bogomil Cove in the Shetland Islands.

Bolívar

Spanish, meaning 'the bank of the river'. Simón Bolívar was a leader in Latin America's struggle for independence from Spain. The bolívar is the currency of Venezuela.

Bond

Old English, meaning 'peasant farmer'. Usually associated with novel and film character James Bond.

Boris

Slavic, meaning 'battle glory'. Boris Johnson is a politican and former Mayor of London.

Bosten

English, meaning 'town by the woods'.

Botolf

English, meaning 'wolf'. St Botwulf of Thorney is the patron saint of travellers and farming.

Bowen

Welsh, meaning 'son of Owen'. The Bowen knot is a common heraldic symbol, and looks like a square with loops at each corner.

Bowie

Gaelic, meaning 'long double-edged sword'.

Boyd

Scottish Gaelic, meaning 'yellow'. Famous Boyds include English historian Boyd Hilton, designer and star of *American Hot Rod* Boyd Coddington and cricketer Boyd Rankin.

Bradley
(abbrev. Brad)

Old English, meaning 'broad' or 'wide'. Brad Pitt is one of America's most famous modern actors. Cyclist

Sir Bradley Wiggins is the winner of multiple Olympic medals and the Tour de France.

Brady

Irish, meaning 'large-chested'.

Bradyn

(alt. Braden, Brayden)

Gaelic, meaning 'descendant of Bradan'.

Bram

Gaelic, meaning 'raven'.

Brandon

(alt. Bran)

Old English, meaning 'gorse'. Brandon Stark is a character in the TV series Game of Thrones.

Brandt

(alt. Brant)

Old English, meaning 'beacon'.

Brannon

Gaelic, meaning 'raven'. Brannon Braga is a TV producer.

Branson

English, meaning 'son of Brand'. Sir Richard Branson is an entrepreneur and adventurer, the founder of the Virgin Group of companies.

Braulio

Spanish, meaning 'shining'.

Brendan

Gaelic, meaning 'prince'. Actor Brendan Fraser is known for his role in The Mummy film series.

Brennan

Gaelic, meaning 'teardrop'. The Brennan family are Ireland's most successful musical family, selling over 100 million records worldwide.

Brenton

English, from Brent, meaning 'hill'. Actor Brenton Thwaites is known for his role in soap opera Home and Away.

Brett

English, meaning 'a brewer'. Singer Brett Michaels is the lead singer of rock group Poison.

Brewster

(alt. Brew, Brewer)

English, meaning 'a brewer'.

Brian

(alt. Bryan, Bryant)

Gaelic, meaning 'high' or 'noble'. Famous Brians include physicist and TV star Professor Brian Cox, actor Brian Blessed and Queen guitar legend Brian May.

Brice

(alt. Bryce)

Latin, meaning 'speckled'.

Brier

French, meaning 'heather'.

Brock

Old English dialect, meaning 'badger'.

Broderick

English, meaning 'ruler'.

Brody

Gaelic, meaning both 'ditch' and 'brother'. It can be used for girls but more commonly for boys.

Brogan

Irish, meaning 'sturdy shoe'. A very old name, being mentioned in texts from the ninth century.

Bronwyn

Welsh, meaning 'white breasted'. More commonly used as a girls' name.

Brook

English, meaning 'stream'.

Brooklyn

From the name of the New York borough. Commonly associated with David and Victoria Beckham's eldest child.

Bruce

Scottish, meaning 'high' or 'noble'. Television presenter the late Sir Bruce Forsyth holds the Guinness World Record for the longest television career for a male entertainer.

Bruno

Germanic, meaning 'brown'. Bruno Tonioli is a judge on *Strictly Come Dancing*, and its American counterpart *Dancing With The Stars*.

Brutus

Latin, meaning 'dim-wit'. The name of Julius Caesar's assassin.

Bryant

English variant of Brian, meaning 'high' or 'noble'.

Bryden
(alt. Brydon)

Irish, meaning 'strong one'.

Bryn

Welsh, meaning 'mount' or 'hill'.

Bryson
(alt. Bryce, Brycen)

Welsh, meaning 'descendant of Brice'.

Bubba

American, meaning 'boy'. Associated with the character Bubba in *Forrest Gump*.

Buck

American, meaning 'goat' or 'deer', specifically a male deer.

Buddy
(abbrev. Bud)

American, meaning 'friend'.

Burdett

Middle English, meaning 'bird'.

Burgess
(alt. Burges, Burgiss, Berje)

English, meaning 'business'.

Burke

French, meaning 'fortified settlement'.

Burl

French, meaning 'knotty wood'.

Buzz

American, shortened form of Busby, meaning 'village in the thicket'. The US astronaut Buzz Aldrin was the second person to set foot on the moon.

Byron

Old English, meaning 'barn'. Made famous by the poet Lord Byron.

C

Boys' names

Cabot
Old English, meaning 'to sail'.

Cadby
(alt. Cadbey, Cadbee, Cadbie)
English, meaning 'soldiers' colony'.

Cade
(alt. Caben, Caden)
English, meaning 'round, lumpy'. A character in the novel Gone With The Wind.

Cadence
Latin, meaning 'with rhythm'. Can be used as a girls' or a boys' name.

Cadogan
Welsh, meaning 'battle glory and honour'. Sir Cadogan is a knight who constantly challenged Gryffindors to duels in J.K. Rowling's Harry Potter books.

Caedmon
Celtic, meaning 'wise warrior'. An early English poet.

Caelan
Gaelic, meaning 'slender'.

Caerwyn
(alt. Carwyn, Gerwyn)
Welsh, meaning 'white fort' or 'settlement'. Carwyn Jones is a former First Minister of Wales.

Caesar
Disputed origin. The Roman military leader and dictator Gaius Julius Caesar favoured the Moorish meaning 'elephant'.

Caetano
Portuguese, meaning 'from Gaeta, Italy'.

Cagney
Irish, meaning 'successor of the advocate'.

Caiden
Arabic, meaning 'companion'. A variant of the name Caden.

Caillou

French, meaning 'pebble'. Name of the main character in a Canadian children's cartoon.

Cain

Hebrew, meaning 'full of beauty'. Brother of Abel in the biblical Book of Genesis.

Cainan

Hebrew, meaning 'possessor' or 'purchaser'.

Cairo

Egypt's capital city. Located near Giza, home of the great pyramids.

Calder

Scottish, meaning 'rough waters'.

Caleb
(alt. Calen; abbrev. Cal)

Hebrew, meaning 'dog'. Caleb was one of 12 spies sent by Moses into Caanan.

Calhoun

Irish, meaning 'slight woods'.

Calix

Greek, meaning 'very handsome'.

Callahan

Irish, meaning 'contention' or 'strife'.

Callum
(alt. Calum)

Gaelic, meaning 'dove'. Often associated with St Columba, one of the Twelve Apostles of Ireland. The name has become popular outside of Scotland and Ireland in recent years.

Calvin
(alt. Kalvin)

French, meaning 'little bald one'. Name of popular fashion designer Calvin Klein.

Camden

Gaelic, meaning 'winding valley'. Also an area of north London.

Cameron

Scottish Gaelic, meaning 'crooked nose'. Name of a Scottish Clan.

Camillo

Latin, meaning 'free born' or 'noble'. A popular Italian name.

Campbell

Scottish Gaelic, meaning 'crooked mouth'. Was first used as a nickname.

Canaan

Hebrew, meaning 'to be humbled'. A region in the Middle East that existed during biblical times.

Candido

Latin, meaning 'candid' or 'honest'. Candido Jacuzzi is the inventor of the jacuzzi tub.

Canon
(alt. Cannon)

French, meaning 'of the church'.

Canton

French, meaning 'dweller of corner'.

Canute
(alt. Cnut, Cnute)
Scandinavian, meaning 'knot'. Name of an 11th-century King of England.

Cappy
Italian, meaning 'lucky'. A nickname for someone with the rank of Captain.

Carden
Old English, meaning 'wool carder'. Carding is the process of combing raw wool fibres to remove tangles and impurities.

Carey
Gaelic, meaning 'love'. Becoming more popular as a girls' as well as a boys' name.

Carl
(alt. Carlo, Carlos)
Old Norse, variant of Charles, meaning 'free man'.

Carlton
Old English, meaning 'free peasant settlement'.

Carmelo
Latin, meaning 'garden' or 'orchard'. Its variant, Carmel, refers to Mount Carmel in Israel, which in biblical times was known for its fruitfulness.

Carmen
Latin/Spanish, meaning 'song'. Name of one of the most famous French operas. Used for both boys and girls.

Carmine
Latin, meaning 'song'. Also a bright red pigment.

Carnell
English, meaning 'defender of the castle'.

Carson
(alt. Carsten)
Scottish, meaning 'marsh-dwellers'.

Carter
Old English, meaning 'transporter of goods'.

Cary
Old Celtic river name. Also means 'love'. Cary Grant was a legendary romantic lead actor in films; Cary Elwes is a British actor.

Case
(alt. Casey)
Irish Gaelic, meaning 'alert' or 'watchful'.

Casimer
Slavic, meaning 'famous destroyer of peace'.

Casper
Persian, meaning 'treasurer'. The name of a friendly ghost in a comic book.

Caspian
English, meaning 'of the Caspy people'. From the Caspian Sea. A literary character from the C.S. Lewis book Prince Caspian.

Cassidy

Irish, meaning 'clever' or 'curly haired'. Originated from the surname, Caiside.

Cassius

(alt. Cassio, Cason, Cash)

Latin, meaning 'empty, hollow'. A name popular during the Roman era. Cassius Clay was the original name of legendary American boxer Muhammad Ali.

Cathal

Celtic, meaning 'battle rule'.

Cato

Latin, meaning 'all-knowing'. Cato the Younger was a Roman politician who opposed Caesar.

Cecil

Latin, meaning 'blind'. Name of famous American movie director Cecil B. DeMille.

Cedar

English, from the name of an evergreen tree.

Cedric

Welsh, meaning 'spectacular bounty'. First appeared in Sir Walter Scott's 1819 novel, *Ivanhoe*.

Celesto

(alt. Celestino, Celindo)

Latin, meaning 'heaven sent'.

Chad

(alt. Chadrick)

Old English, meaning 'warlike, warrior'. Use of this name was rare until it sprang to popularity in the 1960s.

Chaim

(alt. Chayyim)

Hebrew, meaning 'life'.

Champion

English, meaning 'warrior'.

Chandler

Old English, meaning 'candle maker and seller'.

Charles

(abbrev. Chas, Charlie)

Old German, meaning 'free man'. Popularised by Charles the Great (a.k.a. Charlemagne). Prince Charles is heir to the throne of England. Charles Dickens is one of the finest and most enduringly popular English authors.

Chaska

Sioux, the name usually given to a first son.

Chauncey

(alt. Chance)

English, from the word 'chance' meaning 'good fortune'.

Che

Spanish, shortened form of José. Made famous by Che Guevara.

Chesley

Old English, meaning 'camp on the meadow'.

Chesney

English, meaning 'place to camp'. Also used as a girls' name.

Chester

Latin, meaning 'camp of soldiers'. The name of an English city.

Chilton

(alt. Chillron, Chilly, Chilt)

English, meaning 'tranquil'.

Chima

Old English, meaning 'hilly land'.

Christian

English. Christian Bale is an actor and Christian Louboutin is a famous shoe designer.

Christopher

(alt. Christophe; abbrev. Chris, Christy)

Greek, meaning 'Christ bearer'. Christopher Columbus was a famous explorer.

Cian

Irish, meaning 'ancient'. Father of Lug in Irish mythology.

Ciaran

Irish, meaning 'black'. Was the name of two Irish saints.

Cicero

Latin, meaning 'chickpea'. Famous Roman philosopher and orator.

Cimarron

City in western Kansas. Also the name of a novel by Edna Ferber.

Ciprian

Latin, meaning 'from Cyprus'. Popular in Romanian heritage.

Ciro

Spanish, meaning 'sun'. Name of an opera by Francesco Cavalli dating back to 1654.

Clancy

Old Irish, meaning 'red warrior'. Evolved from the surname Mac Fhlannchaidh.

Clarence

Latin, meaning 'one who lives near the river Clare'.

Clark

Latin, meaning 'clerk'. The human identity of the famed superhero Superman (Clark Kent).

Claude

(alt. Claudie, Claudio, Claudius)

Latin, meaning 'lame'. Has been in use since the Middle Ages.

Claus

Variant of Nicholas, meaning 'victorious'.

Clay

English, from the word 'clay'.

Clement
(alt. Clem)

Latin, meaning 'merciful'. Has been used as the name for 14 different popes.

Cleo

Greek, meaning 'glory'. Most commonly used as a name for girls, but also for boys.

Cletus

Greek, meaning 'illustrious'. Used to refer to the third pope, Anacletus.

Clifford
(alt. Clifton; abbrev. Cliff)

English, from the word 'cliff'.

Clint
(alt. Clinton)

Old English, meaning 'fenced settlement'. Name of famous actor/writer/director Clint Eastwood.

Clive

Old English, meaning 'cliff' or 'slope'. Famous Clives include actor Clive Owen and author and broadcaster Clive James.

Clyde

Scottish, from the river that passes through Glasgow. Name of famous American bank robber Clyde Barrow of the duo Bonnie and Clyde.

Coby
(alt. Cody, Colby)

Irish, meaning 'son of Oda'.

Cody

English, meaning 'pillow'. Also a girls' name.

Colden

Old English, meaning 'dark valley'.

Cole
(alt. Coley)

Old French, meaning 'coal black'.

Colin

Gaelic, meaning 'young creature'. Famous Colins include actor Colin Firth and champion rally driver Colin McRae.

Colson

Old English, meaning 'coal black'.

Colton

English, meaning 'swarthy'. Evolved from the Old English name, Cola.

Columbus

Latin, meaning 'dove'. Name of Italian explorer Christopher Columbus.

Colwyn

Welsh, from the river in Wales.

Conan

Gaelic, meaning 'wolf'. Middle name of 'Sherlock Holmes' author, Sir Arthur Conan Doyle.

Conley

Gaelic, meaning 'sensible'.

Connell
(alt. Connolly)
Irish, meaning 'high' or 'mighty'.

Connor
(alt. Conor, Conrad, Conroy)
Irish, meaning 'lover of hounds'. Evolved from the name Conchobhar (King of Ulster).

Constant
(alt. Constantine)
English. A name widely used by Christians as early as the 17th century.

Cooper
Old English, meaning 'barrel maker'.

Corban
Hebrew, meaning 'dedicated and belonging to God'.

Corbett
(alt. Corbin, Corby)
Norman French, meaning 'young crow'.

Cordell
Old English, meaning 'cord maker'.

Corey
(alt. Cory)
Gaelic, meaning 'hill hollow'. Thought to have originated from the Old Norse name Kori.

Corin
Latin, meaning 'spear'. A variant of the German given name Quirin.

Corliss
(alt. Corlis, Corlyss, Corlys)
English, meaning 'benevolent'.

Cormac
Gaelic, meaning 'impure son'. Name given to a third-century Irish king.

Cornelius
(alt. Cornell)
Latin, meaning 'horn'. The head of the Ministry of Magic (Cornelius Fudge) in J.K. Rowling's Harry Potter books.

Cortez
Spanish, meaning 'courteous'.

Corwin
Old English, meaning 'heart's friend' or 'companion'.

Cosimo
(alt. Cosme, Cosmo)
Italian, meaning 'order' or 'beauty'. Given name of Pope Innocent VII (1339–1406).

Coty
French, meaning 'riverbank'. Surname of people who lived near a coast.

Coulter
English, meaning 'young horse'.

Courtney
Old English, meaning 'domain of Curtis'. A given name that has been in use since the 17th century. Used for both boys and girls.

Covey

English, meaning 'flock of birds'.

Cowan

Gaelic, meaning 'hollow in the hill'.

Craig

Welsh, meaning 'rock'. Originally used as a surname by people who lived near a cliff. Craig David is a singer-songwriter and there are two famous sporting Craig Bellamys, one a Welsh footballer and the other an Australian rugby league star.

Crispin

Latin, meaning 'curly haired'. Name of a third-century saint, twin brother of St Crispinian. Patron saints of shoemakers.

Croix

French, meaning 'cross'.

Cruz

Spanish, meaning 'cross'. Made famous by David and Victoria Beckham's son.

Cullen

Gaelic, meaning 'handsome'. Made famous by the *Twilight* book series.

Curran

Gaelic, meaning 'dagger' or 'hero'.

Curtis

(*alt. Curt*)

Old French, meaning 'courteous'. Commonly used in the Middle Ages as a name of a courteous person.

Cutler

Old English, meaning 'knife maker'.

Cyprian

English, meaning 'from Cyprus'.

Cyril

Greek, meaning 'master' or 'Lord'. Name of St Cyril, one of the inventors of the Glagolitic alphabet, the precursor to the Cyrillic alphabet.

Cyrus

Persian, meaning 'Lord'. Cyrus the Great conquered Babylon in 539 BC.

Boys' names

Dabeel
(alt. Dabee, Dabie, Daby)
Sanskrit, meaning 'warrior'.

Daelan
English, meaning 'aware'. Also a girls' name.

Dafydd
(alt. Dai)
Welsh, meaning 'beloved'. Welsh version of David.

Daichi
Japanese, meaning 'great wisdom'.

Daire
(alt. Daer, Daere, Dair)
Irish, meaning 'wealthy'.

Daisuke
Japanese, meaning 'lionhearted'.

Dakari
Swahili, meaning 'happy'.

Dale
Old English, meaning 'valley'.

Dallin
English, meaning 'dweller in the valley'.

Dalton
English, meaning 'town in the valley'.

Daly
Gaelic, meaning 'assembly'.

Damarion
Greek, meaning 'gentle'.

Damian
(alt. Damien, Damon)
Greek, meaning 'to tame, subdue'. Name of a fourth-century patron saint of physicians. Damon Hill is British champion racing driver and Damon Albarn is a musician and the lead singer of Blur.

Dane

Old English, meaning 'from Denmark'.

Daniel

(alt. Dan, Danny)

Hebrew, meaning 'God is my judge'. Daniel was a prophet during biblical times. An enduringly popular name for boys.

Dante

Latin, meaning 'lasting'. Associated with the 13th-century Italian poet Dante Alighieri, author of *The Divine Comedy*.

Darby

Irish, meaning 'without envy'.

Darcy

(alt. Darcey)

Gaelic, meaning 'dark'. Associated with Jane Austen's Mr Darcy, and the parody of this character in *Bridget Jones' Diary*. A name more commonly used for girls in modern times.

Dario

(alt. Darius)

Greek, meaning 'kingly'. Associated with Dario Argento, an Italian film director.

Darnell

Old English, meaning 'the hidden spot'.

Darragh

(alt. Dara)

Irish, meaning 'dark oak'. A popular name in Ireland, now being seen across the UK.

Darrell

(alt. Daryl)

Old English, meaning 'open'. Originated from the Norman French surname d'Airelle.

Darren

(alt. Darrian)

Gaelic, meaning 'great'. Darren Aronofsky is an American film-maker. In the UK the name is well connected with sport, including cricketer Darren Gough.

Darrick

Old German, meaning 'power of the tribe'.

Darshan

Hindi, meaning 'vision'.

Darwin

Old English, meaning 'dear friend'. Often associated with the naturalist Charles Darwin.

Dash

(alt. Dashawn)

American, meaning 'enlightened one'. Associated with one of the characters in Disney Pixar's *The Incredibles*.

Famous male drummers

Dave (Grohl)	Phil (Collins)
John (Bonham)	Ringo (Starr – real name Richard Starkey)
Keith (Moon)	Stewart (Copeland)
Lars (Ulrich)	Tommy (Lee)
Mick (Fleetwood)	Travis (Barker)

Dashiell

French, meaning 'page boy'. Dashiell Hammett was an American author, famous for hard-boiled detective fiction.

Dason

Native American, meaning 'chief'.

David

(alt. Dave, Davey, Davie, Davin)
Hebrew, meaning 'beloved'. Associated with the King of Israel who killed Goliath the giant as a boy.

Davis

Old English, meaning 'son of David'.

Dawson

Old English, meaning 'son of David'. Associated with the main character in the TV show *Dawson's Creek*.

Dax

(alt. Daxton)
French, once a town in south-western France.

Dayal

Sanskrit, meaning 'kind'.

Dayton

Old English, meaning 'David's place'. A city in the US state of Ohio.

Dean

Old English, meaning 'valley'. Dean Koontz is an American author and Dean Martin was a hugely popular singer and entertainer, known as the 'King of Cool'.

Declan

Irish, meaning 'full of goodness'. Associated with St Declan, who was born in the fifth century.

Dedric

Old English, meaning 'gifted ruler'.

Deepak

(alt. Deepan)
Sanskrit, meaning 'illumination'. Associated with doctor and spiritual author Deepak Chopra.

Del

(alt. Delano, Delbert, Dell)
Old English, meaning 'bright shining one'. Associated with the main character in *Only Fools and Horses*.

Delaney
Irish, meaning 'dark challenge'.

Demetrius
Greek, meaning 'harvest lover'. Name of a fourth-century Greek sculptor.

Dempsey
Irish, meaning 'proud'.

Denham
(alt. Denholm)
Old English, meaning 'valley settlement'.

Dennis
(alt. Denis, Denny, Denton)
English, meaning 'follower of Dionysius'. Associated with the comic strip Dennis the Menace. Other famous Dennises include actors Dennis Hopper and Dennis Quaid and footballer Dennis Bergkamp.

Denzil
(alt. Densel, Denzel)
English, meaning 'fort'. Most commonly associated with Oscar-winning actor Denzel Washington.

Deon
Greek, meaning 'of Zeus'.

Derek
English, meaning 'power of the tribe'. Short form for the given name Diderik.

Dermot
Irish, meaning 'free man'. Dermot O'Leary is a prolific TV and radio presenter.

Desmond
Irish, meaning 'from south Munster'. Associated with South African social rights activist Archbishop Desmond Tutu.

Destin
French, meaning 'destiny'.

Deveraux
French, meaning 'from the town of Évreux'.

Devyn
(alt. Devin)
Irish, meaning 'poet'.

Dewey
Welsh, from Dewi (David). One of Disney character Donald Duck's three nephews.

Dexter
(alt. Dex)
Latin, meaning 'right-handed'.

Diallo
(alt. Dialo)
Swahili, meaning 'bold'.

Dick
(alt. Dickie, Dickon, Diccon)
From Richard, meaning 'powerful leader'. Dick is one of Enid Blyton's Famous Five and Dickon is a character in Frances Hodgson Burnett's The Secret Garden.

Didier

French, meaning 'much desired'. St Didier is a saint honoured in the Catholic Church. Famous Didiers include footballers Didier Deschamps and Didier Drogba.

Diego

Spanish, meaning 'supplanter'. Has been in use since the 11th century.

Dietrich

Old German, meaning 'power of the tribe'.

Diggory

English, meaning 'dyke'.

Dilbert

English, meaning 'day bright'. Popularised by the American comic strip of the same name.

Dimitri
(alt. Dimitrios, Dimitris)

Greek, meaning 'prince'. A popular name in Russia.

Dino

Diminutive of Dean, meaning 'valley'. Used as short form for names ending with -dino.

Dion

Greek, short form of Dionysius, the Greek god of wine. Dionysius was the son of Zeus and Semele.

Dirk

Variant of Derek, meaning 'power of the tribe'. A name also used to refer to a dagger.

Divakar

Sanskrit, meaning 'the sun'.

Dominic

Latin, meaning 'Lord'.

Donald
(alt. Don, Donal, Donaldo)

Gaelic, meaning 'great chief'. Famous Donalds include actor Donald Sutherland, businessman-turned-US President Donald Trump and ever-popular Disney character Donald Duck.

Donato

Italian, meaning 'gift'. Given name of Italian sculptor Donatello.

Donnell
(alt. Donnie, Donny)

Gaelic, meaning 'world fighter'.

Donovan

Gaelic, meaning 'dark-haired chief'. Associated with Australian singer and actor Jason Donovan.

Doran

Gaelic, meaning 'exile'.

Dorian

Greek, meaning 'descendant of Doris'. Name of the title character in Oscar Wilde's *The Picture of Dorian Gray*.

Douglas
(alt. Dougal, Dougie)

Scottish, meaning 'black river'. Douglas Adams was the author of *The Hitchhiker's Guide to the Galaxy*.

Doyle

Irish, meaning 'foreigner'.

Draco

(alt. Drake)

Latin, meaning 'dragon'. Made popular by the character Draco Malfoy in J.K. Rowling's *Harry Potter* books.

Drew

Shortened form of Andrew, meaning 'man' or 'warrior'.

Dryden

English, meaning 'dry town'.

Dudley

Old English, meaning 'people's field'. Also the name of Harry Potter's cousin.

Duff

Gaelic, meaning 'swarthy'.

Duke

Latin, meaning 'leader'. The title of a nobleman ruling over a duchy.

Duncan

Scottish, meaning 'dark warrior'. King Duncan is a character in Shakespeare's *Macbeth*.

Dustin

(alt. Dusty)

French, meaning 'brave warrior'. Popularised by American actor Dustin Hoffman.

Dwayne

(alt. Duwayne, Duane)

Irish Gaelic, meaning 'swarthy'.

Dwight

Flemish, meaning 'blond'. Associated with the 34th President of the United States, Dwight D. Eisenhower.

Dwyer

Gaelic, meaning 'dark wise one'.

Dyani

Native American, meaning 'eagle'.

Dylan

(alt. Dillon)

Welsh, meaning 'son of the sea'. Name of the famous Welsh poet Dylan Thomas.

E Boys' names

Eagan
Irish, meaning 'fiery'.

Eamon
(alt. Eamonn, Eames)
Irish, meaning 'wealthy protector'.

Earl
(alt. Earle, Errol)
English, meaning 'nobleman, warrior, prince'. Earl is a title of nobility, used since Anglo-Saxon times.

Ebenezer
(abbrev. Ebb)
Hebrew, meaning 'stone of help'. Ebenezer Scrooge is the main character in Charles Dickens' novel A Christmas Carol.

Edgar
(alt. Elgar)
Old English, meaning 'wealthy spear'. Poet and writer Edgar Allan Poe is known for works such as The Raven.

Edison
English, meaning 'son of Edward'. Thomas Edison was one of America's greatest inventors.

Edmund
(abbrev. Ed)
English, meaning 'wealthy protector'.

Edric
Old English, meaning 'rich and powerful'.

Edsel
Old German, meaning 'noble'. Henry Ford, the automobile magnate, named his son Edsel.

Edward
(alt. Eduardo; abbrev. Ed, Edd, Eddie, Eddy)
Old English, meaning 'wealthy guard'. Edward has become extremely popular since the release of the Twilight series.

Edwin
English, meaning 'wealthy friend'.

Efrain

Hebrew, meaning 'fruitful'. Normally used in Spanish-speaking cultures.

Egan

Irish, meaning 'fire'. Egan, derived from the name Aedhagan, is one of the oldest surnames in Europe.

Eilif

(alt. Elif, Eilyg, Elyf)

Norse, meaning 'immortal'. Eilif Paterssen was a Norwegian painter in the early 20th century.

Einar

Old Norse, meaning 'battle leader'. Still a popular name in Iceland.

Eladio

Greek, meaning 'Greek'. Related to the name Heladio.

Elam

Hebrew, meaning 'eternal'. Elam is mentioned in the Bible as being a son of Shem, and son of Noah.

Elan

French, meaning 'energy and enthusiasm'. Also the name of a river valley in Wales.

Elbert

Old English, meaning 'famous'. Variation of the name Albert.

Eldon

Old English, meaning 'Ella's hill'. Also refers to the town in County Durham, England.

Eldred

(alt. Eldridge)

Old English, meaning 'old venerable counsel'.

Elgin

Old English, meaning 'high minded'. Also refers to the town of the same name in Scotland.

Eli

(alt. Eliah)

Hebrew, meaning 'high'. Eli is a character in the Old Testament of the Bible.

Elias

(alt. Elijah, Elio)

Hebrew, meaning 'the Lord is my God'. Walt Disney's father was Elias Disney. Actor Elijah Wood played Frodo Baggins in the Lord of the Rings films.

Ellery

Old English, meaning 'elder tree'. Ellery Hanley is a former rugby league player and coach for Great Britain.

Elliott

English variant of Elio, meaning 'the Lord is my God'. Made popular by the lead character in the film E.T.

Ellis

Welsh, variant of Elio, meaning 'the Lord is my God'.

Ellison

English, meaning 'son of Ellis'.

Elmer

Old English, meaning 'noble'; Arabic, meaning 'aristocratic'. Elmer the elephant features in a number of children's picture books by author David McKee.

Elmo
(alt. Ellmo, Elmon)

Greek, meaning 'gregarious'.

Elmore

Old English, meaning from 'elm tree' and 'moor'. Elmore Leonard was an American author.

Elon
(alt. Alon)

Hebrew, meaning 'oak tree'. A very old name, it is now not used much outside of Hebrew-speaking communities.

Elroy

French, meaning 'king'.

Elton

Old English, meaning 'Ella's town'. Singer and songwriter Sir Elton John's real name is Reg Dwight.

Elvin

English, meaning 'elf-like'.

Elvis

Figure in Norse mythology. Made famous by the singer Elvis Presley.

Emanuel

Hebrew, meaning 'God is with us'. Features in hymns and carols.

Emeric

German, meaning 'work rule'. St Emeric of Hungary was known for a pure and pious life.

Emile
(alt. Emil, Emiliano, Emilio)

Latin, meaning 'eager'. Emile is Remy the rat's older brother in Disney's film Ratatouille.

Emlyn

Welsh. The name of a town, Newcastle Emlyn, in west Wales.

Emmett

English, meaning 'universal'. Emmett is a member of the Cullen family in the Twilight series.

Emrys

Welsh, meaning 'immortal'. The legendary magician Merlin is said to have been given the name Emrys at birth, and only later adopted his more famous moniker.

Eneco

Spanish, meaning 'fiery one'.

Enoch

Hebrew, meaning 'dedicated'. Enoch was the great-great-grandfather of Noah in the Bible.

Enrico
(alt. Enrique)

Italian, form of Henry, meaning 'home ruler'. Extremely popular name in Italy for boys.

Enzo

Italian, short for Lorenzo, meaning 'laurel'. Enzo Ferrari was the founder of the Ferrari automobile company.

Eoghan
(alt. Eoin)

Irish form of Owen, meaning 'well born' or 'noble'. Eoghan was an Irish king in the fifth century. Eoin Colfer is the author of the young adult fiction series *Artemis Fowl*.

Ephron
(alt. *Effron*)
Hebrew, meaning 'dust'.

Erasmo
(alt. *Erasmus*)
Greek, meaning 'to love'. Erasmus was a Dutch humanist and theologian during the Renaissance period.

Eric
Old Norse, meaning 'ruler'. Often associated with singer and guitarist Eric Clapton.

Ernest
(alt. *Ernesto, Ernie, Ernst*)
Old German, meaning 'serious'. Author Ernest Hemingway is known for his influential novels *A Farewell to Arms* and *The Old Man and the Sea*.

Errol
English, meaning 'boar wolf'. Actor Errol Flynn is best known for his swashbuckler roles and the lead role in *The Adventures of Robin Hood*.

Erskine
Scottish, meaning 'high cliff'. Also a place in Scotland.

Erwin
Old English, meaning 'boar friend'.

Eryx
Greek, meaning 'boxer'. Sometimes used as an alternative spelling for Eric.

Ethan
(alt. *Etienne*)
Hebrew, meaning 'long lived'. Ethan Hawke is an Oscar-nominated actor.

Eugene
Greek, meaning 'well born'.

Evan
(alt. *Ifan*)
Welsh, meaning 'God is gracious'.

Evelyn
German, meaning 'hazelnut'. Evelyn Waugh is the author of *Brideshead Revisited*, *Decline and Fall* and *Scoop*.

Everard
(alt. *Everett*)
Old English, meaning 'strong boar'. Also the name of an old English ale.

Everly
(alt. *Everleigh, Everley*)
English, meaning 'grazing meadow'. Used as a name for boys and girls.

Ewan
(alt. *Euan, Ewald, Ewen, Ewell*)
Old English, from Owen, meaning 'well born' or 'noble'. Actor Ewan McGregor is known for his roles in *Trainspotting*, *Moulin Rouge* and *Star Wars*.

Exton
English, meaning 'on the River Exe'.

Ezra
Hebrew, meaning 'helper'. Ezra Pound was an American poet. George Ezra is a singer-songwriter.

Boys' names

Faber
(alt. Fabir)

Latin, meaning 'blacksmith'. Faber and Faber is a well-known UK publishing house.

Fabian
(alt. Fabien, Fabio)

Latin, meaning 'one who grows beans'. Also associated with the teen pop sensation Fabian in the 1950s and '60s.

Fabrice
(alt. Fabrizio)

Latin, meaning 'works with his hands'. Popular in France. Fabrice Muamba is a former football player who survived an on-pitch heart attack.

Faisal

Arabic, meaning 'resolute'. Faisal II was the last King of Iraq, whose reign ended during the revolution of 1958.

Falco
(alt. Falcon, Falconer, Falke, Faulkner)

Latin, meaning 'falconer'.

Faron

Spanish, meaning 'pharaoh'. Also derived from a Gaelic word for 'thunder'.

Farrell

Gaelic, meaning 'hero'.

Faustino

Latin, meaning 'fortunate'.

Fela
(alt. Felah, Fella, Fellah)

Swahili, meaning 'a man who is warlike'. The name of the famous Nigerian musician Fela Kuti.

Felipe
(alt. Filippo)

Spanish, meaning 'lover of horses'. Formula One driver Felipe Massa has driven for Ferrari and Williams.

Felix
(alt. Felice)

Italian/Latin, meaning 'happy'. Felix the Cat was a popular 20th-century cartoon character.

Fennel

Latin, name of a herb. More commonly used as a girls' name.

Ferdinand
(alt. Fernando)

Old German, meaning 'bold voyager'.

Fergus
(alt. Ferguson)

Gaelic, meaning 'supreme man'.

Ferris

Gaelic, meaning 'rock'. *Ferris Bueller's Day Off* was a runaway hit film during the 1980s.

Fiachra

Irish, meaning 'raven'. St Fiachra is the patron saint of gardeners.

Fidel

Latin, meaning 'faithful'. Fidel Castro was President of Cuba from 1976 to 2008.

Finbarr

Gaelic, meaning 'fair head'. St Finbarr is the patron saint of the City of Cork.

Finian
(alt. Finnian)

Gaelic, meaning 'fair'. St Finnian is an important Irish saint, and a founder of the theory of monasticism.

Finlay
(alt. Finley, Fynlee)

Gaelic, meaning 'fair-haired courageous one'.

Finn
(alt. Fynn)

Finnish, meaning 'from Finland'.

Finnegan

Gaelic, meaning 'fair'. Author James Joyce wrote *Finnegans Wake* as a complex work of comedy.

Fintan

Gaelic, meaning 'little fair one'. A seer in Irish mythology called Fintan supposedly saved one of Noah's granddaughters from the flood.

Fitzroy

English, meaning 'the king's son'. Usually associated with Vice-Admiral Robert Fitzroy, who accompanied Charles Darwin on his famous voyages.

Flavio

Latin, meaning 'yellow hair'. The opera *Flavio* was composed by Handel.

Florencio
(alt. Florentino)

Latin, meaning 'from Florence'.

Florian
(alt. Florin)

Slavic/Latin, meaning 'flower'. St Florian is the patron saint of chimney sweeps, soapmakers and firefighters.

Floyd

Welsh, meaning 'grey haired'.

Flynn

Gaelic, meaning 'with a ruddy complexion'.

Forbes

(alt. Forbs, Forb, Forbe)

Gaelic, meaning 'of the field'.

Forrest

(alt. Forest)

Old English, meaning 'dweller or worker of the forest'.

Fortunato

Italian, meaning 'lucky'.

Foster

Old English, meaning 'woodsman'.

Fotini

(alt. Fotis)

Greek, meaning 'light'.

Francis

(alt. Francesco, Francisco, Franco, François)

Latin, meaning 'from France'. After the election of Pope Francis, Francesco has become the most popular name for boys in Italy.

Frank

(alt. Frankie, Franklin, Franz)

Middle English, meaning 'free landholder'. Also a diminutive of Francis. Famous Franks include footballer Frank Lampard, crooner Frank Sinatra, and film director Frank Capra.

Fraser

(alt. Fraiser)

Scottish, meaning 'of the forest men'.

Frederick

(alt. Friedrich; abbrev. Freddie, Fred)

Old German, meaning 'peaceful ruler'. There is a spelling or pronunciation variation of Frederick in practically every European language.

Furman

Old German, meaning 'ferryman'.

Fyfe

(alt. Fife, Fyffes)

Scottish, meaning 'from Fifeshire'.

Boys' names

Gabino
Latin, meaning 'God is my strength'.

Gabriel
(abbrev. Gabe)
Hebrew, meaning 'hero of God'.
One of the archangels in the Bible.

Gael
(alt. Gale)
English, old reference to the Celts.
Gale is a character in the *Hunger Games* trilogy.

Gaius
(alt. Gaeus)
Latin, meaning 'rejoicing'. Julius
Caesar's full name was Gaius Julius
Caesar.

Galen
Greek, meaning 'healer'. Galen
of Pergamon was a well-respected
ancient Greco-Roman philosopher
and physician.

Galileo
Italian, meaning 'from Galilee'.
Galileo Galilei was an important and
influential physicist and astronomer
during the Scientific Revolution.

Ganesh
Hindi, meaning 'lord of the horde'.
One of the Hindu deities.

Gannon
Irish, meaning 'fair skinned'.
Commonly used as a surname,
particularly in Ireland.

Gareth
(alt. Garth, Garthe, Gart, Garte)
Welsh, meaning 'gentle'.

Garfield
Old English, meaning 'spear field'.
Also the name of the cartoon cat.

Garland
English, as in 'garland of flowers'.

Garnet

English, precious stone, red in colour. Occasionally used for boys, although not as frequently as for girls.

Garrett

Old German, meaning 'spear' or 'ruler'. Ireland's Garret the Great was known as 'the uncrowned King of Ireland' during his time of political power in the 15th century.

Gary
(alt. Garry, Geary)

Old English, meaning 'spear'. Some of Britain's best-loved Garys include Take That member Gary Barlow and football pundit Gary Lineker.

Gaspar
(alt. Gaspard)

Persian, meaning 'treasurer'.

Gaston

French, from the Gascony region in the south of France.

Gavin
(alt. Gawain)

Scottish/Welsh, meaning 'little falcon'.

Gene

Greek, shortened form of Eugene, meaning 'well born'. Famous Genes include actors Gene Kelly and Gene Hackman, and Kiss guitarist Gene Simmons.

Genkei

Japanese, meaning 'honoured'. One of Japan's most famous botanists is Genkei Masamune, who is credited with identifying hundreds of new species.

Gennaro

Italian, meaning 'of Janus'.

Geoffrey
(abbrev. Geoff)

Old German, meaning 'peace'.

George
(alt. Giorgio)

Greek, meaning 'farmer'. Chosen by the Duke and Duchess of Cambridge for their elder son who is third in line to the throne.

Gerald
(alt. Geraldo, Gerard, Gerardo, Gerhard; abbrev. Gerry)

Old German, meaning 'spear ruler'. Former President of the United States Gerald Ford is the only person to have served as both President and Vice President without being elected to either position, thanks to two infamous resignations before him.

Geronimo

Italian, meaning 'sacred name'. Originally the name of a prominent Apache Indian, this has now become a word for 'go-get-'em!'

Gert

Old German, meaning 'strong spear'.

Gervase

Old German, meaning 'with honour'. Gervase Phinn is a widely read author of several humorous books describing his life as a school inspector in Yorkshire.

Giacomo

Italian, meaning 'God's son'. Legendary womaniser Casanova's full name was Giacomo Girolamo Casanova.

Gibson

English, meaning 'son of Gilbert'.

Gideon

Hebrew, meaning 'tree cutter'. Gideon is a figure in the Bible.

Gilbert

(alt. Gilberto)

French, meaning 'bright promise'.

Giles

Greek, meaning 'small goat'.

Gino

Italian, meaning 'well born'.

Giovanni

Italian form of John, meaning 'God is gracious'.

Giri

(alt. Gririe, Giry, Girey)

Sanskrit, meaning 'from the mountain'.

Giulio

Italian, meaning 'youthful'. Composer Giulio Caccini was active during the Baroque era.

Giuseppe

Italian form of Joseph, meaning 'Jehovah increases'.

Glen

(alt. Glenn, Glyn)

English, from the word 'glen'.

Godfrey

German, meaning 'peace of God'.

Gordon

Gaelic, meaning 'large fortification'. Famous Gordons include chef Gordon Ramsay and former prime minister Gordon Brown.

Gottlieb

German, meaning 'good love'. One of Mozart's names at birth was Gottlieb; others included Johannes, Chrisostomus and Wolfgang.

Gower

Welsh, from the area of the Welsh coast, by the Bristol Channel.

Graeme

(alt. Graham)

English, meaning 'gravelled area'.

Grant

English, from the word 'grant'.

Granville

English, meaning 'gravelly town'. Probably the most famous Granville is the character portrayed by David Jason in sitcom *Open All Hours*.

Gray
(alt. Grey)
English, from the word 'grey'.

Grayson
English, meaning 'son of gray'.
Grayson Perry is an artist who won
the Turner Prize in 2003.

Green
English, from the word 'green'.

Gregory
(alt. Gregorio; abbrev. Greg, Greig)
English, from the word 'griffin'. Actor
Gregory Peck was best known for his
role in To Kill A Mockingbird.

Griffin
English. A griffin is a mythical
creature with the body of a lion and
the head and wings of an eagle.

Groves
English, meaning 'inhabits near grove
of trees'.

Gruffudd
(alt. Griffith, Gruffydd; abbrev. Griff,
Gruff)
Welsh, meaning 'strong prince'.
It was a common name among
medieval Welsh royalty.

Grylfi
(alt. Gylfie, Gylfee, Gylffi)
Scandinavian, meaning 'king'.
Gylfi was the first Nordic king in
Scandinavia.

Guido
Italian, meaning 'guide'.

Guillaume
French form of William, meaning
'strong protector'. William the
Conqueror is known as Guillaume le
Conquérant in France.

Gulliver
English, meaning 'glutton'. Gulliver's
Travels, by Jonathan Swift, tells the
story of a surgeon who sets sail for
adventure.

Gunther
German, meaning 'warrior'.

Gurpreet
Sanskrit, meaning 'love of the
teacher'. More commonly used in
Punjabi-speaking communities.

Gustave
(abbrev. Gus)
Scandinavian, meaning 'royal staff'.
Gustave Flaubert is the author of
classics including Madame Bovary.
Also the name given to a legendary
crocodile in Burundi, whose length
is said to be over 20ft and that has
killed as many as 300 humans.

Guy
English. Guy Fawkes is the character
most associated with the Gunpowder
Plot of 1605, which was an attempt
to blow up the Houses of Parliament.

Gwyn
Welsh, meaning 'white'. Commonly
used as a name for girls as well as for
boys.

Boys' names

Habib
Arabic, meaning 'beloved one'.

Hackett
(alt. Hacket, Hackit, Hackitt)
German, meaning 'small hacker'.

Haden
(alt. Haiden)
English, meaning 'hedged valley'.
Also a popular type of mango.

Hades
Greek, meaning 'sightless'. Name of
the god of the underworld in Greek
mythology.

Hadrian
From Hadria, a north Italian city.
Hadrian's Wall in northern England
is named after the Roman Emperor
Hadrian.

Hadwin
Old English, meaning 'friend in war'.

Hakeem
Arabic, meaning 'wise and insightful'.
Hakeem Lyon is a major character in
the musical epic drama *Empire*.

Hal
(alt. Hale, Hallie)
English, nickname for Henry,
meaning 'home ruler'. Used in this
context in Shakespeare's *Henry IV*
plays.

Halim
Arabic, meaning 'gentle'. Al-Halim is
one the names of God in Islam.

Hallam
Old English, meaning 'the valley'.

Hamid
Arabic, meaning 'praiseworthy'.
Hamid Karzai was the elected
president of Afghanistan from 2001
to 2014.

Hamilton
Old English, meaning 'flat-topped hill'.

Hamish

Scottish form of James, meaning 'he who supplants'.

Hamlet

(alt. Hamlett, Hammet, Hamnet)
German, meaning 'village'. A variation of the Danish Amleth, and often associated with Shakespeare's tragedy *Hamlet*.

Hampus

Swedish form of Homer, meaning 'pledge'. Hampus Lindholm is an international ice hockey player, originally from Sweden.

Hamza

Arabic, meaning 'lamb'. Also a letter in the Arabic alphabet.

Han

(alt. Hannes, Hans)
Scandinavian, meaning 'the Lord is gracious'.

Hanif

(alt. Haneef, Haneaf, Haneif)
Arabic, meaning 'devout'. In Islam it usually refers to people who submitted entirely to their religion.

Hank

German, form of Henry, meaning 'home ruler'.

Hansel

German, meaning 'the Lord is gracious'. One of the most famous Grimm fairy tales is the story of Hansel and Gretel.

Hardy

English, meaning 'tough'. Often associated with the author Thomas Hardy, comedic duo Laurel and Hardy and English actor Tom Hardy.

Harlan

English, meaning 'dweller by the boundary wood'. Harlan Coben is the author of several mystery novels.

Harland

Old English, meaning 'army land'. Fast food chain KFC was founded by Colonel Harland David Sanders. The *Titanic* was built at Belfast shipyard Harland and Wolff.

Harley

Old English, meaning 'hare meadow'.

Harmon

Old German, meaning 'soldier'.

Harold

Scandinavian, meaning 'army ruler'. The last Anglo-Saxon King of England was Harold II, whose reign ended after he lost the Battle of Hastings.

Harris

Old English, meaning 'home ruler'.

Harrison

Old English, meaning 'son of Harry' or 'son of Harris'. The middle name of Archie Mountbatten-Windsor.

Harry

Old German, form of Henry, meaning 'home ruler'. Famous Harrys include Harry Potter and One Direction singer Harry Styles.

Hart

Old English, meaning 'stag'.

Harvey

Old English, meaning 'strong and worthy'. The film *Harvey*, starring Jimmy Stewart and Josephine Hull, is about a man whose best friend is an enormous invisible rabbit.

Haskell

Hebrew, meaning 'intellect'.

Hassan

Arabic, meaning 'handsome'. Hassan Rouhani is the current President of Iran.

Haydn
(alt. Hayden, Haydon)

Old English, meaning 'hedged valley'. Franz Joseph Haydn, was one of the most influential and popular composers of the classical period.

Heart

English, from the word 'heart'.

Heath

English, meaning 'heath' or 'moor'. Heath Ledger was a prolific actor, known for his roles in *A Knight's Tale*, *10 Things I Hate About You* and *The Dark Knight*.

Heathcliff

English, meaning 'cliff near a heath'. Made famous by Emily Brontë's novel *Wuthering Heights*.

Heber

Hebrew, meaning 'partner'.

Hector

Greek, meaning 'steadfast'. A Trojan prince and historic fighter in ancient Greek mythology.

Henry
(alt. Henri, Hendrik, Hendrix)

Old German, meaning 'home ruler'. There have been eight Kings of England named Henry.

Henson

English, meaning 'son of Henry'.

Herbert
(alt. Heriberto; abbrev. Bert, Herb)

Old German, meaning 'illustrious warrior'. Herbert Hoover was a President of the United States and founder of the FBI.

Herman
(alt. Herminio, Hermon)

Old German, meaning 'soldier'.

Hermes

Greek, meaning 'messenger'. The messenger of the gods in Greek mythology.

Herschel
(alt. Hirsch)

Yiddish, meaning 'deer'.

Hezekiah

Hebrew, meaning 'God gives strength'. The 13th king of Judah was King Hezekiah.

Hideki

Japanese, meaning 'excellent trees'. The prime minister of Japan during World War II was Hideki Tojo.

Hideo

Japanese, meaning 'excellent name'. One of Japan's most prolific comedians is Hideo Higashikokubaru.

Hilario

Latin, meaning 'cheerful, happy'. Retired goalkeeper Henrique Hilario Meireles Sampaio is usually known just as Hilario.

Hilary
(alt. Hillary)

English, meaning 'cheerful'. Most used now as a girls' name although it can be used for boys, as with politician Hilary Benn.

Hildred

German, meaning 'battle counsellor'.

Hillel

Hebrew, meaning 'greatly praised'. Rabbi Hillel was an important leader in the Jewish faith.

Hilliard

Old German, meaning 'battle guard'.

Hilton

Old English, meaning 'hill settlement'.

Hiram

Hebrew, meaning 'exalted brother'.

Hiro

Spanish, meaning 'sacred name'.

Hiroshi

Japanese, meaning 'generous'.

Hobart

English, meaning 'bright and shining intellect'. Also the name of the capital of Tasmania.

Hodge

English, meaning 'son of Roger'.

Hogan

Gaelic, meaning 'youth'. Wrestling superstar Terry Bollea is better known as Hulk Hogan.

Holden

English, meaning 'deep valley'.

Hollis

Old English, meaning 'holly tree'.

Homer

Greek, meaning 'pledge'. Name of the Greek poet – and of the TV character Homer Simpson.

Honorius

Latin, meaning 'honourable'. Honorius was a Roman emperor in the fifth century BC.

Horace

Latin, common name of the Roman poet Quintus Horatius Flaccus.

Houston

Old English, meaning 'Hugh's town'. Also a city in the state of Texas, USA.

Howard

Old English, meaning 'noble watchman'. Howard Hughes was a businessman, film-maker and aviator and extremely wealthy. Howard Donald is a founding member of enduringly successful boy band Take That.

Howell

Welsh, meaning 'eminent and remarkable'. Also the name of a town in Lincolnshire.

Hoyt

Norse, meaning 'spirit' or 'soul'. Also believed to be an Old English name, meaning someone who lives on a hill.

Hristo

From Christo, meaning 'follower of Christ'. Hristo Stoichkov is acknowledged to be one of the best footballers of his generation, and the best Bulgarian footballer ever.

Hubbell
(alt. Hubble)

English, meaning 'brave hearted'.

Hubert

German, meaning 'bright and shining intellect'.

Hudson

Old English, meaning 'adventurous' or 'son of Hugh'. Also one of the largest rivers in the USA.

Hugh
(alt. Hubert, Hugo, Huw)

Old German, meaning 'soul, mind and intellect'. Famous Hughs include actors Hugh Grant, Hugh Laurie and Hugh Jackman. Huw Stephens is a Welsh TV and radio presenter.

Humbert

Old German, meaning 'famous giant'. Be warned: it's the name and surname of the paedophile protagonist of Vladimir Nabokov's novel *Lolita*.

Humphrey

Old German, meaning 'peaceful warrior'. Actor Humphrey Bogart is best known for his role in the film *Casablanca*.

Hunter

English. Popular name in the USA for boys, yet to take off in the UK.

Hurley

Gaelic, meaning 'sea tide'.

Huxley

Old English, meaning 'Hugh's meadow'.

Hyrum
(alt. Hiram, Hyram)

Hebrew, meaning 'exalted brother'. Hyrum Smith was one of the founders of the Church of Jesus Christ of Latter Day Saints; also known as the Mormons.

Boys' names

Iago

Spanish, meaning 'he who supplants'. Name of the villain in Shakespeare's *Othello*.

Ian
(alt. Ion, Iain)

Gaelic, variant of John, meaning 'God is gracious'. Famous Ians include former cricketer Sir Ian Botham, novelists Ian Fleming and Iain Banks and journalist and satirist Ian Hislop.

Ianto

Welsh, meaning 'gift of God'. Ianto Jones is a featured character in sci-fi drama series *Torchwood*.

Ibaad

Arabic, meaning 'a believer in God'.

Ibrahim

Arabic, meaning 'father of many'. Also the Arabic name for the prophet and father of Islam, Abraham.

Ichabod

Hebrew, meaning 'glory is good'. The protagonist in Washington Irving's short story 'The Legend of Sleepy Hollow' is called Ichabod Crane.

Ichiro

Japanese, meaning 'firstborn son'. A current Japanese superstar baseball player is Ichiro Suzuki.

Idan

Hebrew, meaning 'place in time'.

Idris

Welsh, meaning 'fiery leader'. Actor Idris Elba is known for his roles in *The Wire*, *Luther* and *Mandela: Long Walk to Freedom*.

Ieuan
(alt. Ioan)

Welsh variant of John, meaning 'God is gracious'.

Ignacio

Latin, meaning 'ardent' or 'burning'. More commonly found in South America, particularly Uruguay and Argentina.

Ignatz

German, meaning 'fiery'.

Igor

Russian or Norse origin, meaning 'warrior'.

Ikaika

Hawaiian, meaning 'strong'.

Iku

Japanese, meaning 'nourishing'.

Ilan
(alt. Elan)

Hebrew, meaning 'tree'. Composer Ilan Eshkeri is known for his scores of several films, including *Layer Cake* and *Kick-Ass*.

Ilias

Greek variant of Hebrew Elijah, meaning 'the Lord is my God'.

Imanol

Basque-language variant of Immanuel, meaning 'God is with us'.

Indiana

Latin, meaning 'from India'. Also the film character Indiana Jones and the American state.

Indigo

English, describing a deep blue colour derived from a plant. Used as a boys' and girls' name.

Indio

Spanish, meaning 'indigenous people'.

Ingo

Danish, meaning 'meadow'. Also the name of a tropical plant.

Inigo

Spanish, meaning 'fiery'. Famous Inigos include the 16th-century architect Inigo Jones and a character in the film *The Princess Bride*.

Ian

Welsh, meaning 'gift of God'. Ioan Gruffudd is a Welsh actor.

Ioannis

Greek, meaning 'the Lord is gracious'.

Iovianno

Native American, meaning 'yellow hawk'. More common as a spelling alternative for Giovanni.

Ira

Hebrew, meaning 'full grown and watchful'. In the Hindu faith, Ira-putra is Hanuman the monkey god. Ira Gershwin was a famous 20th-century American lyricist.

Irvin
(alt. Irving, Irwin)

Gaelic, meaning 'green and fresh water'. Composer Irving Berlin is known for songs such as 'White Christmas' and 'Alexander's Ragtime Band'.

Isaac
(alt. Isaak; abbrev. Ike)

Hebrew, meaning 'laughter'. Isaac was the son of Abraham and Sarah in the Bible and the Qur'an. Famous Ikes include singer Ike Turner and former US president Dwight D. Eisenhower (known as Ike).

Isadore
(alt. Isidore, Isidro)

Greek, meaning 'gift of Isis'. Popular name in both ancient Greece and ancient Egypt.

Isai
(alt. Isaiah, Isaias, Izaiah)

Arabic, meaning 'protection and security'.

Iser
Yiddish, meaning 'God wrestler'. Most common in Germany.

Ishedus
Native American, meaning 'on top'.

Ishmael
(alt. Ismael)

Hebrew, meaning 'God listens'. Ishmael was the son of the prophet Abraham and his wife Hagar.

Israel
Hebrew, meaning 'God perseveres'. Also the name of the country.

Istvan
Hungarian variant of Stephen, meaning 'crowned'. Very common in Eastern Europe.

Itai
Hebrew, meaning 'the Lord is with me'. One of the most common names in Israel.

Ivan
Hebrew, meaning 'God is gracious'. Russian Grand Prince Ivan the Terrible conquered so much land to create the vast country of Russia.

Ivanhoe
Russian, meaning 'God is gracious'. Also name of the novel by Walter Scott.

Ivey
English, variant of Ivy usually reserved for boys.

Ivo
French, from the word 'yves', meaning 'yew tree'. Dr Ivo Robotnik is the villain in Sonic the Hedgehog video games.

Ivor
Scandinavian, meaning 'yew'. Welsh-born composer and songwriter Ivor Novello was an influential performer in the first half of the 20th century.

Ivory
Latin, meaning 'white as elephant tusks'. More commonly used as a girls' name.

Izar
Basque, meaning 'star'. The izar is also a piece of Ihram clothing worn during the Islamic Hajj pilgrimage.

Boys' names

Jabari
Swahili, meaning 'valiant'.

Jabez
Hebrew, meaning 'borne in pain'.
Jabez is a well-respected ancestor of
Judah in the Bible.

Jabulani
(alt. Jabulanie, Jabulany, Jabulaney)
Swahili, meaning 'happy one'. The
Jabulani is also a name for a type
of Adidas football used in most
professional Association games.

Jace
(alt. Jaece, Jase, Jayce)
Hebrew, meaning 'healer'.
Sometimes used as a shortened
version of Jason.

Jacek
Polish, meaning 'hyacinth'. Derived
from the Greek name Hyakinthos,
which comes from an ancient myth
about a beautiful boy.

Jacinto
Spanish or Portuguese, meaning
'hyacinth'.

Jack
(alt. Jackie, Jacky)
From the Hebrew John, meaning
'God is gracious'. The UK's most
popular boys' name for 14 years
until fairly recently.

Jackson
(alt. Jaxon, Jaxson)
English, meaning 'son of Jack'.
Jackson Pollock was an abstract
expressionist artist, known for his
large-scale paintings.

Jacob
*(alt. Jacobo, Jaco, Jago; abbrev.
Jake)*
Hebrew, meaning 'he who
supplants'. Ancestor of the tribes of
Israel in the Bible.

Jacques
(alt. Jaquez)

French form of James, meaning 'he who supplants'. Famous Jacques include Jacques Cousteau, the marine explorer, writer and film-maker, and Jacques Villeneuve, the racing driver.

Jaden
(alt. Jadyn, Jaeden, Jaiden, Jaidyn, Jayden, Jaydin)

Hebrew, meaning 'Jehovah has heard'. Actor Will Smith's eldest child is called Jaden Smith, and has an acting career of his own.

Jaeger
(alt. Jager, Jaecer, Jaegar)

German, meaning 'mighty hunter'. Also the name of a British designer clothing line.

Jafar

Arabic, meaning 'stream'. The name of the villain in Disney's *Aladdin*.

Jagger

Old English, meaning 'one who cuts'. Sir Mick Jagger is the lead singer of the Rolling Stones.

Jaheem
(alt. Jaheim)

Hebrew, meaning 'raised up'. R&B singer Jaheim Hoagland goes by the stage name Jaheim.

Jahir

Hindi, meaning 'jewel'.

Jair
(alt. Jairo)

Hebrew, meaning 'God enlightens'.

Jalen
(alt. Jalon, Jaylon, Jaylan)

American, meaning 'healer' or 'tranquil'. The original spelling was probably Galen, in Greek.

Jali

Gujarati, meaning 'latticed screen'. Popular form of architectural detailing throughout India.

Jamar
(alt. Jamarcus, Jamari, Jamarion, Jamir)

Modern variant of Jamaal, meaning 'handsome'. More common in the USA than in Britain.

Jamel
(alt. Jamal, Jamaal, Jamil)

Arabic, meaning 'handsome'. Actor Jamel Debbouze is a French and Moroccan film star.

James
(alt. Jaime; abbrev. Jamie, Jamey, Jim, Jimmy)

English, meaning 'he who supplants'. An enduringly popular name. Famous actors with this name include James Coburn, James Franco, James Corden, Jamie Bell and Jamie Foxx.

Jameson
(alt. Jamison)

English, meaning 'son of James'.

Jamin
(alt. Yamin)

Hebrew, meaning 'son of the right hand'.

Jan
(alt. Janko, János)

Slavic, from John, meaning 'the Lord is gracious'. Jan is also a term of endearment in Arabic, meaning 'dear'. Used for boys and also girls.

Janesh

Hindi, meaning 'leader of people'.

Janus

Latin, meaning 'gateway'. The two-faced Roman god of doors, beginnings and endings.

Japheth
(alt. Japhet)

Hebrew, meaning 'comely'. One of the sons of Noah in the Bible.

Jared
(alt. Jarem, Jaren, Jaret, Jarod, Jarrod)

Hebrew, meaning 'descending'. Actor Jared Leto is known for his roles in *Fight Club*, *American Psycho* and *Dallas Buyers Club*.

Jarlath

Gaelic, from St Iarlaithe mac Loga.

Jarom

Greek, meaning 'to raise and exalt'. One of the prophets in the Book of Mormon.

Jarrell

Variant of Gerald, meaning 'spear ruler'.

Jarrett

Old English, meaning 'spear-brave'. Sometimes used as an alternative spelling to Garrett.

Jarvis

Old German, meaning 'with honour'. Jarvis Cocker is the singer with the band Pulp.

Jason

Greek, meaning 'healer'. Famous Jasons include actor Jason Statham, and the ancient Greek myth of Jason and the Argonauts.

Jasper

Greek, meaning 'treasure holder' or 'speckled stone'. The stone jasper has been used for thousands of years for carved ornaments and jewellery. Jasper Conran is a modern fashion designer.

Javen
(alt. Javan)

Arabic, meaning 'youth'. Javan was one of Noah's grandsons in the Bible.

Javier

Spanish, meaning 'bright'. Actor Javier Bardem is known for his roles in *No Country for Old Men* and the James Bond movie *Skyfall*.

Jay

Latin, meaning 'jaybird'. Jays are a group of bird species in the crow family.

Jeevan

Sanskrit, meaning 'life'. Often used with a prefix such as 'har', to form other names (such as Harjeevan).

Jefferson

English, meaning 'son of Jeffrey'.

Jeffrey

(abbrev. Jeff)

Old German, meaning 'peace'. Famous Jeffreys include author Jeffrey Archer, and actors Jeff Bridges and Jeff Daniels.

Jensen

(alt. Jenson)

Scandinavian, meaning 'son of Jan'. Has increased in popularity in the UK in recent years, probably linked to the rise of Jenson Button, Formula One racing driver.

Jeremiah

(alt. Jeremia, Jeremias, Jeremiya)

Hebrew, meaning 'the Lord exalts'. One of the main prophets in the Bible.

Jeremy

(alt. Jem)

Hebrew, meaning 'the Lord exalts'. Famous Jeremys include actors Jeremy Irons and Jeremy Renner, and presenter Jeremy Clarkson.

Jeriah

Hebrew, meaning 'Jehovah has seen'.

Jericho

Arabic, meaning 'city of the moon'. An ancient and religious city in the Palestinian West Bank.

Jermaine

Latin, meaning 'brotherly'. Jermaine Jackson was one of the original members of the Jackson 5.

Jerome

Greek, meaning 'sacred name'. Famous Jeromes include actor Jerome Flynn, and St Jerome, who was a medieval priest and theologian.

Jerry

English, from Gerald, meaning 'spear ruler'. Famous Jerrys include presenter Jerry Springer, comedian Jerry Seinfeld and the film *Jerry Maguire*.

Jesse

Hebrew, meaning 'the Lord exists'. Jesse James was a Wild West outlaw and train robber in the 1870s.

Jesus

Hebrew, meaning 'the Lord is Salvation' and the Son of God.

Jet

(alt. Jett)

English, meaning 'black gemstone'. Jet is a minor gemstone, formed of fossilised wood.

Jethro

Hebrew, meaning 'eminent'. Famous Jethros include Jethro Tull, the agricultural pioineer, who gave his name to a 1970s rock band, and the father-in-law of Moses in the Bible.

Jim
(alt. Jimmy)

From James, meaning 'he who supplants'. Jim is one of the leading characters in Mark Twain's classic novel *Huckleberry Finn*.

Jiri
(alt. Jiro)

Czech, meaning 'farmer'. More commonly used in Czech-speaking communities as an alternative to George.

Joachim
(alt. Joaquin)

Hebrew, meaning 'established by God'. Also the name of the Virgin Mary's father in the Bible. Actor Joaquin Phoenix is known for his roles in *Gladiator*, *Walk the Line* and *Her*.

Joah
(alt. João)

Hebrew, meaning 'God is gracious'.

Joe
(alt. Joey, Jomar)

From Joseph, meaning 'Jehovah increases'. Usually used as a nickname for Joseph, Joel or Josiah, as well as a name in its own right.

Football players

Aaron (Lennon)

Alan (Shearer)

Ashley (Cole)

Daniel (Sturridge)

Darren (Fletcher)

David (Beckham)

Frank (Lampard)

Gareth (Bale)

Gary (Lineker)

Jack (Wilshere)

Joe (Cole)

Rio (Ferdinand)

Scott (Parker)

Steven (Gerrard)

Wayne (Rooney)

Joel

Hebrew, meaning 'Jehovah is the Lord'.

John
(alt. Johan, Johannes, Johnny)

Hebrew, meaning 'God is gracious'. John the Baptist and the apostle John are major characters in the New Testament of the Bible.

Jolyon

English, meaning 'young'. One of the more prominent characters in the 'Tintin' comic series is Jolyon Wagg.

Jonah
(alt. Jonas)

Hebrew, meaning 'dove'. In the Bible, Jonah was swallowed by a whale.

Jonathan
(alt. Johnathan, Johnathon, Jonathon; abbrev. Jon, Jonny, Jonty)

Hebrew, meaning 'God is gracious'. Famous Jonathans include comedian and TV presenter Jonathan Ross, author Jonathan Swift and actor Jonathan Pryce.

Jordan
(alt. Jory, Judd)

Hebrew, meaning 'down-flowing'. Can be used as a girls' name or a boys' name.

Jorge

Spanish or Portuguese version of George, meaning 'farmer'. Actor Jorge Garcia is known for his role as Hurley in the television series *Lost*.

José

Spanish variant of Joseph, meaning 'God increases'. José Mourinho is a football manager known as 'the special one'.

Joseph
(alt. Josef, Joss)

Hebrew, meaning 'Jehovah increases'. Famous Josephs include two Biblical Josephs: the wearer of the many-coloured coat and the father of Jesus Christ; and the actor Joseph Fiennes.

Joshua
(abbrev. Josh)

Hebrew, meaning 'God is salvation'. Joshua was the leader of the Israelites after Moses' death in the Bible.

Josiah

Hebrew, meaning 'God helps'. One of the kings of Judah in the Bible.

Josué

Spanish variant of Joshua, meaning 'God is salvation'.

Jovan

Latin, meaning 'the supreme God'. More commonly used in Serbia and Macedonia.

Joweese

Native American, meaning 'chirping bird'. Originally used more commonly for girls, it has now become a boys' name.

Joyce

Latin, meaning 'joy'. More commonly used as a girls' name but can be used for boys.

Juan

Spanish variant of John, meaning 'God is gracious'. It is also becoming a popular name for girls in China, with the meaning of 'chapter or scroll' in Mandarin.

Jubal

Hebrew, meaning 'ram's horn'. Also the name of the 'father of music' in the Bible.

Jude
(alt. Judson)

Hebrew, meaning 'praise' or 'thanks'. Famous Judes include St Jude, the patron saint of lost causes, actor Jude Law and Thomas Hardy's novel *Jude the Obscure*.

Julian
(alt. Julio, Julien; abbrev. Juels, Jules, Jools)

Greek, meaning 'belonging to Julius'. The original calendar in the Roman empire was called the Julian calendar. Famous Julians include author Jules Verne, DJ Judge Jules and pianist/presenter Jools Holland.

Julius

Latin, meaning 'youthful'. Julius Caesar was dictator of Rome and the first Roman emperor, ruling in the first century BC.

Junior

Latin, meaning 'the younger one'. Can also be used as a suffix to names to denote a name that has been passed down from father to son (such as Steve Jones Sr and Steve Jones Jr).

Junius

Latin, meaning 'young'. The pseudonym of an anonymous and prolific political writer in the 18th century.

Jupiter

Latin, meaning 'the supreme God'. Jupiter was king of the Roman gods and the god of thunder. Jupiter is also the largest planet in the solar system.

Juraj

Hebrew, meaning 'God is my judge'. More popular in Eastern Europe.

Jurgen

German form of George, meaning 'farmer'. Jurgen Klinsmann was a professional football player in the 1980s and '90s.

Justice

English, from the word 'justice', meaning a set of moral values, ethics and law.

Justin
(alt. Justus)

Latin, meaning 'just and upright'. Famous Justins include singers Justin Timberlake and Justin Bieber, and children's TV presenter Justin Fletcher.

Juwan

Hebrew, meaning 'the Lord is gracious'.

Boys' names

Kabelo
Swahili, meaning 'gift'. Popular name in Botswana.

Kade
Scottish, meaning 'from the wetlands'. More commonly used as a spelling alternative to Cade.

Kadeem
Arabic, meaning 'one who serves'. Actor Kadeem Hardison is known for his role in Tv series *A Different World*.

Kaden
(alt. *Kadin, Kaeden, Kaedin, Kaiden*)
Arabic, meaning 'companion'. Also the name of a town in Germany.

Kadir
Arabic, meaning 'capable and competent'.

Kafka
Czech, meaning 'bird-like'. Often associated with the author Franz Kafka.

Kahekili
Hawaiian, meaning 'the thunder'. Also the name of several kings of Maui.

Kahlil
(alt. *Kalil*)
Arabic, meaning 'friend'. The Lebanese author Kahlil Gibran is known for his work *The Prophet*.

Kai
Greek, meaning 'keeper of the keys'. Kai has meanings in several languages, including 'dog' in Cornish, 'ocean water' in Hawaiian and 'food' in Maori.

Kaito
Japanese, a combination of the words 'sea, ocean' and 'soar, fly'.

Kalani
Hawaiian, meaning 'sky'.

Kale
German, meaning 'free man'. Also the name of a leafy green vegetable.

Kaleb
(alt. Caleb)
Hebrew, meaning 'dog' or 'aggressive'. Kaleb was also the most prominent King of Aksum, the capital of Abyssinia, in the sixth century.

Kalen
Gaelic, meaning 'uncertain'.

Kaleo
Hawaiian, meaning 'the voice'. Kaleo Kanahele is a silver medal-winning American paralympian in volleyball.

Kamari
Sanskrit, meaning 'the enemy of desire'. Also the name of a popular tourist destination in Greece.

Kamden
English, meaning 'winding valley'. Also an alternative spelling for Camden.

Kamil
(alt. Kaamil)
Arabic, meaning 'perfection'. Also a Polish and Slovak name meaning 'religious service attender'.

Kane
Gaelic, meaning 'little battler'.

Kani
Hawaiian, meaning 'sound'.

Kanye
A town in Botswana. Made popular by rapper Kanye West.

Kareem
(alt. Karim)
Arabic, meaning 'generous'.

Karl
(alt. Karson)
Old German, meaning 'free man'.

Kasey
Irish, meaning 'alert'.

Kaspar
Persian, meaning 'treasurer'. Also an alternative spelling for Casper.

Kavon
Gaelic, meaning 'handsome'. More commonly used in the USA.

Kayden
Arabic, meaning 'companion'. Also an alternative spelling for Caden.

Kazimierz
Polish, meaning 'declares peace'. Also the name of a town in Poland.

Kazuki
Japanese, meaning 'radiant hope'. Kazuki Takahashi is a well-known Japanese artist and video game creator.

Kazuo
Japanese, meaning 'harmonious man'. Depending on the characters/spellings used, Kazuo can also mean 'first son' or 'first in leadership'.

Keagan
(alt. Keegan, Kegan)
Gaelic, meaning 'small flame'.

Keane

Gaelic, meaning 'fighter'.

Keanu

Hawaiian, meaning 'breeze'. Actor Keanu Reeves is known for his roles in *Bill & Ted's Excellent Adventure*, *Speed* and *The Matrix* trilogy.

Keary

Gaelic, meaning 'black-haired'. Also used as a girls' name.

Keaton

English, meaning 'place of hawks'. Buster Keaton was a famous American actor and director of silent films.

Keefe
(alt. Keef, Keeffe, Kief, Kiefe)

Gaelic, meaning 'cherished, gentle and kind'.

Keeler

Middle English, meaning 'cool'. Also a term used for a small, shallow tub for bathing.

Keenan
(alt. Kenan)

Gaelic, meaning 'little ancient one'.

Keiji

Japanese, meaning 'govern with discretion'. Also a term sometimes used for police officers.

Keir

Gaelic, meaning 'dark-haired' or 'dark-skinned'. James Keir Hardie was a Scottish socialist and labour leader in the 19th and 20th centuries.

Keith

Gaelic, meaning 'woodland'. Famous Keiths include Rolling Stones band member Keith Richards and chef Keith Floyd.

Kekoa

Hawaiian, meaning 'brave one' or 'soldier'.

Kelby

Old English, meaning 'farmhouse near the stream'.

Kell
(alt. Kellan, Kellen, Kelley, Kelly, Kiel)

Norse, meaning 'spring'. Usually associated with the ancient and lavishly illustrated *Book of Kells* (as well as the cartoon movie).

Kelsey

Old English, meaning 'victorious ship'. Actor Kelsey Grammer is known for his roles in *Cheers* and *Frasier*.

Kelton

Old English, meaning 'town of the keels'. Singer Roy Orbison (of 'Oh, Pretty Woman' fame) had the middle name Kelton.

Kelvin

Old English, meaning 'friend of ships'. A kelvin is a unit of measurement for temperature, using the Kelvin scale.

Kemenes

Hungarian, meaning 'maker of furnaces'. More commonly used in Eastern Europe.

Kendal

Old English, meaning 'the Kent river valley'.

Kendon

Old English, meaning 'brave guard'.

Kendrick

Gaelic, meaning 'royal ruler'. Fairly popular in the USA, where famous Kendricks include hip hop artist Kendrick Lamar and record producer Kendrick Dean.

Kenelm

Old English, meaning 'bold'. St Kenelm was a boy king and martyr, mentioned in *The Canterbury Tales*.

Kenji

Japanese, meaning 'intelligent second son'. Also the name of a period in Japanese history in the 13th century.

Kennedy

Gaelic, meaning 'helmet head'. The Kennedy family are a prominent American-Irish Catholic dynasty, whose members have included President John F. Kennedy.

Kenneth

(abbrev, Ken, Kenny, Kenney)

Gaelic, meaning 'born of fire'. Famous Kenneths include actor Sir Kenneth Branagh and designer brand Kenneth Cole.

Kennison

English, meaning 'son of Kenneth'.

Kent

English, meaning 'rim or border'. From the county of the same name in England.

Kenton

English, meaning 'town of Ken'. Kenton Cool is a British mountaineer and mountain guide. He has climbed Mount Everest 11 times.

Kenya

From the country and mountain in Africa.

Kenzo

Japanese, meaning 'wise'. Kenzo Takada is the Japanese designer who founded the fashion brand Kenzo.

Keola

Hawaiian, meaning 'life'.

Keon

(alt. Kean, Keoni)

Persian, meaning 'King of Kings'. In Hawaiian, the same spelling means 'God is gracious'.

Kepler

German, meaning 'hat maker'.

Kerr

English, meaning 'wetland'. Kerr Smith is an American actor.

Kerry

Irish, from the county of the same name. More commonly a girls' name.

Kerwin
(alt. Kermit)

Gaelic, meaning 'without envy'. Most popular in the USA.

Keshav

Sanskrit, meaning 'beautiful-haired'. One of the names for Vishnu in the Hindu religion.

Kevin

Gaelic, meaning 'handsome beloved'. Famous Kevins include former footballer Kevin Keegan and actors Kevin Kline and Kevin Bacon.

Khalid
(alt. Khaled, Khalif, Khalil)

Arabic, meaning 'immortal'. Actor Khalid Abdalla is known for his roles in *United 93* and *The Kite Runner*.

Kian
(alt. Keyon, Kyan)

Persian, meaning 'king or realm'. In Ireland, the same spelling means 'ancient'.

Kiefer

German, meaning 'barrel maker'. Actor Kiefer Sutherland is best known for his role in the series *24*.

Kieran
(alt. Kiaran, Kieron, Kyron)

Gaelic, meaning 'black'. Famous Kierans include gymnast Kieran Behan and actor Kieran Culkin.

Kijana

Swahili, meaning 'youth'.

Kilby

From the English 'Cilebi', a place in Leicestershire.

Kilian

Irish, meaning 'bright headed'. St Kilian was a bishop in Ireland in the seventh century.

Kimani

Swahili, meaning 'beautiful and sweet'. Kenyan Kimani Maruge held the Guinness World Record for being the oldest person to start primary school, at the ripe old age of 84.

King

English, from the word 'male ruler of state'.

Kingsley

English, meaning 'the king's meadow'. Sir Kingsley Amis was an English novelist.

Kirby

German, meaning 'settlement by a church'. Also the name of a small, pink, bubble-like video game character.

Kirk

Old German, meaning 'church'.

Klaus

German, meaning 'victorious'. Also a shortened form of Nikolaus.

Knightley
(alt. Knightly)

English, meaning 'of the knight's meadows'. An English place name in Staffordshire.

Kobe
(alt. Koda, Kody)
Japanese, meaning 'a Japanese city'.

Kofi
Akan, meaning 'born on Friday'. Kofi Annan was Secretary General of the United Nations from 1997 to 2006.

Kohana
Japanese, meaning 'little flower'. The Kohana cat is a hairless breed of cat.

Kojo
Akan, meaning 'Monday'. Kojo is also a type of computer programming language.

Kolby
Norse, meaning 'settlement'. Often used as a spelling alternative for Colby.

Komal
Hindi, meaning 'soft and tender'.

Korben
(alt. Korbin)
Gaelic, meaning 'a steep hill'. Korben Dallas is the protagonist in the sci-fi film The Fifth Element.

Kramer
German, meaning 'shopkeeper'. Usually associated with the character Kramer in the 1990s sitcom Seinfeld.

Kris
(alt. Krish, Kristoff)
From Christopher, meaning 'Christ bearer'. Can be a short form of Kristopher, Kristian or (for girls) Kristen.

Kurt
German, meaning 'courageous advice'. Famous Kurts include Glee character Kurt, actor Kurt Russell and singer Kurt Cobain.

Kurtis
French, meaning 'courtier'.

Kwame
Akan, meaning 'born on Saturday'. Kwame Nkrumah was the first president of Ghana.

Kyden
English, meaning 'narrow little fire'. Sometimes used as a spelling alternative for Caden.

Kyle
(alt. Kylan, Kyleb, Kyler)
Scottish Gaelic, meaning 'narrow and straight'. Originated from the place name in Scotland.

Kyllion
Irish, meaning 'war'.

Kylo
(alt. Kyloh)
American, from the Latin word for 'sky'. Kylo Ren is a main character in the modern Star Wars trilogy.

Kyree
From Cree, a Canadian tribe. More commonly used in the USA.

Kyros
Greek, meaning 'legitimate power'. Kyros of Constantinople was an important figure in the Orthodox Church in the eighth century.

L Boys' names

Laban
Hebrew, meaning 'white'. Laban is the brother of Rebekah in the Bible.

Lachlan
Gaelic, meaning 'from the land of lakes'. A popular name in Australia.

Lacy
Old French, after the place in France. The feminine equivalent is Lacey.

Laertes
English, meaning 'adventurous'. Ophelia's brother in Shakespeare's *Hamlet*.

Lalit
Hindi, meaning 'beautiful'. The Lalit is one of the melodic aspects of Indian classical music.

Lamar
(alt. Lemar)

Old German, meaning 'water'. Singer Lemar is known for his songs 'Dance (With U)' and 'If There's Any Justice'.

Lambert
(alt. Lambros)

Scandinavian, two elements meaning 'land' and 'brilliant'. The name has been in use since Roman times.

Lamont
Old Norse, meaning 'law man'.

Lancelot
(abbrev. Lance)

Variant of Lance, meaning 'land'. The name of one of the Knights of the Round Table. Cyclist Lance Armstrong won the Tour de France seven times before being stripped of his titles for cheating.

Landen
(alt. Lando, Landon, Langdon, Landen)

English, meaning 'long hill'. Also the name of a town in Belgium.

Lane
(alt. Layne)

English, from the common word meaning 'narrow road'.

Lang
(alt. Langston)
Norse, meaning 'long meadow'.

Lannie
(alt. Lanny)
German, meaning 'precious'. Sometimes used as a nickname for Roland or Orlando, as well as a name in its own right.

Larkin
Gaelic, meaning 'rough' or 'fierce'. Poet Philip Larkin was known for his works The Whitsun Weddings and High Windows.

Laron
French, meaning 'thief'.

Larry
Latin, variant of Laurence, meaning 'man from Laurentum'. Famous Larrys include actor Larry Hagman and presenter Larry King.

Lars
Scandinavian variant of Laurence, meaning 'man from Laurentum'. The founder of Swedish electronics brand Ericsson was called Lars Magnus Ericsson.

Lasse
Finnish, meaning 'girl'. (Still, ironically, a boy's name.) Men with the name Lars are sometimes called Lasse as a nickname in Scandinavia. Finn Lasse Viren was one of the greatest long-distance runners of all time. Lasse Hallström is a Swedish film director.

Laszlo
Hungarian, meaning 'glorious rule'. Derived from the name of King/St Ladislaus I of Hungary.

Lathyn
Latin, meaning 'fighter'. Sometimes also used as a name for girls.

Latif
Arabic, meaning 'gentle'. The female equivalent for girls is Latifa.

Laurel
Latin, meaning 'bay'. One of the founders of Jamaican ska music was Laurel Aitken.

Laurence
(alt. Lawrence; abbrev. Larry)
Latin, meaning 'man from Laurentum'. Actor Sir Laurence Olivier was known for his roles in dozens of Shakespeare productions and Hollywood films.

Laurent
French form of Laurence, meaning 'man from Laurentum'. Laurent-Perrier is a champagne brand.

Lazarus
Hebrew, meaning 'God is my help'. In the Bible, Lazarus was said to have been raised from the dead by Jesus Christ.

Leandro
Spanish, meaning 'lion man'. More commonly used in South America.

Lear

German, meaning 'of the meadow'. Shakespeare's play *King Lear* tells the story of a wealthy king decending into madness.

Lee
(alt. Leigh)

English, meaning 'pasture' or 'meadow'. Famous Lees include comedian Lee Mack, *Harry Potter* character Lee Jordan and assassin Lee Harvey Oswald.

Leib

Yiddish, meaning 'lion'.

Leif
(alt. Liev)

Scandinavian, meaning 'heir'. Actor Liev Schreiber is known for his roles in *X-Men Origins: Wolverine*, the *Scream* trilogy and *Ray Donovan*.

Leith

From the name of a busy port town in Scotland.

Lennox

Gaelic, meaning 'with many elm trees'. Lennox Lewis is a retired world heavyweight boxing champion.

Lenny

Shortened form of Lennox or Leonard, as well as a name in its own right. Lenny Kravitz is a musician and Lenny Godber was a much-loved character in the classic TV series *Porridge*.

Leo
(alt. Leon)

Latin, meaning 'lion'. Also the star sign.

Leonard
(alt. Leonardo)

Old German, meaning 'lion strength'. Famous Leonardos include actor Leonardo DiCaprio and artist and inventor Leonardo da Vinci.

Leopold

German, meaning 'brave people'. Prince Leopold was Queen Victoria and Prince Albert's eighth child, who was known to suffer from the blood disorder haemophilia.

Leroy

French, meaning 'king'. The song 'Bad Bad Leroy Brown' was a hit for R&B singer Jim Croce in 1973.

Leslie
(abbrev. Les)

Scottish Gaelic, from the name of the prominent clan. Also meaning 'holly garden'. Usually spet Lesley when used as a name for girls.

Lester

English, meaning 'from Leicester'. Lester Piggott is one of England's most successful jockeys.

Lewis

English form of French Louis, meaning 'famous warrior'. Famous Lewises include Formula One racing driver Lewis Hamilton, comedian Lewis Black and *Alice in Wonderland* author Lewis Carroll.

Lex

English variant of Alexander, meaning 'defending men'. Lex Luthor is the villain of the *Superman* stories.

Liam

German, meaning 'helmet'. Famous Liams include actor Liam Neeson, singer Liam Gallagher and One Direction member Liam Payne.

Lincoln

English, meaning 'lake colony'.

Linden

European, from the tree of the same name. Less commonly used for girls.

Lindsay

Scottish, meaning 'linden tree'. In recent times used more for girls than for boys.

Linus

Latin, meaning 'lion'. Usually associated with the *Peanuts* cartoon strip character, who is known for carrying a blanket everywhere.

Lionel

English, meaning 'lion'. Famous Lionels include dancer/actor Lionel Blair, singer Lionel Richie and composer Lionel Bart.

Llewellyn

Welsh, meaning 'like a lion'.

Lloyd

Welsh, meaning 'grey-haired and sacred'. Famous Lloyds include actor Roger Lloyd Pack, former prime minister David Lloyd George and composer Andrew Lloyd Webber.

Logan

Gaelic, meaning 'hollow'. Usually associated with sci-fi novel *Logan's Run*. Has risen in popularity following 2017's *Logan* Wolverine film.

London

Pre-Celtic, meaning 'place at the navigable or unfordable river'.

Lonnie

English, meaning 'lion strength'.

Lorcan

Gaelic, meaning 'little fierce one'. Also the name of several kings of Leinster in Ireland.

Louis
(alt. Lou, Louie, Luigi, Luis)

French, meaning 'famous warrior'. The given name of the fifth in line to the throne, Prince Louis Arthur Charles, as well as One Direction's Louis Tomlinson, music manager Louis Walsh and designer brand Louis Vuitton.

Lucas
(alt. Lukas, Luca)

English, meaning 'man from Luciana'. Popular in Brazil – there are several Brazilian footballers with this first name.

Lucian
(alt. Lucio)

Latin, meaning 'light'. Lucian of Samosata was an ancient Greek writer. Lucian Freud was a painter.

Ludwig

German, meaning 'famous warrior'. Ludwig van Beethoven was a hugely influential Classical and Romantic composer.

Luke
(alt. Luc, Luka)

Latin, meaning 'from Lucanus'. Famous Lukes include the Gospel of Luke, *Star Wars* protagonist Luke Skywalker and late actor Luke Perry.

Lupe

Latin, meaning 'wolf'. Rapper Lupe Fiasco is known for his songs 'Superstar' and 'The Show Goes On'.

Luther

German, meaning 'soldier of the people'. Famous Luthers include the German church reformer Martin Luther, US civil rights activist Martin Luther King Jr and singer Luther Vandross.

Lyle

French, meaning 'the island'. Lyle Lovett is an American country singer.

Lyn
(alt. Lyndon)

Spanish, meaning 'pretty'. More commonly used as a name for girls.

Lynton

English, meaning 'town of lime trees'. Also a girls' name.

Boys' names

Mabon
(alt. Maban, Mabery)
Welsh, meaning 'our son'. A character in the King Arthur legend.

Mac
(alt. Mack, Mackie)
Scottish, meaning 'son of'.

Macaulay
Scottish, meaning 'son of the phantom'. Actor Macaulay Culkin shot to fame as a child actor in the *Home Alone* films.

Mace
English, meaning 'heavy staff' or 'club'. Can also be a nickname for Mason.

Mackenzie
Scottish, meaning 'the fair one'. Actor Mackenzie Crook is known for his roles in *The Office*, *Pirates of the Caribbean*, *Game of Thrones* and *The Detectorists*.

Mackland
Scottish, meaning 'land of Mac'.

Macon
French, name of towns in France and Georgia (USA).

Macsen
Scottish, meaning 'son of Mac'.

Madden
(abbrev. Mads)
Irish, meaning 'descendant of the hound'.

Maddox
English, meaning 'good' or 'generous'. Derived from Madoc, a legendary Welsh prince who supposedly discovered America years before Christopher Columbus. Maddox Jolie-Pitt is the eldest son of Angelina and Brad.

Madison
(alt. Madsen)
Irish, meaning 'son of Madden'.

Magnus
(alt. *Manus*)

Latin, meaning 'great'. Famous Magnuses include Magnus Carlsen the chess grand master and former TV presenter Magnus Magnusson.

Maguire
Gaelic, meaning 'son of the beige one'.

Mahabala
Sanskrit, meaning 'great strength'. Also the name of a Buddhist guardian.

Mahesh
Hindi, meaning 'great ruler'. Also one of the names of Lord Shiva in the Hindu faith.

Mahir
Arabic, meaning 'skilful'.

Mahlon
Hebrew, meaning 'sickness'. Found in the Bible.

Mahmoud
Arabic, meaning 'praiseworthy'. Mahmoud Ahmadinejad was the president of Iran until 2013.

Mahoney
Irish, meaning 'bear'.

Major
English, from the word 'major'.

Makal
Alternative to Michael or Mikael, meaning 'close to God'.

Makani
Hawaiian, meaning 'wind'. Also a popular name in Arabic-speaking communities.

Makis
Hebrew, meaning 'gift from God'.

Mako
Hebrew, meaning 'God is with us'.

Malachi
(alt. *Malachy*)

Hebrew, meaning 'messenger of God', the name of a Jewish prophet in the Bible. Also an Irish name.

Malcolm
English, meaning 'Columba's servant'. Famous Malcolms include activist Malcolm X, actor Malcolm McDowell and bestselling author and journalist Malcolm Gladwell.

Mali
Arabic, meaning 'full and rich'. Also the name of a West African republic.

Manfred
Old German, meaning 'man of peace'. The band Manfred Mann is known for the song 'Blinded by the Light'.

Manish
(alt. *Manesh*)

English, meaning 'manly'. Extremely popular name in large parts of India.

Manley
English, meaning 'manly and brave'. Also the name of a Cornish village.

Mannix

Gaelic, meaning 'little monk'. Usually associated with the detective series *Mannix*.

Manoi
(alt. Manos)

Japanese, meaning 'love springing from intellect'. Also the name of a Laotian king.

Manuel

Spanish variation of Hebrew Emanuel, meaning 'God is with us'. Usually associated with the character of Manuel in the sitcom *Fawlty Towers*.

Manzi

Italian, meaning 'steer'. Also the old name for parts of southern China.

Marc
(alt. Marco, Marcos, Marcus, Markel)

French, meaning 'from the god Mars'. Famous Marcs include designer brand Marc Jacobs, singer Marc Bolan and drummer Marc Bell.

Marcel
(alt. Marcelino, Marcello)

French, meaning 'little warrior'. One of the most famous mimes of all time was Frenchman Marcel Marceau.

Marek

Polish variant of Mark, meaning 'from the god Mars'.

Mariano

Latin, meaning 'from the god Mars'. Other theories suggest that Mariano is a tribute to the Virgin Mary.

Mario
(alt. Marius)

Latin, meaning 'manly'. Mario is a popular Nintendo video game character, alongside his brother Luigi. Mario Andretti is a retired Formula One world champion racing driver.

Mark
(alt. Markus)

English, meaning 'from the god Mars'. Famous Marks include the Gospel of Mark, actors Mark Hamill and Mark Wahlberg and author Mark Twain.

Marley
(alt. Marlin)

Old English, meaning 'meadow near the lake'. Sometimes used as a short form of Marlon. Famous Marleys include singer Bob Marley.

Marlo

American, meaning 'bitter'.

Marlon

English, meaning 'like little hawk'. Famous Marlons include actor Marlon Brando, singer Marlon Jackson and comedian Marlon Wayans.

Marshall

Old French, meaning 'caretaker of horses'. Also the name of a group of islands in the Pacific Ocean.

Martin
(abbrev. Marty)

Latin, meaning 'dedicated to Mars'. Famous Martins include actors Martin Freeman and Martin Sheen and director Martin Scorsese.

Marvel

English, from the word 'marvel'. Also the name of the long-running comic book company.

Marvin

Welsh, meaning 'sea friend'. Famous Marvins include singer Marvin Gaye and composer Marvin Hamlish.

Mason

English; a mason is a craftsman in either stonework or brickwork.

Massimo

Italian, meaning 'greatest'. The Massimo family were an ancient Roman family with great influence.

Mathias
(alt. Matthias)

Hebrew, meaning 'gift of the Lord'. Matthias was the apostle chosen to replace Judas in the Bible.

Mathieu

French form of Matthew, meaning 'gift of God'.

Matthew
(alt. Mathew)

Hebrew, meaning 'gift of the Lord'. Famous Matthews include the Gospel of Matthew and actors Matthew McConaughey and Matthew Lewis.

Maurice
(alt. Mauricio)

Latin, meaning 'dark skinned' or 'Moorish'. Children's author Maurice Sendak is best known for his work *Where the Wild Things Are*.

Maverick

American, meaning 'non-conformist leader'. Usually associated with the character Maverick from the *Top Gun* films.

Maximillian
(alt. Maximilian; abbrev. Max, Maxie, Maxim)

Latin, meaning 'greatest'. The name of several Roman emperors. Famous Maxes include actor Max Greenfield, the film *Mad Max: Fury Road*, and cosmetics brand Max Factor.

Maximino

Latin, meaning 'little Max'. More commonly used in Spanish-speaking communities.

Maxwell

Latin, meaning 'Maccus' stream'.

Maynard

Old German, meaning 'brave'. John Maynard Keynes was a highly influential British economist.

Mearl

English, meaning 'my earl'. Was used widely in the 19th century.

Mederic

French, meaning 'doctor'. Most commonly used in Quebec, Canada.

Mekhi

Swahili, meaning 'who is God?' Actor Mekhi Phifer is known for his roles in *ER*, *8 Mile* and *Divergent*.

Melbourne

From the city of the same name in Victoria, Australia.

Melchior

Persian, meaning 'king of the city'. The name of one of the three kings in the biblical story of the birth of Jesus.

Melton

English, meaning 'town of Mel'.

Melville

Scottish, meaning 'town of Mel'.

Melvin

(alt. Melvyn; abbrev. Mel)
English, meaning 'smooth brow'. Famous Melvins include DJ Melvin O'Doom, presenter Melvyn Bragg and actor Melvyn Douglas. Famous Mels include director Mel Brooks and comedian Mel Smith.

Memphis

Greek, meaning 'established and beautiful'. Also the name of a city in Tennessee, USA.

Mercer

English; a mercer was a man who traded or dealt in textiles.

Meredith

Welsh, meaning 'great ruler'. Used equally for girls and boys.

Merle

(alt. Merl, Murl)
French, meaning 'blackbird'.

Merlin

Welsh, meaning 'sea fortress'. Merlin was a magician and wise man in the King Arthur legend.

Merrick

Welsh, meaning 'Moorish'.

Merrill

Gaelic, meaning 'shining sea'.

Merritt

English, from the word 'merit'. Can be used for both boys and girls.

Merton

Old English, meaning 'town by the lake'. Also the name of a London borough.

Meyer

(alt. Mayer)
Hebrew, meaning 'bright farmer'.

Michael

(abbrev. Mick, Micky, Mickey, Mike, Mikey)
Hebrew, meaning 'resembles God'. Famous Michaels include one of the archangels, Formula One racing legend Michael Schumacher, singer Michael Jackson and comedian Michael McIntyre.

Michalis

Greek form of Michael, meaning 'resembles God'.

Michel

French form of Michael, meaning 'resembles God'. Deutscher Michel is also the cartoon personification of Germany (in the same way that Uncle Sam represents the USA).

Michelangelo

Italian, meaning 'Michael's angel'. Name of the famous painter whose work can still be seen in the Sistine Chapel in Rome.

Michele

Italian form of Michael, meaning 'resembles God'. Elsewhere, more commonly used as a girls' name.

Michio

Japanese, meaning 'a man with the strength of three thousand men'. Michio Kaku is a leading theoretical physicist.

Miguel

Spanish form of Michael, meaning 'resembles God'.

Miklos

Greek form of Nicholas, meaning 'victorious'. Sometimes used as an alternative to Michael as well.

Milan

From the name of the Italian city. Also the name of the son of singer-songwriter Shakira.

Miles

(alt. Milo, Milos, Myles)

English, from the word 'miles'. Famous Mileses include trumpeter Miles Davies, singer Miles Kane and *Star Trek: Next Generation* character Miles O'Brien.

Milton

English, meaning 'miller's town'.

Miro

Slavic, meaning 'peace'.

Misha

Russian, meaning 'resembles God'. Its English equivalent is often thought to be Mike, and the feminine version is Mischa.

Mitchell

(abbrev. Mitch)

English, meaning 'who is like God'. Mitchell Mark was a pioneer in motion picture technology.

Modesto

Italian, meaning 'modest'. Also the name of a town in California, USA.

Mohandas

Sanskrit, meaning 'servant'.

Monroe

Gaelic, meaning 'mouth of the river Rotha'.

Monserrate

Latin, meaning 'jagged mountain'. A mountain in Colombia.

Montague
(abbrev. Monty)
French, meaning 'pointed hill'.

Montana
Latin, meaning 'mountain'. Also a state in the USA.

Monte
Italian, meaning 'mountain'. Also the name of a popular card game.

Montgomery
(abbrev. Monty)
Variant of Montague, meaning 'pointed hill'. Monty Don is a well known TV personality and gardener.

Moody
English, from the word 'moody'. Mad Eye Moody is a prominent character in J.K. Rowling's *Harry Potter* series.

Mordecai
Hebrew, meaning 'little man'.

Morgan
Welsh, meaning 'great and bright'. Can be used for both boys and girls. Famous Morgans include actor Morgan Freeman, film maker Morgan Spurlock and musician Morgan Nicholls.

Moritz
Latin, meaning 'dark skinned and Moorish'. Also the German equivalent of Maurice.

Moroccan
Arabic, meaning 'from Morocco'. Also the name of one of Mariah Carey's twins.

Morpheus
Greek, meaning 'shape'. The name of the god of dreams in the epic poem *Metamorphoses* by Roman poet Ovid. Also a character in *The Matrix*.

Morris
Welsh, meaning 'dark skinned and Moorish'.

Morrison
English, meaning 'son of Morris'.

Mortimer
French, meaning 'dead sea'.

Morton
Old English, meaning 'moor town'. The name of several English towns.

Moses
(alt. Moshe, Moshon)
Hebrew, meaning 'saviour'. In the Bible, Moses receives the Ten Commandments from God.

Moss
English, meaning 'near a peat bog'.

Muhammad

(alt. Mohamed, Mohamet, Mohammad, Mohammed; abbrev. Mo)

Arabic, meaning 'praiseworthy'. Acknowledged as the prophet and founder of Islam. Sir Mo Farah is Britain's most decorated field and track athlete.

Muir

Gaelic, meaning 'of the moor'.

Mungo

Gaelic, meaning 'most dear'.

Murphy

Irish, meaning 'sea warrior'.

Murray

Gaelic, meaning 'lord and master'. Famous Murrays include legendary Formula One commentator Murray Walker and tennis star Andy Murray.

Mustafa

Arabic, meaning 'chosen'. Also a name for the prophet Muhammad in the Muslim faith.

Mwita

Swahili, meaning 'humorous one'.

Myron

Greek, meaning 'myrrh'. Myron was a popular sculptor in ancient Greece.

Boys' names

Nairn

Scottish, meaning 'alder-tree river'. From the Scottish town of the same name.

Najee

Arabic, meaning 'dear companion'. Also the name of an influential jazz musician.

Nakia

Arabic, meaning 'pure'. Also used as a name for girls.

Nakul

Sanskrit, meaning 'mongoose'. Choreographer Nakul Dev Mahajan has made a name for himself choreographing both Bollywood and Hollywood films.

Nana
(alt. Nanna)

Ghanaiian, meaning Your Royal Highness.

Naphtali
(alt. Naftali)

Hebrew, meaning 'wrestling'. One of Joseph's brothers in the Bible.

Napoleon

Italian, meaning 'man from Naples'. The French general Napoleon Bonaparte became Emperor of France.

Narciso

Latin, from the myth of Narcissus, who drowned after falling in love with his own reflection.

Nash

English, meaning 'at the ash tree'.

Nasir

Arabic, meaning 'helper'.

Nathan
(alt. Nathaniel; abbrev. Nat, Nate)

Hebrew, meaning 'God has given'.

Naval

Sanskrit, meaning 'wonder'.

Naveen

Sanskrit, meaning 'new'. Actor Naveen Andrews is known for his roles in *Lost*, *The English Patient* and *Rollerball*.

Ned

Used as a short form of Edward, meaning 'wealthy guard', but can be used in its own right. A character in *Game of Thrones* and *The Simpsons*.

Prime ministers' names

Alexander (Alec) (Douglas-Home)

Andrew (Bonar Law)

Anthony (Eden, Blair)

Arthur (Wellesley, Balfour, Chamberlain)

Benjamin (Disraeli)

Boris (Johnson)

Clement (Attlee)

David (Lloyd George, Cameron)

Edward (Heath)

Gordon (Brown)

Harold (Macmillan, Wilson – though neither of their first names was Harold)

James (Callaghan – whose first name was Leonard)

John (Stuart, Russell, Major)

Neville (Chamberlain)

Ramsay (MacDonald – whose first name was James)

Spencer (Crompton, Perceval)

Stanley (Baldwin)

William (Cavendish, Pitt (Elder and Younger), Wyndham, Lamb, Gladstone)

Winston (Churchill)

– and Margaret (Thatcher) and Theresa (May) for girls.

Nehemiah
Hebrew, meaning 'comforter'.

Neil
(alt. Neal, Niall)
Irish, meaning 'champion'.

Neilson
Irish, meaning 'son of Neil'. Also the name of a prominent train manufacturer in Scotland.

Nelson
Variant of Neil, meaning 'champion'. Admiral Horatio Nelson commanded the British navy at the Battle of Trafalgar. Nelson Mandela was the first black president of South Africa.

Nemo
Latin, meaning 'nobody'. Made famous by the Disney animation *Finding Nemo*.

Neo
Latin, meaning 'new'. Neo is the protagonist in *The Matrix* trilogy.

Nephi
Greek, meaning 'cloud'. The Books of Nephi are some of the subdivisions of the Book of Mormon.

Nessim
(alt. Nasim)
Arabic, meaning 'breeze'. Sham el-Nessim is also the first day of spring in Egypt.

Nestor
Greek, meaning 'traveller'. Nestor was the king of Pylos in ancient Greek mythology.

Neville
Old French, meaning 'new village'. Famous Nevilles include former prime minister Neville Chamberlain and *Harry Potter* character Neville Longbottom.

Newland
(alt. Newlands, Newland, Neuland)
English, meaning 'from a new land'. Also the name of several towns in the UK.

Newton
English, meaning 'new town'.

Neymar
Portuguese contraction of Latin names Netuno and Mars. Made popular by Brazilian footballer Neymar de Silva Santos.

Nicholas
(alt. Nicolas, Niklas; abbrev. Nick, Nicky, Niko, Nikos, Nico)
Greek, meaning 'victorious'. An enduringly popular name. Famous Nicholases include St Nicholas, actor Nicolas Cage and the alchemist Nicholas Flamel.

Nigel
Gaelic, meaning 'champion'. Famous Nigels include actor Nigel Hawthorne, photographer Nigel Barker and producer/presenter Nigel Lythgoe.

Nikhil
Sanskrit, meaning 'whole' or 'entire'.

Nikita
Greek, meaning 'unconquered', also Russian. Nikita Khrushchev was leader of the Soviet Union from 1953 to 1964. Also used as a girls' name.

Nikolai
(alt. Nikolay)
Russian variant of Nicholas, meaning 'victorious'. Several Russian emperors were known as either Nicholas or Nikolai.

Nimrod
Hebrew, meaning 'we will rebel'. Also the title of a piece of music by Elgar and the name of a type of aircraft.

Ninian
Gaelic, associated with the fifth-century saint of the same name.

Nissim
Hebrew, meaning 'wonderful things'.

Noah
Hebrew, meaning 'peaceful'. In the Bible, Noah is said to have built an ark to save two of every animal from a flood that covered the Earth.

Noel
French, meaning 'Christmas'. Famous Noels include actor/composer Noel Coward and musician Noel Gallagher.

Nolan
Gaelic, meaning 'champion'.

Norbert
Old German, meaning 'Northern brightness'. Norbert is also the name of Hagrid's pet dragon in J.K. Rowling's *Harry Potter* series.

Norman
Old German, meaning 'Northerner'.

Normand
French, meaning 'from Normandy'.

Norris
Old French, meaning 'Northerner'. Norris McWhirter was the co-author with his brother, Ross, of *The Guiness Book of Records*.

Norton
English, meaning 'Northern town'.

Norval
French, meaning 'Northern town'.

Norwood
English, meaning 'Northern forest'. Also the name of several towns in the UK.

Nova
Latin, meaning 'new'.

Nuno
Latin, meaning 'ninth'.

Nunzio
Italian, meaning 'messenger'. A fairly popular name in Italy.

Boys' names

Oakley

English, meaning 'from the oak meadow'. Also the name of a clothing brand.

Obadiah

Hebrew, meaning 'God's worker'. Used throughout the Bible to indicate a servant of God.

Obama

Swahili, meaning 'crooked'. Made famous by the 44th President of the USA, Barack Obama.

Obed

Hebrew, meaning 'servant of God'. Obed was the grandfather of David in the Bible.

Oberon

(abbrev. Obie)

Old German, meaning 'royal bear'. The Fairy King in Shakespeare's *A Midsummer Night's Dream*.

Obijulu

(alt. Obiajulu)

Swahili, meaning 'one who has been consoled'.

Octave

(alt. Octavian, Octavio)

Latin, meaning 'eight'. An octave is a group of eight notes in a musical scale.

Oda

(alt. Odell, Odie, Odis)

Hebrew, meaning 'praise God'. Oda of Canterbury was archbishop in the 10th century.

Ogden

Old English, meaning 'oak valley'. Ogden Nash was an American humorous poet.

Oisin

(alt. Osian, Ossian)

Celtic, meaning 'fawn'. The name of an ancient Irish poet.

Ola

Norse, meaning 'precious'. Ola Nordmann is the personification of Norway, in the same way Uncle Sam represents the USA.

Olaf
(alt. Olan)

Old Norse, meaning 'ancestor'. The name of the snowman in Disney's *Frozen*.

Oleander

Hawaiian, meaning 'joyous'. Also the name of a highly poisonous flowering shrub.

Oleg
(alt. Olen)

Russian, meaning 'holy'. Oleg the Seer was a Grand Prince of Rus', who ruled large parts of eastern Europe in the tenth century.

Olin

Russian, meaning 'rock'.

Oliver
(abbrev. Ollie)

Latin, meaning 'olive tree'. The UK's most popular boys' name in several recent years.

Olivier

French form of Oliver, meaning 'olive tree'.

Omar
(alt. Omari, Omarion)

Arabic, meaning 'speaker'. Extremely popular name in Sunni communities.

Ondrej

Czech, meaning 'manly'. The English equivalent is Andrew.

Ora

Latin, meaning 'hour'.

Oran
(alt. Oren, Orrin)

Gaelic, meaning 'light and pale'.

Orion

Greek, from the legend of a massive hunter who was sent to spend eternity as a star constellation.

Orlando
(alt. Orlo)

Old German, meaning 'old land'. Famous Orlandos include actor Orlando Bloom, the Shakespearean character Orlando in *As You Like It* and the city of Orlando in Florida, USA.

Orpheus

Greek, meaning 'beautiful voice'. Orpheus was an ancient Greek musician and charmer, who tried to rescue his wife from the underworld.

Orrick

English, meaning 'sword ruler'.

Orson

Latin, meaning 'bear'. Film director Orson Welles was known for his radio play *The War of the Worlds*, and films *Citizen Kane* and *Touch of Evil*.

Orville

Old French, meaning 'gold town'. Orville and Wilbur Wright were the American brothers credited with building the first successful aeroplane.

Osaka

From the Japanese city.

Osborne

(alt. Osbourne)

Norse, meaning 'bear god'.

Oscar

Old English, meaning 'spear of the Gods'. Oscar Wilde was an Irish poet and writer, best known for his ready wit.

Osias

Hebrew, meaning 'salvation'. Osias Beert was an influential still-life painter in the 17th century.

Oswald

German, meaning 'God's power'. Oswald the Lucky Rabbit was Walt Disney's original cartoon creation before Mickey Mouse was born.

Othello

Old German, meaning 'wealth'. From the character in Shakespeare's play *Othello*.

Otis

German, meaning 'wealth'. Singer Otis Redding was known for his songs '(Sittin' on) The Dock of the Bay', 'Respect' and 'Try A Little Tenderness'.

Otten

German, meaning 'son of Otto'.

Otto

(alt. Otha, Otho)

German, meaning 'wealthy'. Famous Ottos include Anne Frank's father, Otto Frank, and Prussian leader Otto von Bismarck.

Ovid

Latin, meaning 'sheep'. Associated with the Roman poet, author of *Metamorphoses*.

Owain

(alt. Owen)

Welsh, meaning 'noble-born'. Owain Ddantgwyn was a prince of Wales and a contender to be the real King Arthur.

Oz

Hebrew, meaning 'strength'. As well as the fictional land of Oz in the story *The Wizard of Oz*, this is also a slang term for Australia.

Boys' names

Pablo
Spanish, meaning 'little'. Spanish painter and sculptor Pablo Picasso was one of the most influential artists of the 20th century.

Paco
Native American, meaning 'eagle'. Also a Spanish alternative for Francisco.

Padma
Sanskrit, meaning 'lotus'. Also used as a name for girls.

Padraig
Irish, meaning 'noble'. The English equivalent is Patrick.

Panos
Greek, meaning 'all holy'.

Paolo
(alt. Paulo)
Italian, meaning 'little'. Paolo Nutini is a singer and Paulo Coelho is a Brazilian author.

Paresh
Sanskrit, meaning 'supreme spirit'.

Paris
From France's capital city. Also the Trojan prince in Homer's *Iliad* and Juliet's suitor in Shakespeare's *Romeo and Juliet*. Originally a boys' name, but now also used as a name for girls.

Pascal
Latin, meaning 'Easter child'.

Patrice
French form of Patrick, meaning 'noble'. Also a name given to girls.

Patrick
(abbrev. Pat, Paddy)
Irish, meaning 'noble'. The patron saint of Ireland. Sir Patrick Stewart is an English actor with a long and distinguished career on both stage and screen.

Patten
English, meaning 'noble'.

Paul

Hebrew, meaning 'small'. Pauls include the biblical Paul the Apostle, singers Paul Simon and Paul McCartney and artist Paul Cézanne.

Pavel

Latin, meaning 'small'. The English equivalent is Paul.

Pax

Latin, meaning 'peace'. From the Roman goddess of peace.

Paxton

English, meaning 'town of peace'.

Payne

Latin, meaning 'peasant'.

Payton

Latin, meaning 'peasant's town'.

Pedro

Spanish form of Peter, meaning 'rock'. Several kings of Portugal and Aragon have been named Pedro.

Penn

English, meaning 'hill'. Famous Penns include magician Penn Jillette and American actor Penn Badgley.

Percival

(abbrev. Percy)

French, meaning 'pierce the valley'. One of the Knights of the Round Table.

Perez

Hebrew, meaning 'breach'. One of Judah's sons in the Bible.

Pericles

Greek, meaning 'far-famed'. Pericles was an influential ancient Greek general and statesman.

Perrin

Greek, meaning 'rock'.

Perry

English, meaning 'rock'. Perry is an alcoholic drink made from pears.

Pervis

English, meaning 'purveyor'.

Pesah

(alt. Pesach, Pesasch)

Hebrew, meaning 'spared'. Pesach is the Hebrew name for the Jewish festival of Passover.

Peter

(abbrev. Pete)

Greek, meaning 'rock'. St Peter was one of Jesus's disciples in the Bible. Famous Peters include Peter Pan, film director Sir Peter Jackson, and Spiderman's real persona, Peter Parker.

Petros

Greek form of Peter, meaning 'rock'.

Peyton

Old English, meaning 'fighting man's estate'.

Philemon

Greek, meaning 'affectionate'. From the New Testament of the Bible.

Philip

(alt. Phillip; abbrev. Phil, Phill, Pip)

Greek, meaning 'lover of horses'. Famous Philips include Prince Philip, Philip the Apostle in the Bible and author Philip Pullman. Pip is usually associated with the lead character in Charles Dickens' novel *Great Expectations*.

Philo

Greek, meaning 'love'. Philo of Alexandria was an ancient Roman Jewish philosopher.

Phineas

(alt. Pinchas)

Hebrew, meaning 'oracle'. Phineas was an ancient Greek king of Thrace.

Phoenix

Greek, meaning 'dark red'. In ancient Greek mythology, a phoenix is a bird that has the power to regenerate itself from its ashes.

Pierre

French form of Peter, meaning 'rock'. A popular French name.

Piers

Old English form of Peter, meaning 'rock'. Journalist and TV presenter Piers Morgan is known for his work with various tabloid newspapers and *Britain's Got Talent*.

Pierson

Variant of Piers, meaning 'son of Piers'.

Placido

Latin, meaning 'placid'. Tenor opera singer Placido Domingo is known for his vast array of operatic roles and performances with Luciano Pavarotti and José Carreras.

Pradeep

Hindi, meaning 'light'.

Pranav

Sanskrit, meaning 'spiritual leader'. Pranava is another way of saying 'Om' in Sanskrit.

Presley

Old English, meaning 'priest's meadow'. Usually associated with music legend Elvis Presley.

Preston

Old English, meaning 'priest's town'. Also the name of a city in England. Preston Sturges was an Oscar-winning playwright.

Primo

Italian, meaning 'first'. Also used as a slang term for 'good' or 'excellent'.

Primus

Latin, meaning 'first'. Primus is often used in cartoons and comic books as a name for villains or superheroes, including in *Transformers* and Marvel comics.

Prince

English, from the word 'prince'. As well as a title of nobility, this name is often associated with the late singer Prince.

Proctor
(alt. Prockter, Procter)
Latin, meaning 'steward'.

Prospero

Latin, meaning 'prosperous'. Prospero is the protagonist in Shakespeare's play *The Tempest*.

Pryor
English, meaning 'first'.

Psalm

Old English, meaning 'hymn'. The name of Kanye West and Kim Kardashian-West's fourth child.

Ptolemy

Greek, meaning 'aggressive' or 'warlike'. Claudius Ptolemy was an ancient Greek mathematician and astronomer.

Purvis
(alt. Purves, Purviss)
French, meaning 'purveyor'.

Boys' names

Qabil
(alt. Quabil)

Arabic, meaning 'accepter'. Qabil is the Arabic name for Cain, who was one of the sons of Adam and Eve in the Bible.

Qadim
(alt. Qaadim, Qadem, Qadeem, Quadim)

Arabic, meaning 'organiser, convenor'. Often used with the prefix 'al', to form Al-Qadim.

Qadir
(alt. Quadir)

Arabic, meaning 'powerful'.

Qino
(alt. Quino)

Chinese, meaning 'handsome'. Also used in Spanish-speaking communities.

Quaid

Irish, meaning 'fourth'.

Qued

Old English, meaning 'bad or ugly'. Also an old name for the devil.

Quemby

Norse, meaning 'from the woman's estate'.

Quentin
(alt. Quinten, Quintin, Quinton, Quintus)

Latin, meaning 'fifth'. Famous Quentins include illustrator Quentin Blake and film director Quentin Tarantino.

Quillan

Gaelic, meaning 'sword'.

Quillon

Gaelic, meaning 'club'. The quillon is the bar on a sword where the handle meets the blade.

Quincy

Old French, meaning 'estate of the fifth son'. Jazz and soul legend Quincy Jones is known for his long career of music production, songwriting and performing.

Quinlan

Gaelic, meaning 'fit, shapely and strong'.

Quinn

Gaelic, meaning 'counsel'. Usually associated with the character from *Glee*.

Quinton

English, meaning 'queen's community'.

Boys' names

Radames
Slavic, meaning 'famous joy'. A character in the Verdi opera *Aïda*.

Rafael
(alt. Raphael; abbrev. Rafa, Rafe, Rafer, Raffi)
Hebrew, meaning 'God has healed'. One of the archangels in the Bible. Rafael Nadal is a Spanish tennis player who has held the world No. 1 ranking.

Ragnar
Old Norse, meaning 'strong counsellor'. Ragnar Lothbrok is a lead character in Amazon Prime's *Vikings*.

Raheem
(alt. Rahim)
Arabic, meaning 'merciful and kind'.

Rahm
Hebrew, meaning 'mercy'.

Rahul
(alt. Raoul, Raul)
Sanskrit, meaning 'efficient'. Rahul was Buddha's son.

Raiden
(alt. Rainen)
From the Japanese god of thunder. It also refers to the combination of lightning and thunder.

Rainer
Old German, meaning 'warrior from the gods'. Rainer Hersch is a British classical music comedian.

Raj
Sanskrit, meaning 'kingdom'. Also a Polish term for 'heaven'.

Rajesh
(alt. Ramesh)
Sanskrit, meaning 'ruler of kings'. Popular in both India and Nepal.

R

Raleigh

Old English, meaning 'deer's meadow'. Sir Walter Raleigh was an Elizabethan explorer and politician.

Ralph

Old English, meaning 'wolf'. Famous Ralphs include actor Ralph Fiennes, fashion brand Ralph Lauren and cartoon character Ralph from *The Simpsons*.

Ram

English, from the word for a male sheep.

Ramiro

Spanish, meaning 'judicious'. A popular name for boys in Argentina.

Ramone

Spanish, meaning 'wise supporter' or 'romantic'. The Ramones were an American rock band.

Ramsey
(alt. Ramsay)

Old English, meaning 'wild garlic island'. Ramsay MacDonald was the UK's first-ever Labour prime minister.

Randall
(alt. Randal, Randolph; abbrev. Randy)

Old German, meaning 'wolf shield'. Randy Newman is an American singer-songwriter and film composer. In modern English, randy can also mean amorous.

Raniel

English, meaning 'God is my happiness'. Can also be used as an alternative to Daniel.

Ranjit

Sanskrit, meaning 'influenced by charm'. Several Indian cricketers have been called Ranjit.

Rannoch

Gaelic, meaning 'fern'. Also an area in the Scottish Highlands.

Rashad

Arabic, meaning 'good judgement'.

Rashid
(alt. Rasheed)

Sanskrit, meaning 'rightly guided'. Ar-Rashid, meaning The Guide, is one of God's names in the Islamic tradition.

Rasmus

Greek, meaning 'beloved'. Usually used as a shortened form of Erasmus.

Raven

English, from the word 'raven', referring to the black bird.

Ravi

Hindi, meaning 'sun'. Ravivar is the Hindi word for Sunday.

Rawlins

French alternative of Roland, meaning 'renowned land'.

Raymond
(alt. Rayner; abbrev. Ray)

English, meaning 'adviser'. Illustrator and author Raymond Briggs is known for *The Snowman*. Famous Rays include singer Ray Charles and actors Ray Liotta and Ray Winstone.

Raz

Hebrew, meaning 'secret' or 'mystery'.

Reagan

Irish, meaning 'little king'.

Reginald
(abbrev. Reggie)

Latin, meaning 'regal'. Singer Elton John's birth name was Reginald Kenneth Dwight. Reggie Yates is a British actor and TV and radio presenter.

Regis

Latin, meaning 'of the king'.

Reid

Old English, meaning 'by the reeds'.

Reilly
(alt. Rilee, Rileigh, Riley, Ryle, Rylea, Rylei)

Irish, meaning 'courageous'. A very common first name and surname in Ireland.

Remington

English, meaning 'ridge town'.

Remus

Latin, meaning 'swift'. Famous Remuses include the ancient Roman myth of Romulus and Remus, and the character of Remus Lupin in J.K. Rowling's *Harry Potter* series.

Rémy

French, meaning 'from Rheims'.

Ren

Shortened form of Reginald, meaning 'regal'. According to Confucianism, Ren is also the feeling of satisfaction or pleasure after doing something nice for someone else.

Renato

Latin, meaning 'rebirth'.

René

French, meaning 'rebirth'. Traditionally only a name for boys, René is now often given to girls as well – in place of Renée.

Reno

Latin, meaning 'renewed'. Also a gambling city in Nevada, USA.

Reuben
(alt. Ruben)

Spanish, meaning 'a son'. The son of Jacob and eldest brother of Joseph in the Bible.

Reuel

Hebrew, meaning 'friend of God'.

Rex

Latin, meaning 'king'.

Rey

Spanish, meaning 'king'. In Telugu, Rey also means 'friend'.

Reynold

Latin, meaning 'king's adviser'. As a surname, Reynold can be traced back to pre-Norman times.

Rhodes

German, meaning 'where the roses grow'. Also the name of a Greek island and city.

Rhodri

Welsh, meaning 'ruler of the circle'. Rhodri the Great was a Welsh king in the ninth century.

Rhys

(alt. Reece)

Welsh, meaning 'enthusiasm'. Famous Rhyses include actors Rhys Ifans, Griff Rhys Jones and Jonathan Rhys Meyers.

Ricardo

Spanish form of Richard, meaning 'powerful leader'.

Richard

(abbrev. Rich, Richie, Ritchie, Rick, Ricki, Ricky, Dick, Dicky)

Old German, meaning 'powerful leader'. A popular name through many decades, it has dropped off in usage in recent years. Famous Richards include three kings of England. Famous Rickys include actor, writer and comedian Ricky Gervais and singer-songwriter Ricky Wilson.

Ridley

English, meaning 'cleared wood'. Film director Sir Ridley Scott is known for his films *Alien*, *Thelma & Louise* and *Gladiator*.

Rigby

English, meaning 'valley of the ruler'.

Ringo

English, meaning 'ring'. Usually associated with Beatles drummer Ringo Starr, whose birth name is Richard Starkey.

Rio

Spanish, meaning 'river'. Footballer Rio Ferdinand played for Manchester United and England.

Riordan

Gaelic, meaning 'bard'.

Rishi

Sanskrit, meaning 'scribe'. In ancient India, Rishis were the scribes who kept records of hymns and scientific advancement.

River

English, from the body of water. Actor River Phoenix was known for his roles in *Stand By Me*, *Indiana Jones and the Last Crusade* and *My Own Private Idaho*.

Roald

Scandinavian, meaning 'ruler'. Author Roald Dahl is one of the best-loved children's authors of all time, penning books such as *Charlie and the Chocolate Factory*, *Matilda* and *The Witches*.

Robert
(abbrev. Rob, Robbie, Bob, Bobby, Dobbin)

Old German, meaning 'bright fame'. Famous Roberts include Scottish king Robert the Bruce and actors Robert Pattinson and Robert de Niro. Famous Robs include actor Rob Lowe and comedian Rob Brydon. Famous Robbies include singer Robbie Wiliams, actor Robbie Coltrane and poet Robert 'Robbie' Burns.

Roberto

Italian form of Robert, meaning 'bright fame'.

Robin

English, from the word for the small, flame-breasted bird. Famous Robins include comedian Robin Williams, singer Robin Thicke and outlaw legend Robin Hood.

Robinson

English, meaning 'son of Robin'. Usually associated with the novel and title character *Robinson Crusoe*, by Daniel Defoe.

Rocco
(alt. Rocky)

Italian, meaning 'rest'. Rocco Ritchie is the son of Madonna and film director Guy Ritchie.

Rockwell

English, meaning 'of the rock well'.

Rod

Shortened form of Rhodri, Roderick and Rodney. Famous Rods include singer Rod Stewart and journalist Rod Liddle.

Roderick
(abbrev. Rod, Roddy)

German, meaning 'famous power'. Impressionist Rory Bremner's real name is Roderick Bremner.

Rodney
(abbrev. Rod, Roddy)

Old German, meaning 'island near the clearing'. Also a much-loved character in *Only Fools And Horses*.

Rodrigo

Spanish form of Roderick, meaning 'famous power'.

Roger

Old German, meaning 'spear man'. Famous Rogers include athlete Sir Roger Bannister, The Who singer Roger Daltrey and tennis player Roger Federer.

Roland
(alt. Rowland)

Old German, meaning 'renowned land'. Also puppet character Roland Rat.

Rolf

Old German, meaning 'wolf'.

Rollie
(alt. Rollo)

Old German, meaning 'renowned land'. Often used as a shortened version of Rolf or Roland.

Roman

Latin, meaning 'from Rome'.

Romeo

Latin, meaning 'pilgrim to Rome'. Made famous by Shakespeare's play *Romeo and Juliet*. Romeo is the second son of David and Victoria Beckham.

Ronald
(abbrev. Ron, Ronnie)

Norse, meaning 'mountain of strength'. Hollywood actor Ronald Reagan became the 40th president of the United States.

Ronan

Gaelic, meaning 'little seal'. Singer Ronan Keating is known for his career with boy band Boyzone.

Rory

English, meaning 'red king'. Famous Rorys include comedian Rory Bremner, actor Rory MacGregor and comedian Rory McGrath.

Ross
(alt. Russ)

Scottish, meaning 'cape'. Famous Rosses include actor Ross Kemp and comedian Ross Noble.

Rowan
(alt. Roan, Rohan)

Gaelic, meaning 'little red one'. Also reference to the rowan tree. Sir Rowan Atkinson is the comedian, writer and actor best known for his roles in *Blackadder* and as *Mr Bean*.

Roy

Gaelic, meaning 'red'. Famous Roys include England football manager Roy Hodgson and singer Roy Orbison.

Rudolph
(abbrev. Rudy)

Old German, meaning 'famous wolf'. Usually associated with the Christmas reindeer with a shiny red nose.

Rufus

Latin, meaning 'red-haired'. Famous Rufuses include presenter Rufus Hound, actor Rufus Sewell and singer Rufus Wainwright.

Rupert

Variant of Robert, meaning 'bright fame'.

Ruslan

Russian, meaning 'like a lion'.

Russell

Old French, meaning 'little red one'. Famous Russells include comedian Russell Brand, screenwriter Russell T. Davies and astrologer Russell Grant.

Rusty

English, meaning 'ruddy'. Most commonly used in the USA as a name for boys.

Ryan

Gaelic, meaning 'little king'. Famous Ryans include actors Ryan Gosling and Ryan Reynolds and footballer Ryan Giggs.

Ryder

English, meaning 'horseman'.

Rye

English, from the word 'rye'. Also a type of grain.

Ryker

From Richard, meaning 'powerful leader'.

Rylan

English, meaning 'land where rye is grown'. Presenter Rylan Clark-Neale is known for several reality TV programmes, including *Celebrity Big Brother*.

Ryley

Old English, meaning 'rye clearing'. More commonly used as a spelling alternative to Riley.

Rym

Arabic, meaning 'antelope'.

Ryu

Japanese, meaning 'dragon'. A Ryu can also refer to a discipline, such as a martial art, or school of thought.

Boys' names

Saar
Hebrew, meaning 'tempest'.

Saber
(alt. Sabre)
French, meaning 'sword'.

Sagar
Bengali, meaning 'sea'.

Sage
English, meaning 'wise'. Also a herb.

Sakari
Native American, meaning 'sweet'. Most commonly used in Finnish-speaking communities.

Salil
Sanskrit, meaning 'from the water'.

Salim
(alt. Saleem)
Arabic, meaning 'secure'. The Salim Khan family are a Bollywood dynasty, with dozens of members involved as actors, directors, producers or writers.

Salvador
Spanish, meaning 'saviour'. Artist Salvador Dali was known for his surrealist paintings.

Salvatore
Italian, meaning 'saviour'.

Samir
Arabic, meaning 'pleasant companion'.

Samson
Hebrew, meaning 'son of Sam'. Character with supernatural strength in the Bible.

Samuel
(abbrev. Sam, Sama, Sammie, Sammy)
Hebrew, meaning 'God is heard'. Famous Samuels include a prophet in the Bible and actor Samuel L. Jackson.

Sandeep
(alt. Sundeep)

Hindi, meaning 'lighting the way'. Popular in Hindu and Sikh communities.

Sandro

Italian, a shortened form of Alessandro, meaning 'defending men'.

Sandy

Shortened form of Alexander, meaning 'defender of mankind'. Famous Sandys include TV presenter Sandy Toksvig and pro golfer Sandy Lyle.

Sanjay

Hindi, meaning 'victory'. Famous Sanjays include *The Simpsons* character Sanjay, politician Sanjay Gandhi and Hindu narrative *Mahabharata* character Sanjaya.

Santiago

Spanish, meaning 'St James'. Also the name of the capital city of Chile.

Santino

Spanish, meaning 'little St James'. Santino was also the name of the first chimpanzee recognised to have forward-planning skills, in 2009.

Santo
(alt. Santos)

Latin, meaning 'saint'. Also the name of at least 10 separate football clubs around the world, including in Brazil, Mexico and Cape Town.

Sasha
(alt. Sacha)

Shortened Russian form of Alexander, meaning 'defending men'. DJ Sasha is known for his remixes of popular songs by Madonna and The Chemical Brothers. Sasha Baron Cohen is a successful comedian and actor.

Scott
(alt. Scottie)

English, meaning 'from Scotland'. Scott Mills is a radio DJ and TV presenter.

Seamus

Irish variant of James, meaning 'he who supplants'. Irish poet and playwright Seamus Heaney was awarded the Nobel Prize for literature.

Sean
(alt. Shaun, Shawn)

Variant of John, meaning 'God is gracious'. The name originated in the Middle Ages, when French invaders reached Ireland and the Irish began pronouncing the French name Jean as Sean. Famous Seans include legendary Bond actor Sean Connery.

Sebastian
(alt. Sébastien; abbrev. Seb)

Greek, meaning 'revered'. Famous Sebastians include the crab character in Disney's *The Little Mermaid*, novelist Sebastian Faulks and Sebastian Vettel, the Formula One world champion racing driver.

Sergio
(alt. Serge)

Latin, meaning 'servant'. Popular name for boys in parts of Cameroon, Belgium and Haiti.

Seth

Hebrew, meaning 'appointed'. Famous Seths include the third son of Adam and Eve in the Bible, and actors Seth MacFarlane and Seth Greene.

Severus

Latin, meaning 'severe'. Best known now as the character Severus Snape in J.K. Rowling's *Harry Potter* series.

Seymour

English, from Saint-Maur in northern France. Famous fictional Seymours include Seymour of *The Little Shop of Horrors* and Principal Seymour Skinner in *The Simpsons*.

Shalen

Arabic, meaning 'tribal leader'.

Shane

Variant of Sean, meaning 'God is gracious'. Famous Shanes include presenter Shane Richie, novelist Shane Briant and film director Shane Meadows.

Sharif

Arabic, meaning 'honoured'. Also a name for descendants of one of Muhammad's grandchildren.

Shea

Gaelic, meaning 'admirable'.

Shelby

Norse, meaning 'willow'. Also the name of a type of Mustang car.

Sherlock

English, meaning 'fair haired'. Usually associated with the fictional detective Sherlock Holmes.

Sherman

Old English, meaning 'shear man'. Also a type of World War II tank.

Shmuel

Hebrew, meaning 'his name is God'. The English equivalent is Samuel.

Shola

Arabic, meaning 'energetic'. Can be used for boys and girls. Shola Ameobi is a footballer who has played for Fleetwood Town and for Nigeria.

Sidney
(alt. Sydney; abbrev. Sid)

English, meaning 'wide meadow'.

Sigmund

Old German, meaning 'victorious hand'. Neurologist Sigmund Freud was known for his vast work of psychoanalysis.

Silvanus
(alt. Silvio)

Latin, meaning 'woods'. Silvanus was an ancient Roman deity of woods and fields.

Simba
(abbrev. Sim)

Swahili, meaning 'lion'. Usually associated with the character of Simba in Disney's *The Lion King*.

Simon
(alt. Simeon)

Hebrew, meaning 'to hear'. Famous Simons include music producer Simon Cowell and actor Simon Pegg.

Sinbad
(alt. Sindbad)

Persian, meaning 'Lord of Sages'. Also a literary merchant adventurer.

Sindri

Norse, meaning 'dwarf', from ancient Norse mythology.

Sipho

Swahili, meaning 'the unknown one'.

Sire

English, from the word 'sire'. Used as a form of address or title for reigning kings.

Sirius

Hebrew, meaning 'brightest star'. Name of Harry Potter's godfather, Sirius Black, in J.K. Rowling's *Harry Potter* series.

Skipper

English, meaning 'ship captain'.

Skyler
(alt. Skylar)

English, meaning 'scholar'. Can be a boys' or girls' name. Now often associated with female *Breaking Bad* character Skyler White.

Solomon
(alt. Shlomo)

Hebrew, meaning 'peace'. One of the most important kings in the Bible and Torah.

Sonny

American English, meaning 'son'. Singer Sonny Bono was half of the duo Sonny and Cher.

Soren

Scandinavian, meaning 'brightest star'. Also the name of a town in Germany.

Spencer

English, meaning 'guardian'. Actor Spencer Tracy was a star of Hollywood's golden era.

Spike

English, from the word 'spike'. Famous Spikes include film director Spike Lee and comedian and writer Spike Milligan (though neither was actually given the name Spike).

Stamos

Greek, meaning 'reasonable'.

Stanford

English, meaning 'stone ford'. Stanford University in the USA is one of the most well-known Ivy League universities.

Stanley
(abbrev. Stan)

English, meaning 'stony meadow'. Famous Stanleys include children's character Flat Stanley, film director Stanley Kubrick and actor Stanley Tucci.

Stavros

Greek, meaning 'cross'.

Stellan

Latin, meaning 'starred'. More commonly used in Swedish-speaking communities.

Steno

German, meaning 'stone'.

Stephen
(alt. Steven, Stefan, Stefano, Steffan; abbrev. Steve, Stevie)

English, meaning 'crowned'. Famous Stephens include actor Stephen Fry, physicist Stephen Hawking and author Stephen King. Famous Stevens include film director Steven Spielberg, Apple founder Steve Jobs and actor Steve Coogan.

Stewart
(alt. Stuart)

English, meaning 'steward'. The House of Stewart was the longest-surviving royal line in the Scottish monarchy. Famous Stuarts include DJ Stuart Maconie, football manager Stuart Pearce and film director Stuart Townsend.

Stoney

English, meaning 'stone like'. More commonly used as a surname.

Storm

English, from the word 'storm'.

Sven

Norse, meaning 'boy'. In the UK, Sven is usually associated with former England football manager Sven-Goran Eriksson.

Syed
(alt. Sayyid)

Arabic, meaning 'lucky'. Also a way of describing decendants of one of Muhammad's grandchildren.

Sylvester

Latin, meaning 'wooded'. Usually associated with the cartoon cat or actor Sylvester Stallone.

Syon

Sanskrit, meaning 'followed by good'. Also the name of a large historical stately home in England.

Boys' names

Tacitus

Latin, meaning 'silent, calm'. From the ancient Roman historian and senator.

Tad

English, from the word 'tadpole'. Also a shortened form of Thaddeus.

Taine

Gaelic, meaning 'river'.

Taj

Sanskrit, meaning 'crown'. Usually associated with the Indian palace the Taj Mahal.

Takashi

Japanese, meaning 'praiseworthy'.

Takoda

Sioux, meaning 'friend to everyone'. Most commonly used in the USA.

Talbot
(alt. Tal)

English, meaning 'command of the valley'. An aristocratic name.

Tamir

Arabic, meaning 'tall and wealthy'.

Taran
(alt. Taron)

Welsh, meaning 'thunder'. Actor Taron Egerton is best known for *Eddie the Eagle*, *Kingsman* and *Rocketman*.

Taras
(alt. Tarez)

Scottish, meaning 'crag'. Taras was the son of Poseidon in ancient Greek mythology.

Tarek
(alt. Tarik, Tariq)

Arabic, meaning 'to strike'.

Tarian

Welsh, meaning 'shield'. Also the name of a breed of Welsh pony.

Tarquin

Latin, from the Roman clan name. Author Tarquin Hall is known for his works *To the Elephant Graveyard* and *Salaam Brick Lane*.

Tarun

Hindi, meaning 'young'. Bollywood star Tarun Kumar Bhatti is known simply as Tarun.

Tatanka

Lakota, meaning 'buffalo'. Legendary Native American leader Sitting Bull's Western name was Tatanka Lyotake.

Tate

English, meaning 'cheerful'.

Taurean

English, meaning 'bull like'. Also used as a term for people born under the Taurus star sign.

Tavares

English, meaning 'descendant of the hermit'. Also found as a last name in Portuguese-speaking communities.

Tave
(alt. Tavian, Tavis, Tavish)

French, from Gustave, meaning 'royal staff'. In Nordic cultures the name also means 'guarantor'.

Tavor

Hebrew, meaning 'misfortunate'. Also the name given to a type of assault rifle.

Taylor

English, meaning 'tailor'. Actor Taylor Lautner appeared in the *Twilight* films. Now used as often for girls as for boys.

Names of poets

Andrew (Marvell)

Benjamin (Zephaniah)

Geoffrey (Chaucer)

Hugo (Williams)

John (Donne, Keats, Milton, Cooper Clarke)

Percy (Bysshe Shelley)

Robert (Burns)

Ted (Hughes)

Walt (Whitman)

William (Blake, Wordsworth)

Ted
(alt. Teddy)

Shortened form of Edward, meaning 'wealthy guard'. Famous Teds include *Father Ted*, and the *Ted* films.

Tennessee

Native American, meaning 'river town'. Also the name of a state in the USA.

Terence
(alt. Terrill, Terrence; abbrev. Terry)

English, meaning 'tender'. Terence was an ancient Roman playwright of comedies.

Tex

English, meaning 'Texan'. More commonly used in the USA.

Thabo

Swahili, meaning 'filled with happiness'. Thabo Mbeki was the president of South Africa from 1999 to 2008.

Thaddaeus
(abbrev. Thad, Thadd)

Greek, meaning 'courageous heart'.

Thane
(alt. Thayer)

Scottish, meaning 'landholder'.

Thelonious

Latin, meaning 'ruler of the people'. Thelonious Monk was an influential jazz pianist and composer.

Theodore
(abbrev. Theo)

Greek, meaning 'God's gift'. St Theodore was a warrior and martyr of the Eastern Orthodox Church.

Theophile
(alt. Theophilus)

Latin, meaning 'God's love'.

Theron

Greek, meaning 'hunter'.

Thierry

French variant of Terence, meaning 'tender'. Striker Thierry Henry played for Arsenal and France.

Thomas
(abbrev. Thom, Tom, Tomaz, Tommy)

Aramaic, meaning 'twin'. An enduringly popular name. Thomas the Tank Engine is one of the most long-standing popular children's characters of book and screen.

Thomson
(alt. Thomsen)

English, meaning 'son of Thomas'. The spelling Thomsen also means 'twin' in Aramaic.

Thor

Norse, meaning 'thunder'. Thor was an ancient Nordic god of thunder and lightning.

Tiago

From Santiago, meaning 'St James'. Used as a shortened form of Santiago as often as a name in its own right, particularly in Portuguese-speaking communities.

Tibor

Latin, from the river Tiber. In Hungary, the name can also mean 'a short meeting'.

Tieman
(alt. Tiemann)

Gaelic, meaning 'lord'.

Tien

Vietnamese, meaning 'first'.

Timothy
(abbrev. Tim, Timmy)

Greek, meaning 'God's honour'. Famous Timothys include actors Timothy Spall, Timothy Olyphant and Timothy Dalton.

Tito
(alt. Titus)

Latin, meaning 'defender'. Usually associated with Tito Jackson, an original member of the Jackson 5.

Tobias
(alt. Toby)
Hebrew, meaning 'God is good'.

Tod
(alt. Todd)
English, meaning 'fox'. Several fictional characters are called Tod or Todd, including Todd Flanders in *The Simpsons*, Todd Alquist in *Breaking Bad* and Todd Grimshaw in *Coronation Street*.

Tonneau
French, meaning 'barrel'. A tonneau is also a word used for the rear section of a car, particularly old-fashioned cars.

Tony
Shortened form of Anthony, from the old Roman family name. Famous Tonys include footballer Tony Adams, former prime minister Tony Blair and comedian, historian and TV presenter Tony Robinson.

Torin
Gaelic, meaning 'chief'. Actor Torin Thatcher was known for his numerous stage roles and films, including *Great Expectations* and *Mutiny on the Bounty*.

Torquil
Gaelic, meaning 'helmet'. In Scandinavia the name is also derived from Thor, the god of thunder and lightning.

Tory
(alt. Torey)
Norse, meaning 'Thor'.

Toshi
Japanese, meaning 'reflection'. More commonly used in Japanese-speaking communities.

Travis
French, meaning 'crossroads'.

Trevelyan
Cornish, meaning 'of the house of Eden'.

Trevor
Welsh, meaning 'great settlement'. Famous Trevors include inventor Trevor Baylis, DJ Trevor Nelson and politician and presenter Trevor Phillips.

Trey
(alt. Tyree)
French, meaning 'three'. Sometimes used as a nickname for a third-born child or person whose name ends in III, such as Microsoft founder Bill Gates, whose birth name is William Henry Gates III.

Tristan
(alt. Tristram)
Celtic, from the Celtic hero. One of the knights of the Round Table.

Troy
Gaelic, meaning 'descended from the soldier'. Troy was a legendary city in ancient Greece.

Tudor

Variant of Theodore, 'God's gift'.
The Tudors were a family dynasty
who ruled England during the 16th
century, including Henry VIII and
Elizabeth I.

Tyler

English, meaning 'tile maker'. The
name can be traced back to the 14th
century and English rebel Wat Tyler,
leader of the Peasants' Revolt.

Tyrell

French, meaning 'puller'. Usually
associated with the House of Tyrell
from *Game of Thrones*.

Tyrone

Gaelic, meaning 'Owen's county'.
Also the name of a county in
Northern Ireland.

Tyson

English, meaning 'son of Tyrone'.
Became popular after the rise of
Mike Tyson, the boxer known for his
aggressive fighting style.

Boys' names

Uberto
(alt. Umberto)
Italian, variant of Hubert, meaning 'bright or shining intellect'. Several kings of Italy were called Umberto.

Udath
(alt. Udathel)
Sanskrit, meaning 'noble'.

Udo
German, meaning 'power of the wolf'.

Ugo
Italian form of Hugo, meaning 'soul, mind and intellect'. Also the name of a town in Japan.

Ulf
German, meaning 'wolf'. Also the name of a Danish Viking chief.

Ulrich
German, meaning 'noble ruler'.

Ultan
Irish, meaning 'from Ulster'. St Ultan was an Irish monk in the seventh century.

Ulysses
Greek, meaning 'wrathful'. Made famous by the mythological voyager of ancient Greece.

Unwyn
(alt. Unwin, Unwine)
English, meaning 'unfriendly'.

Old name, new fashion

Bertrand	Norris
Dexter	Pierce
Felix	Reginald
Hector	Ulysses
Jefferson	Winston

Upton
English, meaning 'high town'.

Urho
Finnish, meaning 'brave'.

Uri
(alt. Uriah, Urias)
Hebrew, meaning 'my light'. Magician Uri Geller is known for his illusions of psychokinesis and telepathy.

Uriel
Hebrew, meaning 'angel of light'. One of the archangels in the Bible.

Usher
English. Made famous by the American R&B star.

Uttam
Sanskrit, meaning 'best'. Actor Uttam Kumar is known as one of the great Bollywood actors of the 20th century.

Uzi
(alt. Uzzi, Uzziah)
Hebrew, meaning 'God is my strength'. Also the name of an Israeli type of submachine gun.

Boys' names

Vaclav
Czech, meaning 'receives glory'. The English form is Wenceslaus.

Vadim
Russian, meaning 'scandal maker'. Vadim the Bold was a legendary warrior in Eastern Europe during the ninth century.

Valdemar
German, meaning 'renowned leader'. Valdemar was a king of Sweden during the 13th century.

Valente
Latin, meaning 'valiant'. More commonly used as a surname, particularly in Italy and Portugal.

Valentine
(alt. Valentin, Valentino; abbrev. Val)
English. St Valentine was a Roman saint associated with the tradition of courtly love, and whose day is celebrated on 14 February. The Spanish variant is Valentin and the Italian is Valentino.

Valerio
Italian, meaning 'to be strong'. Originally a surname in Italy, Valerio is now also being given as a first name to boys.

Valia
Sanskrit, meaning 'king of the monkeys'. Also used as a girls' name.

Van
Dutch, meaning 'son of'. Also a shortened form of Ivan, as with singer Van Morrison.

Vance
English, meaning 'marshland'.

Vangelis
Greek, meaning 'good news'. Vangelis is a modern Greek composer of various music, and is known for his work on films such as *Chariots of Fire*, *Blade Runner* and *Alexander*.

Varro

Latin, meaning 'strong'. There are several ancient Roman generals and poets known as Varro, most of whom were related to each other.

Varun

Hindi, meaning 'water god'. Shortened form of Varuna, who is the Hindu god of all water.

Vasilis

Greek, meaning 'kingly'.

Vaughan
(alt. Vaughn)

Welsh, meaning 'little'.

Vernell

French, meaning 'green and flourishing'. More commonly used in the USA.

Verner

Scandinavian form of the German Werner, meaning 'army defender'.

Vernon
(alt. Vernie)

French, meaning 'alder grove'.

Versilius

Latin, meaning 'flier'. Also the name of a fashionable part of Tuscany, Italy.

Vester

Latin, meaning 'wooded'. Also the name of a manufacturer of guitars.

Vibol

Cambodian, meaning 'man of plenty'.

Victor
(alt. Viktor)

Latin, meaning 'champion'. Author Victor Hugo is known for his novels *Les Miserables* and *The Hunchback of Notre-Dame*.

Vidal
(alt. Vidar)

Spanish, meaning 'life giving'. Hairdresser Vidal Sassoon owned a chain of salons and a range of styling products.

Vijay

Hindi, meaning 'conquering'. Bollywood star Joseph Vijay Chandrasekhar is known simply as Vijay.

Vikram

Hindi, meaning 'sun'. Bollywood star Vikram Kennedy Vinod Raj is known simply as Vikram.

Ville

French, meaning 'town'. The word is used to describe towns or cities throughout France and the UK, usually as a suffix – such as Carville in Yorkshire.

Vincent
(abbrev. Vin, Vince, Vinnie)

English, meaning 'victorious'. Famous Vincents include actor Vince Vaughn, artist Vincent van Gogh and footballer-turned-actor Vinnie Jones.

Virgil

Latin, meaning 'staff bearer'. Ancient Roman poet of the same name.

Vito

Spanish, meaning 'life'. Usually associated with the character Vito Corleone from *The Godfather*.

Vittorio

Italian, meaning 'victory'. The English equivalent is Victor.

Vitus

Latin, meaning 'life'. St Vitus's day was traditionally celebrated with dancing, which led to naming a neurological condition that looks like uncontrolled dancing as 'St Vitus Dance'.

Vivek

Sanskrit, meaning 'wisdom'. Bollywood star Vivekananthan is known simply as Vivek.

Vivian

Latin, meaning 'lively'. Commonly given to both boys and girls.

Vladimir
(abbrev. Vlad)

Slavic, meaning 'prince'. Famous Vladimirs include Russian President Vladimir Putin and legendary warrior Vlad the Impaler – who was also known as Dracula.

Volker

German, meaning 'defender of the people'.

Von

Norse, meaning 'hope'. In Germany, 'von' also means 'of' or 'from', and is used in names to denote origin, such as Ulrich von Liechtenstein.

Boys' names

Wade

English, meaning 'to move forward' or 'to go'. Wade Robson is a prolific choreographer of contemporary dance.

Waldemar

German, meaning 'famous ruler'. A common name for German princes during the Middle Ages.

Walden

English, meaning 'valley of the Britons'. Title of Henry Thoreau's famous book reflecting on simple living off the land.

Waldo

Old German, meaning 'rule'. Famous in the USA for the line of 'Where's Waldo?' books, known as 'Where's Wally?' in the UK.

Walker

German, meaning 'a fuller of cloth'. Most common in late 1800s and early 1900s in America.

Wallace

English, meaning 'foreigner' or 'stranger'. The man of the man-and-dog duo known to children everywhere as Wallace and Gromit.

Walter

(abbrev. Walt, Wally)
German, meaning 'ruler of the army'.

Ward

English, meaning 'guardian'.

Wardell

Old English, meaning 'watchman's hill'.

Warner

German, meaning 'army guard'. Best known for the movie studio Warner Brothers Entertainment, which has released blockbusters such as *Batman* and *Superman*.

Warren

German, meaning 'guard' or 'the game park'. Warren Buffett, an American businessman and philanthropist, is known as one of the richest people in the world.

Warwick

English, meaning 'farm near the weir'. The name of a historic town in England with a castle and a university.

Washington

English, meaning 'clever' or 'clever man's settlement'. The surname of the first president of the USA.

Wasim

Arabic, meaning 'attractive' or 'full of grace'.

Wassily

Greek, meaning 'royal' or 'kingly'. Wassily Kandinsky was an influential Russian painter of abstract art.

Watson

English, meaning 'son' or 'son of Walter'. The right-hand man of the famous fictional detective Sherlock Holmes.

Waverley

(alt. Waverly)

English, meaning 'meadow of aspens'. A common name for towns and cities in the USA.

Waylon

English, meaning 'land by the road'. American Waylon Jennings has been a popular country singer for decades.

Wayne

English, meaning 'a cartwright'. Famous Waynes include footballer Wayne Rooney, comedian Wayne Brady and rapper Lil Wayne.

Webster

English, meaning 'weaver'.

Weldon

English, meaning 'from the hill of well' or 'hill with a well'.

Wendell

(alt. Wendel)

German, meaning 'a wend'. American novelist and poet Wendell Berry has penned dozens of works throughout his career.

Werner

German, meaning 'army guard'.

Werther

German, meaning 'a soldier in the army'.

Weston

English, meaning 'from the west town'.

Wheeler

English, meaning 'wheel maker'.

Whitley
English, meaning 'white wood'.

Whitman
Old English, meaning 'white man'.

Whitney
Old English, meaning 'white island'.
Can be used as a boys' or girls'
name.

Wilber
(alt. Wilbur)
Old German, meaning 'bright will'.
As one of the Wright brothers, Wilbur
helped to invent the first powered
aeroplanes.

Wildon
English, meaning 'wooded hill'.

Wiley
Old English, meaning 'beguiling'
or 'enchanting'. The stage name
of English rapper and songwriter
Richard Kylea Cowie.

Wilford
Old English, meaning 'the ford by the
willows'.

Wilfred
(alt. Wilfredo, Wilfrid; abbrev. Wilf)
English, meaning 'to will peace'.

Wilhelm
German, meaning 'strong-willed
warrior'.

Wilkes
(alt. Wilkie)
Old English, meaning 'strong-willed
protector' or 'strong and resolute
protector'.

Willem
Dutch, meaning 'strong-willed
warrior'.

William
(abbrev. Wil, Will, Willie, Willy, Bill,
Billy)
Old German, meaning 'strong-willed
warrior'. Famous Williams include
Prince William, playwright William
Shakespeare and rapper Will.i.am.

Willis
English, meaning 'server of William'.

Willoughby
Old Norse and Old English, meaning
'from the farm by the trees'.

Wilmer
English (Teutonic), meaning
'famously resolute'. Wilmer
Eduardo Valderrama is an American
actor. Wilmer Allison was a tennis
champion in the 1930s.

Wilmot
English, meaning 'resolute mind'.

Wilson
English, meaning 'son of William'.
Wilson Pickett was an American
R&B, soul and rock 'n' roll singer-
songwriter.

Wilton

Old Norse and English, meaning 'from the farm by the brook' or 'from the farm by the streams'. A town in Wiltshire with a history dating back to the eighth century.

Windell

German, meaning 'wanderer' or 'seeker'. Windell Middlebrooks is an American actor.

Windsor

Old English, meaning 'river bank' or 'landing place'.

Winfield

English, meaning 'from the field of Wina'.

Winslow

Old English, meaning 'victory on the hill'.

Winter

Old English, meaning 'to be born in the winter'.

Winthrop

Old English, meaning 'village of friends'.

Winton

Old English, meaning 'a friend's farm'.

Wirrin

Aboriginal, meaning 'a tea tree'.

Wistan

Old English, meaning 'battle stone' or 'mark of the battle'. St Wistan was martyred in AD 840 and has his feast day on 1 June.

Wittan

Old English, meaning 'farm in the woods' or 'farm by the woods'. The Witan were a group of advisers to the king that operated from the seventh to 11th centuries.

Wolf
(alt. Wolfe)

English, meaning 'strong as a wolf'.

Wolfgang

Teutonic, meaning 'the path of wolves'. Wolfgang Amadeus Mozart was one of the most important composers of the classical period.

Wolfrom

Teutonic, meaning 'raven wolf'.

Wolter

Dutch, a form of Walter, meaning 'ruler of the army'. Wolter Kroes is a Dutch singer.

Woodburn

Old English, meaning 'a stream in the woods'.

Woodrow
(abbrev. Woody)

English, meaning 'from the row of houses by the wood'. Woodrow Wilson was the 28th president of the USA. Woody is also the well-known cowboy in *Toy Story*.

Woodward

English, meaning 'guardian of the forest'.

Worcester

Old English, meaning 'from a Roman site'.

Worth

American, meaning 'worth much' or 'wealthy place' or 'wealth and riches'.

Wren

Old English, meaning 'tiny bird'. Often associated with the species of small birds found throughout the world.

Wright

Old English, meaning 'to be a craftsman' or 'from a carpenter'.

Wyatt

Teutonic, meaning 'from wood' or 'from the wide water'. Famous Wyatts include wild-west sheriff Wyatt Earp and comedian Wyatt Cenac.

Wyclef

(alt. Wycleff, Wycliff, Wycliffe)

English, meaning 'inhabitant of the white cliff'. Wyclef Jeanelle Jean is an American-Haitian rapper best known for his role in The Fugees.

Wynn

(alt. Wyn)

Welsh, meaning 'very blessed' or 'the fair blessed one'. Also used in old English to mean 'friend'.

Popular song names

Alfie ('Alfie' – Lily Allen)

Carmen ('Carmen' – Lana Del Ray)

Diana ('Diana' – One Direction)

George ('Oh George' – Foo Fighters)

Maddie ('Alone With You (Maddie's Song)' – Ne Yo)

Mary ('Blind Mary' – Gnarls Barkley)

Simone ('Simone' – Goldfrapp)

Stephen ('Hey Stephen' – Taylor Swift)

Wyatt ('Lullaby for Wyatt' – Sheryl Crow)

Boys' names

Xadrian

American, a combination of X and Adrian, meaning 'from Hadria'.

Xander

Greek, meaning 'defender of the people'. A short form of Alexander.

Xannon

American, meaning 'descendant of an ancient family'.

Xanthus

Greek, meaning 'golden-haired'. One of the horses belonging to Achilles.

Xavier

(alt. Xzaviar)

Spanish, meaning 'the new house'. A name originating from the Catholic saint, Francis Xavier.

Xenon

Greek, meaning 'the guest'. Also one of the noble gases.

Xerxes

Persian, meaning 'ruler of the people' or 'respected king'. A king who attempted to invade the Greek mainland, but failed.

Xeven

Slavic, meaning 'lively'.

Xylander

Greek, meaning 'man of the forest'.

Boys' names

Yaal
Hebrew, meaning 'ascending' or 'one to ascend'.

Yadid
Hebrew, meaning 'the beloved one'.

Yadon
Hebrew, meaning 'against judgement'. Name of one of the many Pokemon characters.

Yahir
Spanish, meaning 'handsome one'. A Mexican singer.

Yaholo
Native American, meaning 'yells'.

Yair
Hebrew, meaning 'the enlightening one' or 'illuminating'.

Yakiya
Hebrew, meaning 'pure' or 'bright'.

Yanis
(alt. Yannis)
Greek, a form of John, meaning 'gift of God'.

Yarden
Hebrew, meaning 'to flow downward'. The Hebrew name Jordan comes from Yarden.

Ye
Chinese, meaning 'bright one' or 'light'.

Yehuda
(alt. Yehudi)
Hebrew, meaning 'to praise and exalt'. Often translated to mean Judah. Judah was a son of Jacob in the Bible.

Yered
Hebrew, a form of Jared, meaning 'descending'.

Yerik

Russian, meaning 'God-appointed one'.

Yerodin

Swahili, meaning 'studious'.

Yervant

Armenian, meaning 'king of people'.

Yitzak

(alt. Yitzaak)

Hebrew, meaning 'laughter' or 'one who laughs'.

Ynyr

Welsh, meaning 'to honour'.

Yobachi

Swahili, meaning 'one who prays to God' or 'prayed to God'.

Yogi

Sanskrit, meaning 'master of oneself'. Popularised by the American cartoon character, Yogi Bear.

Yoloti

Aztec, meaning 'heart'.

Yona

Native American, meaning 'bear'; Hebrew, meaning 'dove'. A name used to refer to ancient people who spoke Greek.

York

Celtic, meaning 'yew tree' or 'from the farm of the yew tree'. Used as a surname by people originating from the city of York.

Yosef

Hebrew form of Joseph, meaning 'Jehovah increases'.

Yuri

Aboriginal, meaning 'to hear'; Japanese, meaning 'one to listen'; Russian, a form of George, meaning 'farmer'. Name of a South Korean pop singer.

Yuuta

Japanese, meaning 'excellent'.

Yves

French, meaning 'miniature archer' or 'small archer'. Yves Saint Laurent was a famous French fashion designer.

Z

Boys' names

Zachariah
(alt. Zachary, Zecheriah; abbrev. Zac, Zach)
Hebrew, meaning 'remembered by the Lord' or 'God has remembered'.

Zad
Persian, meaning 'my son'.

Zada
(alt. Zadan, Zadin, Zadun)
Dutch, meaning 'a man who sowed seeds'.

Zadok
Hebrew, meaning 'righteous one'. The priest who anointed Solomon, made famous in Handel's anthem.

Zador
Hungarian, meaning 'violent demeanour'.

> **Long names**
> Alexander
> Bartholomew
> Christopher
> Demetrius
> Giovanni
> Montgomery
> Obadiah
> Roberto
> Salvatore
> Zachariah

Zafar
Arabic, meaning 'triumphant'. Zafar Younis is a character from the BBC drama *Spooks*.

Zaid
Swahili, meaning 'increase the growth' or 'growth'.

Zaide

Yiddish, meaning 'the elder ones'. An unfinished opera by Mozart.

Zain
(alt. Zane)

Arabic, meaning 'the handsome son'.

Zaire

Swahili, meaning 'river'. Formerly the name of a country in Africa, now known as Democratic Republic of the Congo.

Zander

Greek, meaning 'defender of my people'.

Zarek

Persian, meaning 'God protect our king'. A Marvel comic book character created by Stan Lee and Gene Colan.

Zoltan
(alt. Zoltin)

Hungarian, meaning 'life'. Zoltan Karpathy is a character from the musical *My Fair Lady*.

Zuma

Arabic, meaning 'peace'.

Part three

Girls' names A–Z

Baby names vary widely in spelling and pronunciation. To simplify things, this book usually lists each name only once: under the most common initial and spelling. If a name has an alternative spelling with a different initial, it may be listed under that letter also.

Girls' names

Abigail
(alt. Abagail, Abbiegayle, Abbigail, Abigale, Abigayle; abbrev. Abbey, Abbi, Abi, Abie)

Hebrew, meaning 'my father's joy'. Found in the Bible. Abbey Clancy is a model and TV presenter. Abi Morgan is a screenwriter of films, including *The Iron Lady* and *Shame*.

Abilene
(alt. Abilee)

Latin and Spanish for 'hazelnut'; Greek meaning 'plain' or 'meadow', it is the name of an ancient area of Syria.

Abina
(alt. Abena)

Akan, meaning 'born on Tuesday'.

Abra
Sanskrit, meaning 'clouds'. Female variation of Abraham.

Abril
Spanish for the month of April.

Acacia
Greek, meaning 'point' or 'thorn'. Also a type of flowering tree and shrub.

Ada
(alt. Adair)

Hebrew, meaning 'adornment'. The mathematician Ada Lovelace is generally considered to be the world's first computer programmer, in the 19th century.

Adalee
Derived from German, meaning 'noble'. Sometimes used as a contraction of Ada and Lee.

Adalia
Hebrew, meaning 'God is my refuge'. Also the name of a type of ladybird.

Addison
(alt. Addisyn, Addyson; abbrev. Addie)

English, meaning 'son of Adam'. Used equally for girls and boys.

Adelaide
(alt. Adelaida; abbrev. Addie)

German, meaning 'noble'. Popular after the rule of William IV and Queen Adelaide of England in the 19th century. Also an Australian city and name of Australian actor Adelaide Kane.

Adele
(alt. Adela, Adelia, Adell, Adella, Adelle; abbrev. Addie)

German, meaning 'noble'. Award-winning singer-songwriter Adele Laurie Blue Adkins is better known as simply 'Adele'.

Adeline
(alt. Adalyn, Adalynn, Adelina, Adelyn)

Variant of Adelaide, meaning 'noble'.

Adeola
(alt. Adeolah, Adeolla)

Nigerian, meaning 'weaver of a crown of honour'.

Aderyn

Welsh, meaning 'bird'. Also the name of several places in Wales.

Adesina

Swahili, meaning 'she paves the way'. Often given to a firstborn daughter in Nigerian communities.

Adia

Variant of Ada, meaning 'adornment'. Usually associated with the song 'Adia'.

Adina
(alt. Adena)

Hebrew, meaning 'high hopes' or 'precious'. Found in the Bible.

Adira

Hebrew, meaning 'noble' or 'powerful'.

Adrienne
(alt. Adrian, Adriana, Adriane, Adrianna, Adrianne)

Feminine form of Adrian, from the Latin, meaning 'from Hadria'.

Aegle

Greek, meaning 'brightness' or 'splendour'. Also the name of several characters in ancient Greek mythology.

Aerin

Name of a character in J.R.R. Tolkien's *Lord of the Rings* trilogy.

Aerith

American, from a character in the computer game *Final Fantasy VII*.

Aero
(alt. Aeron)

Greek, meaning 'flight'.

Aerolynn

Combination of the Greek Aero, meaning 'flight', and the English Lynn, meaning 'waterfall'.

Afia
(alt. Aafia, Aff, Affi)

Arabic, meaning 'a child born on Friday'.

Africa

Celtic, meaning 'pleasant'. Also the name of the continent.

Afsaneh

Persian, meaning 'a fairy tale'.

Afsha

Persian, meaning 'one who sprinkles light'.

Afton

Originally the name of a river in Ayrshire, Scotland, or a town on the Isle of Wight.

Agatha

(abbrev. Aggie)

Greek and Latin, meaning 'good'. St Agatha was a third-century Christian saint, patron saint of fire, earthquakes and bells, among other things. Crime writer Agatha Christie is the world's best-selling novelist.

Aglaia

(alt. Aglaya, Aglaja)

Greek, meaning 'brilliance'. In Greek mythology, one of the Three Graces. Also the name of a kind of mahogany tree, an opera, an 18th-century British ship and a saint.

Agnes

Greek, meaning 'virginal' or 'pure'. St Agnes of Rome is the patron saint of chastity and girls, among other things.

Agrippina

Latin, meaning 'born feet first'. The name of several influential women of ancient Rome.

Aida

Arabic, meaning 'reward' or 'present'. Also the name of an opera by Giuseppe Verdi.

Aidanne

(alt. Aden, Aidan, Aidanne, Aiden, Aidenne)

Feminine form of Aidan, from the Gaelic, meaning 'fire'.

Ailbhe

Irish, meaning 'noble' or 'bright'. Has also been used as a boys' name.

Aileen

(alt. Aelinn, Aleen, Aline, Alline, Eileen)

Gaelic variant of Helen, meaning 'light'. Aileen Cust was the first female veterinarian in Great Britain.

Ailith

(alt. Ailish)

Old English, meaning 'seasoned warrior'. Rare since the Middle Ages.

Ailsa

Scottish, meaning 'pledge from God'. Also the name of a Scottish island, Ailsa Craig.

Aimee

(alt. Aimie, Amie)

French form of Amy, meaning 'beloved'. Famous Aimees include actor Aimee Garcia and singer Aimee Mann.

Aina
Scandinavian, meaning 'forever'.

Aine
(alt. Aino)
Celtic, meaning 'happiness'. Aine was a Celtic goddess of summer and prosperity.

Ainsley
(alt. Ansley)
Old English, meaning 'meadow' or 'clearing'. Also variant of an old Scottish last name used as a first name. Both a girls' and a boys' name. Ainsley Hayes was a leading character in TV hit The West Wing.

Aisha
(alt. Aeysha, Aysha)
Arabic, meaning 'woman'; Swahili, meaning 'life'. Aisha was one of the prophet Muhammad's wives.

Aishwarya
Variant of the Arabic Aisha, meaning 'woman'. Actor Aishwarya Rai Bachchan is one of the most recognisable Bollywood stars.

Aislinn
(alt. Aislin, Aisling, Aislyn, Alene, Allene)
Irish Gaelic, meaning 'dream'.

Aiyanna
(alt. Aiyana)
Native American, meaning 'forever flowering'.

Aja
Hindi, meaning 'goat'. Also Scandinavian.

Aka
(alt. Akah, Akkah)
Maori, meaning 'loving one' or 'affectionate'.

Akela
(alt. Akilah)
Hawaiian, meaning 'noble'. Also the wolf pack leader Akela in Rudyard Kipling's The Jungle Book.

Akilina
Greek or Russian, meaning 'eagle'.

Akiva
Hebrew, meaning 'protect and shelter'.

Alaina
(alt. Alane, Alani, Alayna, Aleena)
Feminine form of Alan, from the Gaelic for 'rock'. Also used as a spelling alternative to Eleanor.

Alana
(alt. Alanna, Alannah)
Gaelic, meaning 'beauty'; Hawaiian, meaning 'beautiful offering'; Old German, meaning 'precious'.

Alanis
(alt. Alarice)
Variant of Alaina, meaning 'rock'. Canadian-American Alanis Morissette is a multi-award-winning singer.

Alba

Latin, meaning 'white'. Also the Gaelic word for Scotland. Name of the central character in the novel *The Time Traveller's Wife*.

Alberta

(alt. Albertha, Albertine)

Feminine of Albert, from the Old German for 'noble, bright, famous'. Also the name of a province in Canada.

Albina

Latin, meaning 'white' or 'fair'. Also the name of an Etruscan goddess of the dawn.

Alda

German, meaning 'old' or 'prosperous'. St Alda was an Italian mystic in the 11th century, who took care of the sick.

Aldis

English, meaning 'battle-seasoned'. Used most commonly for boys but also for girls.

Aleah

Arabic, meaning 'high'; also Persian, meaning 'one of God's beings'. Often used as a spelling alternative for Aliyah.

Alesha

(alt. Alisha, Alysha)

Variant of Alice, meaning 'nobility'. Alesha Dixon is a British singer, dancer, model and TV presenter.

Aleta

(alt. Aletha)

Greek, meaning 'footloose'. Usually associated with the character of Queen Aleta Ellis in the comic strip *The Legend of Prince Valiant*.

Alethea

(alt. Aletheia)

Greek, meaning 'truth'. The first use of this name was in the 17th century.

Alexandra

(alt. Alejandra, Alejhandra, Aleksandra, Alessandra, Alexandria; abbrev. Alex, Alexa, Alexi, Alexia, Alexina)

Feminine form of Alexander, meaning 'defender of mankind'. Also one of the names of the ancient Greek goddess Hera.

Alexis

(alt. Alexus, Alexys)

Greek, meaning 'helper'. Alexis was also an ancient Greek comic poet and an ancient Greek sculptor.

Aleydis

Variant of Alice, meaning 'noble' or 'nobility'. Also an alternative name for St Alice of Scharbeek, patron saint of the blind and paralysed.

Alfreda

(alt. Alfre)

Feminine form of Alfred, from Old English, meaning 'elf' or 'magical counsel'. Alfreda Benge is a lyricist and illustrator and Alfreda Hodgson is a singer.

Ali
(alt. Allie, Ally)
Shortened version of Alexandra, Aliyah, Alison or Alice, as well as a name in its own right.

Alibeth
Variant of Elizabeth, meaning 'consecrated to God'. More commonly used in the Middle Ages.

Alice
(alt. Alicia, Alize, Alyce, Alys, Alyse)
English, meaning 'noble' or 'nobility'. Usually associated with *Alice in Wonderland* by Lewis Carroll. Famous Alicias include singer Alicia Keys and actor Alicia Silverstone. Also the birth name of actor Jodie Foster.

Alida
(alt. Aleida)
Latin, meaning 'small winged one'. More commonly used in Dutch-speaking communities.

Alienor
(alt. Aliana)
Variant of Eleanor, from the Greek for 'light'. Also a spelling variation used by Queen Eleanor of Aquitaine in the 12th century.

Aliki
(alt. Alika)
Variant of Alice, meaning 'noble' or 'nobility'. Actor Aliki Vougiouklaki was considered to be one of Greece's greatest actors of the 20th century.

Alima
Arabic, meaning 'cultured'.

Alina
(alt. Alena)
Variation of Helen, meaning 'light'. More commonly used in Brazil, France, Italy, and Spain.

Alison
(alt. Allison, Allisyn, Allyson, Alyson)
Variant of Alice, meaning 'noble' or 'nobility'. Originally the name was Alis in the Middle Ages, with the suffix 'on', which means 'little'.

Alivia
Variant of Olivia, meaning 'olive tree'. More commonly used in the USA.

Aliya
(alt. Aaliyah, Aleah, Alia, Aliah, Aliyah)
Arabic, meaning 'exalted' or 'sublime'.

Alla
Variant of Ella or Alexandra.

Allegra
Italian, meaning 'joyous'. Allegra Byron was the lovechild of the poet Lord Byron. Allegra Versace is the heiress to the Versace fashion empire.

Allura
French, from the word for entice, meaning 'the power of attraction'.

Allyn
Feminine form of Alan, meaning 'rock'.

Alma

Three possible origins: from Latin meaning 'giving nurture', or Italian meaning 'soul' or Arabic meaning 'learned'.

Almeda
(alt. Almeta)

Latin, meaning 'ambitious'. Also the name of a district in Barcelona, Spain.

Almera
(alt. Almira)

Feminine of Elmer, from the Arabic for 'aristocratic' and the Old English for 'noble'.

Alohi

Variant of the Hawaiian greeting Aloha, meaning 'love and affection'. More commonly used in the USA.

Alona
(alt. Alora)

Hebrew, meaning 'oak tree'.

Alpha

The first letter of the Greek alphabet, usually given to a first-born daughter.

Alta

Latin, meaning 'elevated'. Also the name of many towns throughout Europe and the USA.

Altagracia

Spanish, meaning 'grace'. Alta Gracia is also the name of a city in Argentina.

Althaea
(alt. Altea, Altha, Althea)

Greek, meaning 'healing power'. Althaea was a prominent character in Greek mythology.

Alva

Spanish, meaning 'blonde' or 'fair skinned'. In Norway and Sweden it is considered the feminine form of Alf, which means 'elf'.

Alvena
(alt. Alvina)

Old English, meaning 'elf friend'. In Old German, it is considered the feminine form of Adelwin, which means 'noble friend'.

Alvia
(alt. Alyvia)

Variant of Olivia, meaning 'olive tree'; also variant of Elvira, from the ancient Spanish city.

Alyssa
(alt. Alisa, Alissa, Allyssa, Alysa)

Greek, meaning 'rational'. Usually associated with the flower alyssum.

Amabel

Variant of Annabel, meaning 'grace and beauty'.

Amadea

Feminine form of Amadeus, meaning 'love God'. More commonly used in German-speaking communities.

Amal

Arabic, meaning 'hope and aspiration'.

Amalia

Hebrew, meaning 'labour of love';
German, meaning 'work'.

Amana

Hebrew, meaning 'loyal and true'.
Also the name of a type of tulip.

Amanda

(alt. Amandine)

Latin, meaning 'much loved'. Famous
Amandas include presenter and actor
Amanda Holden, and actors Amanda
Bynes and Amanda Seyfried.

Amara

(alt. Amani)

Greek, meaning 'lovely forever'.
Actor Amara Miller is known for her
role in the film *The Descendants*.

Amarantha

Contraction of Amanda and
Samantha, meaning 'much loved
listener'. Also associated with the
amaranth plant.

Amari

(alt. Amaris, Amasa, Amata, Amaya)

Hebrew, meaning 'pledged by God'.
Also the name of a province in
Greece.

Amaryllis

(alt. Ameris)

Greek, meaning 'fresh'. Usually
associated with the flowering plant.

Amber

French, from the word for the semi-
precious stone of the same name.
Famous Ambers include actors
Amber Heard and Amber Benson.

Amberly

Contraction of Amber and Leigh,
meaning 'stone' and 'meadow'.

Amboree

(alt. Amber, Ambree)

American, meaning 'precocious'.
More commonly used in the USA.

Amelia

(alt. Aemilia, Amalie, Amelie)

Greek, meaning 'industrious'.
Famous Amelias include flying legend
Amelia Earhart, and two 18th-
century British princesses.

America

From the country of the same name.
Actor America Ferrera is known for
her roles in *Ugly Betty* and *How to
Train Your Dragon*.

Amethyst

Greek, from the word for the
precious stone of the same name.

Amina

(alt. Aamina)

Arabic, meaning 'honest and
trustworthy'. Also the name of an
influential Nigerian princess in the
17th century. Aamina Sheik is a
Pakistani–American actor and model.

Amira
(alt. Amiya, Amiyah)
Arabic, meaning 'a high-born girl';
Hebrew, meaning 'rich princess'.

Amity
Latin, meaning 'friendship and
harmony'. Also a name of a faction
in the novel *Divergent*.

Amory
Variant of the Spanish name Amor,
meaning 'love'. Also used as a boys'
(more commonly) and girls' name
in America during the late 1800s to
early 1900s, probably then derived
from the French Ameury.

Amy
*(alt. Aimee, Amee, Ami, Amie,
Ammie, Amya)*
Latin, meaning 'beloved'. Famous
Amys include actor Amy Adams,
Winter Olympic skeleton gold
medallist Amy Williams and singer
Amy Winehouse.

Anafa
Hebrew, meaning 'heron'.

Anaïs
Persian, meaning 'love'.

Ananda
Hindi, meaning 'bliss'. Also the name
of one of the Buddha's disciples.

Anastasia
(alt. Athanasia)
Greek, meaning 'resurrection'.
The Grand Duchess Anastasia of
Russia, was killed in the Bolshevik
Revolution of 1917.

Anat
Jewish, meaning 'water spring'.
Name of a Semitic goddess.

Anatolia
Greek, meaning 'east sunrise'. The
name of a large area within Turkey.
Also a Christian saint.

Andrea
(alt. Andreia, Andria, Andrina)
Feminine form of Andrew, from the
Greek term for 'a man's woman'.
Famous Andreas include singer
Andrea Corr and writers Andrea Levy
and Andrea Dworkin.

Andromeda
Greek, meaning 'leader of men'.
From the heroine of an ancient
Greek legend.

Anemone
Greek, meaning 'breath'. Also the
name of a type of flowering plant.

Angela
*(alt. Angel, Angeles, Angelia, Angelle;
abbrev. Angie)*
Greek, meaning 'messenger from
God' or 'angel'. Famous Angelas
include actor Angela Lansbury and
German Chancellor Angela Merkel.

Angelica
*(alt. Angelina, Angeline, Angelique,
Angelise, Angelita, Anjelica, Anjelina)*
Latin, meaning 'angelic'. Famous
Angelicas include actor Anjelica
Huston and *Rugrats* cartoon
character Angelica Pickle.

Angelina
(alt. Anjelina)

Derived from Angela, meaning 'messenger from God' or 'angel'. Famous Angelinas include actor Angelina Jolie and book and TV mouse Angelina Ballerina.

Anise
(alt. Anisa, Anissa)

French, from the liquorice-flavoured plant of the same name. Feminine form of Anis, a boys' name common in Tunisia and Morocco.

Anita
(alt. Anitra)

Variant of Ann, meaning 'grace'. Famous Anitas include actor Anita Dobson, *Body Shop* founder Anita Roddick and singer Anita Baker.

Anna
(alt. Ana, Anne)

Derived from Hannah, which is Hebrew, meaning 'grace'. Taken from the name of Anna the prophetess in the Bible. Anna Maxwell Martin is a BAFTA award-winning English actor.

Annabel
(alt. Anabel, Anabelle, Annabell, Annabella, Annabelle)

Contraction of Anna and Belle, meaning 'grace' and 'beauty'.

Annalise
(alt. Annalee, Annaliese, Annalisa, Anneli, Annelie, Annelies, Annelise)

Combination of Anna and Lise, meaning 'grace' and 'pledged to God'. More commonly used in the USA and parts of Scandinavia.

Anne
(alt. Ann, Annie)

Derived from Hannah, meaning 'grace'. Famous Annes include actor Anne Hathaway and two wives of Henry VIII, Anne Boleyn and Anne of Cleeves.

Annemarie
(alt. Annamae, Annamarie, Annelle, Annmarie, Anne-Marie)

Combination of Anne and Mary, meaning 'grace' and 'star of the sea'. Actor Anne-Marie Duff is known for her roles in *Shameless* and *The Virgin Queen*.

Annette
(alt. Annetta)

Derived from Hannah, which is Hebrew, meaning 'grace'. Famous Annettes include actors Annette Bening, Annette Crosby and Annette Funicello.

Annis

Greek, meaning 'finished or completed'. May also be a variant of Agnes. In English mythology the Black Annis is a blue-faced witch who eats children.

Annora

Latin, meaning 'honour'. More commonly used in Eastern European communities.

Anoushka
(alt. Anousha, Anushka)

Variant of Anne, meaning 'grace'. Most popular in Russia, Greece and India.

Anthea
(alt. Anthi)

Greek, meaning 'flower-like'. Famous Antheas include presenters Anthea Turner and Anthea Redfern, and director Anthea Benton.

Antigone

In ancient Greek mythology, Antigone was the daughter of Oedipus.

Antoinette
(alt. Antonetta, Antonette, Antonietta)

Both a variation of Ann and the feminine form of Anthony, meaning 'invaluable grace'. Usually associated with 18th-century French queen consort Marie Antoinette. Often shortened to Toni.

Antonia
(alt. Antonella, Antonina)

Latin, meaning 'invaluable'. Also the name of dozens of influential ancient Roman women.

Anwen

Welsh, meaning 'very fair'. Usually associated with the character of Anwen Williams in the TV series *Torchwood*.

Anya
(alt. Aanya, Aniya, Aniyah, Aniylah, Anja)

Russian, meaning 'favour' or 'grace'; Sanskrit, meaning 'the inexhaustible'. Anya Hindmarch is known for designing fashion accessories.

Aoife

Gaelic, meaning 'beautiful joy'. Usually associated with the goddess Esuvia.

Apollonia

Feminine form of Apollo, the Greek god of the sun. St Apollonia was a virgin martyr in the third century and is the patron saint of dentistry.

Apple

From the name of the fruit. Famous Apples include the technology company Apple Inc, and Gwyneth Paltrow's daughter.

April
(alt. Avril)

Latin, meaning 'opening up'. Also the name of the month, which has associations with the goddess Venus.

Aquilina
(alt. Aqua, Aquila)

Spanish, meaning 'like an eagle'. St Aquilina was a child martyr in the third century.

Ara

Arabic, meaning 'brings rain'. Also the name of a star constellation. Used as both a girls' and a boys' name.

Arabella

Latin, meaning 'answered prayer'. Also the name of an opera by Richard Strauss.

Araceli
(alt. Aracely)

Spanish, meaning 'altar of Heaven'.

Araminta
(abbrev. Minnie, Minty)
Hebrew, meaning 'lofty'.

Araylia
(alt. Araelea)
Latin, meaning 'golden'. Associated with aralia, a genus of trees and shrubs.

Arcadia
(alt. Acadia)
Greek, meaning 'paradise'. Also the name of a daughter of the ancient Roman Emperor Arcadius. Acadia was a French colony in what is now Canada.

Ardelle
(alt. Ardell, Ardella)
Latin, meaning 'burning with enthusiasm'. Ardelle Kloss was an early leading American ice skater.

Arden
(alt. Ardis, Ardith)
Latin, meaning 'burning with enthusiasm'.

Arella
(alt. Areli, Arely)
Hebrew, meaning 'angel'. More commonly used in the USA.

Aretha
Greek, meaning 'woman of virtue'. Aretha Franklin was an awrd-winning soul singer.

Aria
(alt. Ariah)
Hebrew, meaning 'lioness', and Italian, meaning 'melody'.

Ariadne
Greek and Latin, meaning 'the very holy one'. In ancient Greek mythology, Ariadne was the daughter of King Minos.

Ariana
(alt. Aaryanna, Ariane, Arianna, Arianne, Arienne)
Derived from the Welsh word for 'silver'. Also the name of a large geographical area in ancient Greek times, covering most of modern-day Afghanistan. Ariana Grande is a popular singer and actor.

Ariel
(alt. Ariela, Ariella, Arielle)
Hebrew, meaning 'lioness of God'. Character in Disney's *The Little Mermaid*.

Arlene
(alt. Arleen, Arlie, Arline, Arly)
Gaelic, meaning 'pledge'. Arlene Phillips is known for her appearances on *Strictly Come Dancing* and *So You Think You Can Dance*, as well as her work as a choreographer.

Armida
Latin, meaning 'little armed one'. Taken from the character of Armida in the epic poem *La Gerusalemme liberata*.

Artemisia
(alt. Artemis; abbrev. Artie, Arti)
Greek and Spanish, meaning 'perfect'. Also the name of a legendary female naval commander in Persia during the fifth century.

Arwen
Welsh, meaning 'fair' or 'fine'. Also an Elven character in J.R.R. Tolkien's *Lord of the Rings* trilogy.

Arya
Fictional brave tomboy character from George R.R. Martin's *A Song of Ice and Fire* series of novels and TV series *Game of Thrones*.

Ashanti
From the geographical area in Ghana, Africa. Singer Ashanti Shequoiya Douglas is better known as just 'Ashanti'.

Ashby
English, meaning 'ash tree farm'.

Ashley
(alt. Ashely, Ashlee, Ashleigh, Ashli, Ashlie, Ashly)
English, meaning 'ash tree meadow'. Also a boys' name. Famous female Ashleys include actors Ashley Jensen and Ashley Judd, and singer Ashley Roberts.

Ashlynn
(alt. Ashlyn)
Irish Gaelic, meaning 'dream'. Also a spelling variation for Aislinn.

Ashton
(alt. Ashtyn)
Old English, meaning 'ash tree town'. Used as a girls' and boys' name, but most commonly for boys.

Asia
From the name of the continent. Also a name for an Oceanid in ancient Greek mythology.

Asma
(alt. Aasmah, Asmara)
Arabic, meaning 'high-standing'. Aasmah Mir is a BBC TV presenter and radio journalist. Asmara is the capital city of Eritrea.

Aspen
(alt. Aspynn)
From the name of the tree. Also the name of a city in the US state of Colorado.

Assumpta
(alt. Asumpta, Assunta)
Irish, meaning 'assumption'; Italian, meaning 'raised up'. Assumpta Serna is a Spanish actor. Several Irish actors have this given name.

Asta
(alt. Asteria, Astor, Astoria)
Greek or Latin, meaning 'star-like'. Also the name of a type of moth.

Astrid
Old Norse, meaning 'beautiful like a God'. Swedish uthor Astrid Lundgren is known for her children's novels such as *Pippi Longstocking*.

Atara

Hebrew, meaning 'diadem' or 'crown'. Also the name of a type of butterfly.

Athena
(alt. Athenais)

Greek, meaning 'wise'. From the ancient Greek goddess of wisdom, mathematics and arts and crafts.

Aubrey
(alt. Aubree, Aubriana, Aubrie)

French, meaning 'elf ruler'. Originally a name for boys, it is now far more common for girls.

Audrey
(alt. Audra, Audrie, Audry, Autry, Audrina)

English, meaning 'noble strength'. St Etheldreda was known as St Audrey, and was an English princess in the seventh century. Famous Audreys include actors Audrey Hepburn and Audrey Tautou.

Augusta
(alt. August, Augustine)

Feminine form of the Ancient Roman name Augustus, which is Latin, meaning 'venerated'.

Aura
(alt. Aurea)

Greek or Latin, meaning either 'soft breeze' or 'gold'.

Aurelia
(alt. Aurelie)

Latin, meaning 'gold'. The name of various Ancient Roman women, including Julius Caesar's mother.

Aurora
(alt. Aurore)

Latin, meaning 'dawn'. In ancient Roman mythology, Aurora was the goddess of sunrise.

Austine
(alt. Austen, Austin)

Feminine form of Austin, which is Latin, meaning 'venerated'.

Autumn

Latin, from the name of the harvest season. Canadian-born Autumn Phillips is granddaughter-in-law to Queen Elizabeth II.

Ava
(alt. Avah, Avia, Avie)

Latin, meaning 'like a bird'. Ava Gardner was an iconic American actor during the 1950s to 1970s.

Avalon
(alt. Avalyn, Aveline)

Celtic, meaning 'island of apples'. The name comes from a mythological island in the legend of King Arthur.

Axelle

Greek, meaning 'father of peace'. More commonly used in French- and Flemish-speaking communities.

Aya
(alt. Ayah)
Hebrew, meaning 'bird'.

Ayanna
(alt. Ayana)
Swahili, meaning 'beautiful flower'.

Azalea
(alt. Azalia)
Latin, meaning 'dry earth'. Also the name of a type of flowering shrub. Often associated with Australian singer Iggy Azalea.

Aziza
Hebrew, meaning 'mighty', or Arabic, meaning 'precious'.

Azure
(alt. Azaria)
French, meaning 'sky-blue'.

Girls' names

Babette

French version of Barbara, from the Greek word meaning 'foreign'. Babette Cole is an author of children's books.

Badia

(alt. Badiyn, Badea)

Arabic, meaning 'elegant'.

Bailey

(alt. Baeli, Bailee)

English, meaning 'law enforcer'. Used as a girls' and boys' name, but more commonly for boys in recent years.

Bambi

Shortened version of the Italian Bambina, meaning 'child'. Usually associated with the cartoon Disney character.

Barbara

(alt. Barbra; abbrev. Barb, Barbie)

Greek, meaning 'foreign'. Famous Barbaras include actor Barbara Windsor, singer Barbra Streisand and Barbara McClintock, who won a Nobel Prize for genetics.

Basma

Arabic, meaning 'smile'.

Bathsheba

Hebrew, meaning 'daughter of the oath'. Usually associated with the story of Bathsheba and King David in the Bible. Also a character in the novel *Far From the Madding Crowd*.

Bay

(alt. Baya, Bae)

From the bay tree, or the indentation in a coastline (e.g. Byron Bay). More commonly used for boys.

Beata

Latin, meaning 'blessed'. Can be used as a shortened form of Beatrice or as a name in its own right.

Beatrice

(alt. Beatrix, Beatriz, Bellatrix, Betrys)

Latin, meaning 'blessed' or 'voyager'. A recent rapid riser in the Top Names list. Famous Beatrices include children's book author Beatrix Potter and Princess Beatrice, granddaughter of Queen Elizabeth II.

Becky

(alt. Becca, Beccie, Beccy, Beckie)

Shortened form of Rebecca, meaning 'joined', used as a name in its own right.

Belinda

(alt. Belen, Belina)

Contraction of Belle and Linda, meaning 'beautiful'. Famous Belindas include singer Belinda Carlisle and actor Belinda Stewart-Wilson.

Bella

(alt. Belle)

Latin, meaning 'beautiful'. Usually associated with the character of Isabella (Bella) Swan from the *Twilight* series or Belle from Disney's film *Beauty and the Beast*.

Belva

Latin, meaning 'beautiful view'. The inspiration for one of the characters in the musical *Chicago* was real-life murderer Belva Gaertner.

Movie inspirations

Bella (*Twilight*)

Elsa (*Frozen*)

Fiona (*Shrek*)

Holly (*Breakfast at Tiffany's*)

Lara (*Tomb Raider*)

Maria (*The Sound of Music*)

Marla (*Fight Club*)

Mary (*Mary Poppins*)

Nina (*Black Swan*)

Pandora (*Avatar*)

Rey (*Star Wars*)

Trinity (*The Matrix*)

Bénédicta

(abbrev. Bennie, Benny)

Feminine form of Benedict, which is Latin, meaning 'blessed'. Benedicta Henrietta of the Palatinate is a common ancestor of present-day monarchs.

Benita

(alt. Bernita)

Spanish, meaning 'blessed'.

Berit

(alt. Beret)

Scandinavian, meaning 'splendid' or 'gorgeous'.

Bernadette
(alt. Bernadine; abbrev. Bernie)

French, meaning 'courageous'. St Bernadette was known for her visions of the Virgin Mary.

Bernice
(alt. Berenice, Berniece, Burnice)

Greek, meaning 'she who brings victory'. The name of Herod's daughter in the Bible.

Bertha
(alt. Berta, Berthe, Bertie)

German, meaning 'bright'. There are four saints called Bertha, all from the early Middle Ages.

Beryl

Greek, meaning 'pale green gemstone'. Beryl Reid was a classic British actor and Beryl Cook was a 20th-century English artist.

Bess
(alt. Bessie)

Shortened form of Elizabeth, meaning 'consecrated to God'. Queen Elizabeth I has the nickname Good Queen Bess. Bessie Smith was a blues singer.

Beth

Hebrew, meaning 'house'. Also shortened form of Elizabeth, meaning 'consecrated to God'.

Bethany
(alt. Bethan)

Hebrew, referring to a geographical location found in the Bible. The name has seen a return to popularity in recent years.

Bethel

Hebrew, meaning 'house of God'. Also the name of a city in the Bible.

Bettina

Spanish or German version of Elizabeth, meaning 'consecrated to God'.

Betty
(alt. Betsy, Bette, Bettie, Bettye)

Shortened version of Elizabeth, meaning 'consecrated to God', also used in its own right. Famous Bettys include cartoon character Betty Boop and actor Betty White.

Beulah

Hebrew, meaning 'married'. Also the name for a place that exists between Earth and Heaven.

Beverly
(alt. Beverlee, Beverley)

English, meaning 'beaver stream'. Beverley Knight is a British soul singer, actor and TV personality.

Bevin

Celtic, meaning 'fair lady'.

Beyoncé

Modern American, from the singer. Beyoncé's name was created by her parents as a tribute to her mother's maiden name, which was Beyince. However, some sources say the name is Swahili, meaning 'beyond others'.

Bianca
(alt. Blanca)

Italian, meaning 'white'. Famous Biancas include activist Bianca Jagger, model Bianca Gascoigne, the character of Bianca from Shakespeare's Othello and the long-running EastEnders character of that name.

Bibiana

Greek, meaning 'alive'. St Bibiana was a Roman virgin and martyr during the fourth century.

Bijou

French, meaning 'jewel'.

Billie
(alt. Bill, Billy, Billye)

Shortened version of Wilhelmina, meaning 'determined' as well as a name in its own right. Billie Holiday was an iconic jazz singer. Billie Piper is a singer turned actor.

Bina

Hebrew, meaning 'knowledge'.

Birdie
(alt. Birdy)

English and Swedish, meaning 'little bird'.

Birgit
(alt. Birgitta)

German, meaning 'power and strength'. Used as a variation of Bridget.

Blaer

Icelandic, meaning 'light breeze'.

Blair

Scottish Gaelic, meaning 'flat, plain area'. Blair Waldorf is the main character in Gossip Girl, the novel series, TV series and film.

Blaise

French, meaning 'lisp' or 'stutter'. Also common as a boys' name.

Blake
(alt. Blakely, Blakelyn)

Old English, meaning 'dark, black'. More commonly used as a boys' name. Actor Blake Lively is best known for her role in the TV series Gossip Girl.

Blanche
(alt. Blanch)

French, meaning 'white or pale'. Extremely common in the Middle Ages, Blanche saw an increase in popularity before World War II, but hasn't been widely used since then.

Blodwen

Welsh, meaning 'white flower'.

Blossom

English, meaning 'flower-like'.

Blythe
(alt. Blithe, Bly)

English, meaning 'happy and carefree'. Actor Blythe Danner is known for her roles in *Will & Grace*, *Meet the Parents*, and for being the mother of Gwyneth Paltrow.

Bobbi
(alt. Bobbie, Bobby)

Shortened version of Roberta, meaning 'bright fame', as well as a name in its own right. Usually associated with the cosmetics brand Bobbi Brown.

Bonamy
(alt. Bomani, Bonamia, Bonamea)

Derived from French, meaning 'close friend'.

Bonita

Spanish, meaning 'pretty'.

Bonnie
(alt. Bonny)

Scottish, meaning 'fair of face'. Actor Bonnie Langford was a child star who grew up to appear in West End musicals and *Dr Who*.

Brandy
(alt. Brandee, Brandi, Brandie)

From the name of the liquor created by distilling wine. Singer Brandy is known for her various pop songs as well as her role in *Moesha*.

Branwen

Welsh, meaning 'a white crow'.

Brea
(alt. Bree, Bria)

Shortened form of Brianna, meaning 'strong', but used in its own right. Also the name of a god in ancient Irish mythology.

Brenda

Old Norse, meaning 'sword'. Can also be used as a feminine form of Brendan.

Brianna
(alt. Breana, Breanna, Breanne)

Irish Gaelic, meaning 'strong'. More commonly used in the USA.

Bridget
(alt. Bridgett, Bridgette, Brigette, Brigid, Brigitta, Brigitte)

Irish Gaelic, meaning 'strength and power'. Famous Bridgets include actor Bridget Fonda, Brigitte Bardot, Brigitte Nielsen and the protagonist in the novel *Bridget Jones's Diary* by Helen Fielding.

Brier
(alt. Briar)

French, meaning 'heather'.

Brit
(alt. Britt, Britta)

Celtic, meaning 'spotted' or 'freckled'. Usually a shortened form of Brittany, though it can be used in its own right. Actors Britt Ekland and Britt Robertson are both Brittanys.

Britannia

Latin, meaning 'Britain'. Britannia is the female personification of Great Britain.

Brittany

(alt. Britany, Britney, Britni, Brittani, Brittanie, Brittney, Brittni, Brittny)

Latin, meaning 'from England', though the name also refers to a region of France. Famous Brittanys include actor Brittany Murphy and singer Britney Spears.

Brontë

Greek, meaning 'the sound of thunder'.

Bronwen

(alt. Bronwyn)

Welsh, meaning 'fair breast'. In Wales it is common to give the spelling Bronwen to girls and Bronwyn to boys.

Brooke

(alt. Brook)

English, meaning 'small stream'. Brooke Shields is an American actor and model and Brooke Vincent is a British TV actor.

Brooklyn

(alt. Brooklynn)

From the name of a New York borough. More commonly used as a boys' name.

Brunhilda

(alt. Brunhilde, Brynhildr)

German, meaning 'armour-wearing fighting maid'. Brynhildr, from which Brunhilda and Brunhilde orginated, was an important character in Old German mythology.

Bryn

(alt. Brynn)

Welsh, meaning 'mount' or 'hill'. Used more commonly as a boys' name.

Bryony

(alt. Briony)

English, from the name of bryonia, a European vine. Bryony Hannah is an Olivier-nominated British actor and star of Call the Midwife.

Buffy

A shortened form of Elizabeth, meaning 'consecrated to God'. Usually associated with the protagonist of the sci-fi series Buffy the Vampire Slayer.

Girls' names

Cadence
Feminine form of Caden, from Latin, meaning 'with rhythm'

Cadew
Derived from French, meaning 'gift'; English, meaning 'coarse woollen fabric'.

Cai
Vietnamese, meaning 'feminine'.

Caitlin
(alt. Cadyn, Caitlann, Caitlyn, Caitlynn, Katelin, Katelyn, Katelynn, Katlin, Katlyn)
Greek, meaning 'pure'. Caitlin Moran is a British broadcaster, newspaper columnist and author.

Calandra
Greek, meaning 'lark'. The calandra lark is a small bird found in Mediterranean countries. Calandra is also the name of an asteroid belt.

Calantha
(alt. Calanthe)
Greek, meaning 'lovely flower'. Also refers to dozens of flowering shrubs.

Caledonia
Latin, meaning 'from Scotland'. Also an old name for Scotland.

Calia
American, meaning 'renowned beauty'. Also refers to several species of shrubs and trees.

Calista
(alt. Callista, Callisto, Kallista)
Greek, meaning 'most beautiful'. Actor Calista Flockhart is known for her roles in Ally McBeal and Brothers and Sisters.

Calla
Greek, meaning 'beautiful'. Also refers to a type of white-flowered plant.

Callie
(alt. Caleigh, Cali, Calleigh, Cally)
Greek, meaning 'beauty'. Can also be a derivative of Carol, Caroline or Carolyn, as in screen-writer Callie Khouri, who is known for *Thelma & Louise* and *Nashville*.

Calliope
Greek, meaning 'beautiful voice'. From the muse of epic poetry in ancient Greek mythology.

Camas
Native American, from the root and bulb of the same name.

Cambria
Welsh, from the alternative name for Wales.

Camden
(alt. Camdin, Camdyn)
English, meaning 'winding valley'. More popular as a boys' name.

Cameo
Italian, meaning 'skin'. A cameo in the acting world usually refers to a small part played by a big star.

Cameron
(alt. Camryn, Kameron, Kamron)
Scottish Gaelic, meaning 'bent nose'. More often used as a boys' name but also occasionally for girls, as with actor Cameron Diaz.

Camilla
(alt. Camille, Camelia, Camellia, Camila, Camillia)
Latin, meaning 'spiritual serving girl'. Camilla, Duchess of Cornwall, is married to Prince Charles. The French form, Camille, is often also used for boys.

Candace
(alt. Candice, Candis, Kandice; abbrev. Candy, Candi, Kandy, Kandi)
Latin, meaning 'brilliant white'. In the African ancient kingdom of Kush, Candace was the title given to queens and queen mothers.

Candida
Latin, meaning 'white', associated with purity and salvation. Unfortunately, also the name of a fungal infection.

Candra
Latin, meaning 'glowing'. The Candra family dynasty ruled eastern Bengal in the 10th century. Also the name of an immmortal villainess in Marvel comics.

Canei
Greek, meaning 'pure'. Also refers to a type of shrub.

Caoimhe
Celtic, meaning 'gentle' or 'precious'. Can be pronounced as 'kyva' or 'keeva', depending on where in Ireland it is used.

Caprice

Italian, meaning 'ruled by whim'. Caprice Bourret is a model best known simply as 'Caprice'.

Cara

Latin, meaning 'darling'. Cara Delevingne is a top model.

Caren

(alt. Carin, Caron, Caryn)

Greek, meaning 'pure'. Comedian Whoopi Goldberg's real name is Caryn Elaine Johnson.

Carey

(alt. Cari, Carie, Carrey, Carri, Carrie, Cary)

Gaelic, meaning 'love'. Carey Mulligan is an English actor. Can also be used for boys.

Carina

(alt. Corina)

Italian, meaning 'dearest little one'. Also the name of a star constellation.

Carissa

(alt. Carisa)

Greek, meaning 'grace'. Also the name of a type of shrub.

Carla

(alt. Charla)

Feminine of the Old Norse Carl, meaning 'free man'. Singer Carla Bruni Sarkozy is married to the former president of France Nicolas Sarkozy.

Carlin

(alt. Carleen, Carlene)

Gaelic, meaning 'little champion'.

Carlotta

(alt. Carlota)

Italian form of Charlotte, meaning 'little and feminine'. Also the name of a character in *The Phantom of the Opera*.

Carly

(alt. Carlee, Carley, Carli, Carlie, Karlie, Karly)

Feminine form of Charles, from the German meaning 'free man'. Famous Carlys include singers Carly Simon and Carly Rae Jepson, and model Karlie Kloss.

Carmel

(alt. Carmela, Carmelita, Carmella)

Hebrew, meaning 'God's vineyard'. Mount Carmel is a place mentioned in the Bible.

Carmen

(alt. Carma, Carmina)

Latin, meaning 'song'. Usually associated with the opera *Carmen* by Georges Bizet.

Carol

(alt. Carole, Carrol, Carroll, Caryl)

Shortened form of Caroline, from the German meaning 'man', but commonly used in its own right. Famous Carols include singer Carole King, former Poet Laureate Carol Ann Duffy and TV personality Carol Vorderman.

Caroline
(alt. Carolann, Carolina, Carolyn, Carolynn)
German, meaning 'man'. Famous Carolines include TV presenter, Caroline Flack and the late writer, actor and comedian Caroline Aherne.

Carrington
English, meaning 'Charles's town'.

Carys
(alt. Cerys)
Welsh, meaning 'love'. Singer and radio presenter Cerys Matthews was a founder member of the band Catatonia.

Casey
(alt. Kacey, Kaci, Kacie, Kacy, Kasey, Kasie, Kassie)
Irish Gaelic, meaning 'watchful'. Used especially in the USA and for both girls and boys.

Cassandra
(alt. Casandra, Cassandre, Kassandra)
Greek, meaning 'one who prophesies doom' or 'entangler of men'. Usually associated with the seer in ancient Greek mythology and sister of Helen of Troy. Cassandra Clare is the pen name of bestselling author Judith Rumelt.

Cassia
(alt. Casia, Casie, Cassie)
Greek, meaning 'cinnamon'. Cassia Leo is an American author.

Cassidy
Irish, meaning 'clever' or 'curly-haired'. Cassidy Wolf is a former American teen beauty queen.

Cassiopeia
(alt. Cassiopia, Cassiopea)
Greek, from the constellation and the ancient Greek myth about a vain queen.

Catalina
(alt. Catarina, Caterina)
Spanish version of Catherine, meaning 'pure'.

Catherine
(alt. Catharine, Cathrine, Cathryn, Katharine, Katherine, Kathryn)
Greek, meaning 'pure'. Famous Catherines include Catherine, Duchess of Cambridge, actor Catherine Zeta Jones, and two wives of King Henry VIII.

Cathleen
(alt. Kathleen)
A spelling variation for Kathleen, the Irish version of Catherine, meaning 'pure'. Actor Cathleen Nesbitt was known for her roles in dozens of West End and Broadway productions.

Cathy
(alt. Caitie, Cathey, Cathi, Cathie, Caty, Cato, Caitia, Kathie, Kathy)
Shortened form of Catherine, meaning 'pure'. Can be used in its own right. Author Cathy Cassidy is known for her young adult fiction.

Catrina
(alt. Caitrina, Catriona)
Greek, meaning 'pure'.

Cayley
(alt. Cayla, Caylee, Caylen)
American, meaning 'pure'.

Cecilia
(alt. Cecile, Cecelia, Cecily, Cicely, Cicily; abbrev. Celia)
Latin, meaning 'blind one'.
Associated with the song 'Cecilia' by Simon and Garfunkel.

Celena
Greek, meaning 'goddess of the moon'. A spelling alternative to the Spanish name Selena.

Celeste
(alt. Celestina, Celestine)
Latin, meaning 'heavenly'. American Celeste Holm was an Oscar-winning actor in films and on Broadway.

Celia
Latin, meaning 'heaven'. British actor Celia Imrie has starred in numerous films and television series.

Celine
(alt. Celia, Celina)
French version of Celeste, meaning 'heavenly'. Canadian Celine Dion is one of the most enduringly successful singers in pop music history.

Cerise
French, meaning 'cherry'. The colour cerise is a deep, pinky red.

Chanah
(alt. Chana)
Hebrew, meaning 'grace'. Usually used as a spelling alternative to Hannah.

Chandler
(alt. Chandell)
English, meaning 'candle maker'. Most commonly used as a boys' name.

Chandra
(alt. Chanda, Chandry)
Sanskrit, meaning 'like the moon'. Chandra is a god of the moon in Hinduism.

Chanel
(alt. Chanelle)
French, meaning 'pipe'. Usually associated with the designer and fashion brand Coco Chanel.

Chantal
(alt. Chantel, Chantelle, Chantilly)
French, meaning 'stony spot'. Chantelle Houghton was the first non-celebrity to win *Celebrity Big Brother* and is now a TV personality and columnist.

Chardonnay
French, from the wine variety of the same name.

Charis
(alt. Charissa, Charisse)
Greek, meaning 'grace'. Charis is one of the Graces in ancient Greek mythology.

Charity

Latin, meaning 'brotherly love'. Of the classic trio of names, Faith, Hope and Charity, this has been the least used.

Charlene
(alt. Charleen, Charline)

German, meaning 'man'. Famous Charlenes include singer Charlene Spiteri, actor Charlene McKenna and Kylie Minogue's character in Aussie soap Neighbours.

Charlotte
(alt. Charnette, Charolette, Charlize; abbrev. Charlie, Charly)

French, meaning 'little and feminine'. Famous Charlottes include author Charlotte Brontë, singer Charlotte Church and, fourth in line to the throne, Princess Charlotte.

Charmaine

Latin, meaning 'clan'. The name possibly comes from Charmian, who was a favourite servant of Cleopatra.

Charnelle
(alt. Charnell, Charnel, Charnele)

American, meaning 'sparkles'. The spelling Charnel refers to a building that houses human remains, often located near a church.

Chastity

Latin, meaning 'purity'.

Chava
(alt. Chaya)

Hebrew, meaning 'beloved'.

Chelsea
(alt. Chelsee, Chelsey, Chelsi, Chelsie, Chelsy)

English, meaning 'port or landing place'. Chelsea Clinton is the only child US political royalty Bill and Hillary Clinton.

Cher

French, meaning 'beloved'. Cher is an American singer and actor.

Cherie
(alt. Cheri, Cherise)

French, meaning 'dear'. Cherie Blair is a barrister and wife of former British prime minister Tony Blair.

Cherish
(alt. Cherith)

English, meaning 'to treasure'.

Chermona

Hebrew, meaning 'sacred mountain'. Sometimes used as a feminine form of Sherman.

Cherry
(alt. Cherri)

English, meaning 'cherry fruit'.

Cheryl
(alt. Cheryle)

English, meaning 'little and womanly'. Singer Cheryl found fame with girl group Girls Aloud and has been a judge on The X Factor.

Chesney

English, meaning 'place to camp'. Used as both a girls' and a boys' name.

Cheyenne
(alt. Cheyanne)

Native American, from the tribe of the same name from the state of Wyoming in the USA.

Chiara
(alt. Ceara, Chiarina)

Italian, meaning 'light'.

China

From the Asian country of the same name.

Chiquita

Spanish, meaning 'little one'.

Chloe
(alt. Cloe)

Greek, meaning 'pale green shoot'. Sometimes spelled with an accent on the 'e'. Famous Chloes include the fashion house Chloé, actors Chloë Moretz and Chloë Sevigny.

Chloris

Greek, meaning 'pale'. Chloris was a nymph in ancient Greek mythology.

Christabel

Latin and French, meaning 'fair Christian'. The title of a poem by Samuel Taylor Coleridge.

Christina
(alt. Christine, Christiana, Cristina; abbrev. Chris, Chrissy, Christa, Christie, Christy, Crissy, Cristy)

Greek, meaning 'anointed Christian'. Feminine form of Christian, and a tribute to Jesus Christ. Christina Aguilera is a world famous pop singer.

Chuma

Aramaic, meaning 'warmth'.

Ciara

Irish, meaning 'dark beauty'. Ciara Princess Harris, known simply as Ciara, is an American singer, dancer, actor and model.

Cierra
(alt. Ciera)

Irish, meaning 'black'. Usually used as a spelling alternative to Sierra.

Cinderella

French, meaning 'little ash-girl'. Most often associated with the fairy tale.

Cinnamon

Greek, from the exotic spice of the same name.

Citlali
(alt. Citlalli)

Nahuatl, meaning 'star'. An ancient Aztec name.

Citrine

Latin, from the gemstone of the same name.

Claire
(alt. Clare, Clara, Claira)

Latin, meaning 'bright'. A very popular name, especially in 1960s and '70s Britain. Famous Claires include actors Claire Danes and Claire Foy, and sports presenter Clare Balding.

Clarabelle
(alt. Clarabella, Claribel)
Contraction of Clara and Isobel, meaning 'bright' and 'consecrated to God'. Clarabelle is a Disney cow character and Clarabella is the title of a Beatles song.

Clarissa
(alt. Clarice, Clarisse)
Variation of Claire, meaning 'bright'. One of the longest novels in English is the 18th-century *Clarissa, or, The History of a Young Lady*, by Samuel Richardson.

Clarity
Latin, meaning 'lucid'.

Claudette
Latin, meaning 'lame'. The first female prime minister of Haiti was Claudette Werleigh. Claudette Colvin was a pioneer of the American civil rights movement.

Claudia
(alt. Claudie, Claudine)
Latin, meaning 'lame'. TV presenter and film critic Claudia Winkleman co-presents *Strictly Come Dancing*; Claudia Schiffer is a supermodel.

Clematis
Greek, meaning 'vine'. Also the name of a type of flowering plant.

Clementine
(alt. Clemency, Clementina, Clemmie)
Latin, meaning 'mild and merciful'. Also the name of the sweet orange fruit.

Cleopatra
(alt. Cleo, Clio, Cliona)
Greek, meaning 'her father's renown'. Cleopatra was the last acting Pharaoh of ancient Egypt.

Clodagh
Irish, meaning 'river'.

Clotilda
(alt. Clothilda, Clothilde, Clotilde)
German, meaning 'renowned battle'. St Clotilde was known for her works of charity in the fifth century.

Clover
English, from the flower of the same name.

Coco
Spanish, meaning 'help'. Usually associated with the fashion designer Coco Chanel.

Cody
English, meaning 'pillow'. Used more commonly for boys.

Colleen
(alt. Coleen)
Irish Gaelic, meaning 'girl'. TV presenter Colleen Nolan was the youngest of the singing sisters The Nolans.

Collette
(alt. Colette)
Greek and French, meaning 'people of victory'. Author Sidonie-Gabrielle Colette is known for her novel *Gigi*.

Connie
(alt. Konnie)

Latin, meaning 'steadfast'. Also used as a shortened version of Constance. Kanak Asha Huq, known as Konnie, is a former *Blue Peter* presenter.

Constance
(alt. Constanza)

Latin, meaning 'steadfast'. Oscar Wilde's wife was Constance Lloyd.

Consuelo
(alt. Consuela)

Spanish, meaning 'comfort'. The name originated from a Spanish name for the Virgin Mary, Our Lady of Consolation.

Cora

Greek, meaning 'maiden'.

Coral
(alt. Coralie, Coraline, Corelia, Corene)

Latin, from the marine life of the same name.

Corazon

Spanish, meaning 'heart'. Also a slang term in Spanish meaning 'darling'.

Cordelia
(alt. Cordia, Cordie)

Latin, meaning 'heart'. Also the name of a tragic character in Shakespeare's play *King Lear*.

Corey
(alt. Cori, Corrie, Cory)

Irish Gaelic, meaning 'the hollow'. Used more commonly, for boys.

Corinne
(alt. Corin, Corinna, Corrine)

French version of Cora, from the Greek meaning 'maiden'. Famous Corinnes include singer-songwriter Corinne Bailey Rae and fashion photographer Corinne Day.

Corliss

English, meaning 'cheery'.

Cornelia

Latin, meaning 'like a horn'. Also the name of several important women in the ancient Roman empire.

Cosette

French, meaning 'people of victory'. Also the heroine in *Les Misérables*.

Cosima
(alt. Cosmina)

Feminine form of Cosmo, from the Greek for 'order'. Cosima Lawson is the daughter of celebrity chef Nigella Lawson.

Courtney
(alt. Cortney)

English, meaning 'court-dweller'. Actor Courtney Cox is known for her roles in *Friends* and *Cougar Town*.

Creola

French, meaning 'American-born, English descent'. Usually associated with the Creole people and language.

Crescent

French, meaning 'increasing'. Usually associated with the shape of the same name.

Cressida

From the Trojan heroine in Greek mythology.

Crystal
(alt. *Christal, Chrystal, Cristal, Kristal, Kristel*)

Greek, meaning 'ice'. Can also be spelled using a K in all forms.

Csilla

Hungarian, meaning 'defences'. More commonly used in Eastern European countries.

Cyd

Shortened form of Sidney, meaning 'wide island'. Dancer and actor Cyd Charisse was known for her roles in *Singin' in the Rain*, *The Band Wagon* and *Silk Stockings*.

Cynara

Greek, meaning 'thistly plant'. Also the name of a type of thistle plant.

Cynthia
(abbrev. *Cinda, Cindi, Cyndi, Cindy*)

Greek, meaning 'goddess from the mountain'. Also the name of an ancient Greek goddess of the moon. Famous Cindys include actor Cynthia Nixon (who played Miranda in *Sex in the City*), supermodel Cindy Crawford and Cyndi Lauper the singer, songwriter and actor.

Cyra

Persian, meaning 'sun'. Also the name of a type of ladybird.

Cyrilla

Latin, meaning 'lordly'. Also the name of a type of flowering plant.

Girls' names

Dacey
Irish Gaelic, meaning 'from the south'.

Dada
Swahili, meaning 'curly haired'.

Daelan
English, meaning 'aware'. More commonly used as a boys' name.

Dagmar
German, meaning 'day's glory'. Dagmar was the stage name of one the first major television stars, Virginia Egnor.

Dagny
Nordic, meaning 'new day'.

Dahlia
Scandinavian, from the flowering plant of the same name.

Dai
Welsh, meaning 'darling'; Japanese meaning 'large, great'. Rarely used for girls.

Daisy
(alt. Dasia)
English, meaning 'eye of the day'. Also the common flower. Daisy has seen a rise in popularity in recent years.

Flower names
Acacia	Lily
Daisy	Petunia
Flora	Poppy
Hyacinth	Primrose
Lilac	Rose

Dakota
Native American, meaning 'allies'. There are two American states named after the Dakota people. Actor Dakota Johnson stars in the film version of *50 Shades of Grey*.

Dalia
(alt. Dalila)

Hebrew, meaning 'delicate branch'. Also the name of a goddess of property in ancient Lithuanian mythology.

Dallas

Scottish Gaelic, from the village of the same name. Also the name of a city in Texas, USA.

Damaris

Greek, meaning 'calf'. Found in the Bible.

Damica
(alt. Damika)

French, meaning 'friendly'. Often used as a spelling alternative to Danica.

Damita

Spanish, meaning 'little noblewoman'.

Dana
(alt. Dania, Danna, Dayna)

English, meaning 'from Denmark'; Persian, meaning 'a perfect and valuable pearl'. Actor Dana Delany played one of the *Desperate Housewives*.

Danae

Greek, from the ancient Greek mythological heroine of the same name.

Danica
(alt. Danika)

Latin, meaning 'from Denmark'. Danica Patrick made waves as one of the most successful female racing drivers in history.

Danielle
(alt. Danelle, Daniela, Daniella, Danila, Danyelle; abbrev. Dani, Danii)

Feminine form of Daniel, which is Hebrew for 'God is my judge'. Model Danielle Lloyd is known for her glamour modelling and *Big Brother* career.

Danita

English, meaning 'God will judge'. More commonly used in the USA.

Daphne
(alt. Dafne, Daphna)

Greek, meaning 'laurel tree'. Daphne was a water nymph in ancient Greek mythology.

Dara

Hebrew and Persian, meaning 'wisdom'. Found in the Bible. Used for both girls and boys.

Darby
(alt. Darbi, Darbie)

Irish, meaning 'a park with deer'.

Darcy
(alt. Darcey, Darci, Darcie)

Irish Gaelic, meaning 'dark'. Ballerina Dame Darcey Bussell is one of the reasons behind the recent rise in popularity of the name in the UK.

Daria

Greek, meaning 'rich'. Usually associated with the teenage cartoon character Daria.

Darla

English, meaning 'darling'. Actor Darla Hood was known for her roles as a child star in the 1930s and '40s.

Darlene
(alt. Darleen, Darline)

American, meaning 'darling'. Actor Darlene Gillespie was one of the original Mickey Mouse Club members.

Darva

Slavic, meaning 'honeybee'. Also the name of several locations in Iran.

Daryl
(alt. Darrell, Darryl)

English, originally used as a surname. Famous Daryls include actor Daryl Hannah; Darrell Rivers was the central character in Enid Blyton's classic Malory Towers books.

Dascha
(alt. Dasha)

Russian, meaning 'of the sea'. Actor Dascha Polanco is known for her role in the US television series Orange is the New Black.

Davina

Hebrew, meaning 'loved one'. English TV presenter Davina McCall is the best-known owner of the name.

Dawn
(alt. Dawna)

English, meaning 'to become day'. Dawn French is one of the most successful comedy actors and writers of recent decades.

Daya

Hebrew, meaning 'bird of prey'. Also the term used for a form of teaching in the Sikh religion.

Deanna
(alt. Dayana, Deana, Deanna, Deanne)

English, meaning 'girl from the valley'. Singer and actor Deanna Durbin was a Hollywood star in the 1930s and '40s. Deanna Troi was a central female character in Star Trek.

Deborah
(alt. Debbra, Debora, Debra, Debrah, Dvora; abbrev. Debbi, Debbie, Debby)

Hebrew, meaning 'bee'. Also the name of a prophetess in the Bible. Among the many famous Deborahs are actor Deborah Kerr and entrepreneur Deborah Meaden, star of Dragons' Den.

December

Latin, meaning 'tenth month'.

Decima
(alt. Decia)

Latin, meaning 'tenth'. Also the name of a goddess in ancient Roman mythology.

Dee

Welsh, meaning 'swarthy'.

Deidre
(alt. Deidra, Deirdre)

Irish, meaning 'raging woman'.
Deirdre Barlow was one of *Coronation Street*'s longest-running characters.

Deja
(alt. Dejah)

French, meaning 'already'. The commonly used French phrase *déjà vu* means 'already seen'.

Delaney

Irish Gaelic, meaning 'offspring of the challenger'.

Delia

Greek, meaning 'from Delos'. Delia Smith is one of the most enduringly successful stars of cookery TV programmes and books.

Delilah
(alt. Delina)

Hebrew, meaning 'seductive'. Famous Delilahs include the lover of Samson in the Bible, and the song 'Delilah' by Tom Jones.

Della
(alt. Dell)

Shortened form of Adele, meaning 'noble'. Used as a name in its own right. Donald Duck's twin sister is called Della Duck.

Delores
(alt. Deloris, Dolores, Doloris)

Spanish, meaning 'sorrows'. In Spanish, the shortened form of Delores is Lolita or Lola.

Delphine
(alt. Delpha, Delphia, Delphina, Delphinia)

Greek, meaning 'dolphin'. More commonly used in French-speaking communities.

Delta

Greek, meaning 'fourth child'. Also the name of the fourth letter of the Greek alphabet.

Demelza

Cornish, from the hamlet of the same name in Cornwall. Made popular by the *Poldark* character.

Demetria
(alt. Demetrice, Dimitria)

Greek, from the ancient Greek mythological heroine of the same name.

Demi

French, meaning 'half'. American actor Demi Moore is a star of Hollywood films across several decades.

Dena
(alt. Deena)

English, meaning 'from the valley'. Also the name of a mountain range in Iran.

Denise
(alt. Denice, Denisa, Denisse)

French, meaning 'devoted to Bacchus'. Denise is the feminine French form of Dionysius, the ancient Greek god of wine.

Derora

Hebrew, meaning 'stream'. Also the name of a clan in India.

Desdemona

Greek, meaning 'wretchedness'. A character in Shakespeare's play *Othello*.

Desiree
(alt. Desirae, Des'ree)

French, meaning 'much desired'. Singer Des'ree adapted her name from Desiree, her given name.

Desma

Greek, meaning 'blinding oath'. More commonly used as a shortened version of Desdemona.

Destiny
(alt. Destany, Destinee, Destiney, Destini)

French, meaning 'fate'.

Deva

Hindi, meaning 'God-like'. Deva is also a name for several Buddhist, Hindu and New Age spiritual entities or people.

Devinne
(alt. Devin)

Feminine form of Devin, which is Irish Gaelic for 'poet'.

Devon

English, from the southern English county of the same name.

Diamond

English, meaning 'brilliant'.

Diana
(alt. Dian, Diane, Dianna, Dianne)

Roman, meaning 'divine'. Famous Dianas include Princess Diana, singing legend Diana Ross and Diana the Roman goddess of hunting.

Diandra

Greek, meaning 'two males'.

Dilys

Welsh, meaning 'reliable'. Famous Dilyses include actor Dilys Watling and actor and screenwriter Dilys Laye.

Dimona

Hebrew, meaning 'south'. Also the name of a town in the Bible, now situated in modern Israel.

Dinah
(alt. Dina)

Hebrew, meaning 'justified'.

Dionne

Greek, from the mythological heroine of the same name. Famous Dionnes include singers Dionne Warwick and Dionne Bromfield.

Divine

Italian, meaning 'heavenly'.

Dixie

French, meaning 'tenth'. Usually used as a term for the South of the USA.

Dodie

Hebrew, meaning 'well-loved'. Author Dodie Smith is best known for her children's novel *101 Dalmations*.

Dolly

(alt. Dollie)

Shortened form of Dorothy, meaning 'gift of God'. Can be used in its own right. Dolly Parton is the world-famous country and western singer.

Dominique

(alt. Domenica, Dominica, Domonique)

Latin, meaning 'Lord'. Usually associated with the song 'Dominique' by Soeur Sourire, a singing nun.

Donata

(alt. Donatella)

Latin, meaning 'given', also Italian for 'gift'. Donatella Versace is a leading Italian fashion designer and vice president of the Versace empire.

Donna

(alt. Dona, Donnie)

Italian, meaning 'lady'. Singer Donna Summer had a string of hits in the 1970s and '80s.

Dora

Greek, meaning 'gift'. Usually associated with the cartoon character Dora the Explorer.

Dorcas

Greek, meaning 'gazelle'. Also found in the Bible.

Doreen

(alt. Doren, Dorene, Dorine)

Greek, meaning 'gift'. In Irish Gaelic, the suffix 'een' indicates that a child has the same name as a parent.

Doria

Greek, meaning 'of the sea'. Also the name of an influential Genoese family in the 12th century.

Doris

(alt. Dorris)

Greek, from the region of the same name. Actor and singer Doris Day was a big star in the 1940s and '50s, and was also a leading animal rights campaigner.

Dorothy

(alt. Dorathy, Doretha, Dorotha, Dorothea, Dorthy; abbrev. Dolly, Dot, Dottie, Dotty)

Greek, meaning 'gift of God'. Famous Dorothys include the central character in *The Wizard of Oz* and Dorothy Hodgkin, who won a Nobel Prize for chemistry.

Dorrit

(alt. Dorit)

Greek, meaning 'gift of God'. Usually associated with the novel *Little Dorrit* by Charles Dickens.

Dory

(alt. Dori)

French, meaning 'gilded'. Usually associated with the character from the Disney films *Finding Nemo* and *Finding Dory*.

Dove
(alt. Dovie)

English, from the bird of the same name. Often used as a symbol for peace.

Drew

Greek, meaning 'masculine'. Actor Drew Barrymore became a child star when she appeared in *E.T.*.

Drusilla
(alt. Drucilla)

Latin, meaning 'of the Drusus clan'. Found in the Bible.

Dulcie
(alt. Dulce, Dulcia)

Latin, meaning 'sweet'. Actor Dulcie Gray was known for her roles on stage and screen in the mid-20th century.

Dusty
(alt. Dusti)

Old German, meaning 'brave warrior'. Singer Dusty Springfield was a 1960s star.

Names of Poets
Amy (Lowell)
Anne (Sexton)
Carol Ann (Duffy)
Charlotte (Smith)
Emily (Dickinson)
Flew (Adcock)
Gwyneth (Lewis)
Pam (Ayres)
Ruth (Padel)
Sylvia (Plath)
Wendy (Cope)

E

Girls' names

Eadlin
(alt. Eadlinn, Eadlyn, Eadlen, Edlin)
Anglo-Saxon, meaning 'royalty'. Can also be a nickname for Adeline.

Earla
English, meaning 'leader'. Also a variation of the German name Herlinde, meaning 'shield'.

Eartha
English, meaning 'Earth'. Singer Eartha Kitt was best known for her hit 'Santa Baby'.

Easter
From the festival of the same name.

Ebba
English, meaning 'fortress of riches'. One of the Top 10 names for baby girls in Sweden.

Ebony
(alt. Eboni)
Latin, meaning 'deep black wood'.

Echo
Greek, meaning 'reflected sound'. From the mythological nymph of the same name.

Eda
(alt. Edda)
English, meaning 'wealthy and happy'. An ancient goddess of time and wealth.

Edelmira
Spanish, meaning 'admired for nobility'. Feminine form of Edelmiro.

Eden
Hebrew, meaning 'pleasure'. In the Bible, the Garden of Eden was humankind's first home on Earth.

Edina
Scottish, meaning 'from Edinburgh'. Actor Jennifer Saunders's character in *Absolutely Fabulous* was named Edina Monsoon.

Edith
(alt. Edyth; abbrev. Edie)
English, meaning 'prosperity through battle'. Pulitzer Prize-winner Edith Wharton is the author of *The Age of Innocence*. Actor Edie Falco starred in TV hit *The Sopranos*.

Edna
Hebrew, meaning 'enjoyment'. Australian comedian Barry Humphries is best known for his alter ego Dame Edna Everage.

Edrea
English, meaning 'wealthy and powerful'. Edrea Vorsal was a soprano opera singer.

Edris
(alt. Edriss, Edrys)
Anglo-Saxon, meaning 'prosperous ruler'. Sometimes used as a feminine form of Idris.

Edwina
English, meaning 'wealthy friend'. Edwina Currie was a controversial British politician.

Effie
Greek, meaning 'pleasant speech'. Effie Trinket is a key character in the 'Hunger Games' trilogy, known for her outrageous fashion sense.

Eglantine
French, from the shrub of the same name covered in tiny roses.

Eibhlín
Irish Gaelic, meaning 'shining and brilliant'. Eibhlín Dubh Ní Chonaill was an Irish poet and noblewoman.

Eileen
Irish, meaning 'shining and brilliant'. English version of Eibhlín, and often associated with the song 'Come on Eileen' by Dexys Midnight Runners.

Ekaterina
(alt. Ekaterini)
Slavic, meaning 'pure'.

Elaine
(alt. Elaina, Elayne)
French, meaning 'bright, shining light'. Singer and performer Elaine Paige is a star of West End musical theatre and radio presenter.

Elba
Italian, from the island of the same name.

Elberta
English, meaning 'highborn'.

Eldora
Spanish, meaning 'covered with gold'. Eldora is also the name of a small 'ghost' town in Florida, USA, which has remained uninhabited for over 100 years.

Eldoris
(alt. Eldoriss, Eldorys)
Greek, meaning 'woman of the sea'. Usually found as a variation of Doris.

Eleanor
(alt. Elana, Elena, Elanor, Eleanora)

Greek, meaning 'light'. Queen Eleanor of Aquitaine was married to England's King Henry II, and one of the most influential, wealthy and powerful women of medieval times.

Electra
(alt. Elektra)

Greek, meaning 'shining'. Also a character from an ancient Greek myth. In psychology, Electra is the female counterpart of Oedipus.

Elfrida
(alt. Elfrieda)

English, meaning 'elf power'. Elfrida Andrée was a 19th-century composer and conductor, and the first female organist to be recognised in Sweden.

Eliana
(alt. Eliane)

Hebrew, meaning 'Jehovah is God'. Becoming increasingly popular thanks to the growing trend for names for girls ending in -a.

Elise
(alt. Elisa, Elissa)

French, meaning 'my vow to God'. Commonly associated with Beethoven's 'Für Elise', a piano solo.

Elizabeth
(alt. Elisabet, Elisabeth, Elizabella, Elizabelle, Elsbeth, Elspeth, Elisha; abbrev. Beth, Eliza, Libby, Liz, Lizzie, Lizzy)

Hebrew, meaning 'consecrated to God'. Two queens of England have been named this: Elizabeth I ruled from 1558 to 1603, and Elizabeth II has been on the throne since 1952. Enduringly popular, especially with its many shortened forms.

Elke
(alt. Elkie)

German, meaning 'nobility'. Singer Elkie Brooks had several hits in the 1980s.

Ella

German, meaning 'completely'. Now becoming a name in its own right, Ella is traditionally a shortened version of Eleanor, Elizabeth and Ellen.

Elle

French, meaning 'she'. Elle Macpherson was one of the original supermodels in the 1980s, and known as 'The Body'.

Ellema
(alt. Ellemah, Elema, Ellemma, Elemah)

Swahili, meaning 'dairy farmer' or 'milking a cow'.

Ellen
(alt. Elin, Eline, Ellyn)

Greek, meaning 'shining'. Ellen DeGeneres is a popular actor and TV host.

Ellice
(alt. Elyse)

Greek, meaning 'the Lord is God'.

Ellie
(alt. Elie)

Shortened form of Eleanor which can be used in its own right. Singer and Brit Award winner Ellie Goulding is actually an Elena.

Elma
(alt. Elna)

Latin, meaning 'soul'. Elma Napier was the first woman to be elected to a Caribbean parliament, in 1940.

Elmira
(alt. Elmyra)

Arabic, meaning 'aristocratic lady'. Elmyra Duff is a character in the cartoon *Tiny Toons*.

Elodie

French, meaning 'marsh flower'. Élodie Bouchez-Bangalter is a French actor.

Eloise
(alt. Elois, Eloisa, Elouise)

French, meaning 'renowned in battle'. Also a shortened version and English spelling of French name Héloïse.

Elsa
(alt. Else, Elsie)

Hebrew, meaning 'consecrated to God'. Elsa the Snow Queen is one of the lead characters in Disney's *Frozen*.

Elva

Irish, meaning 'noble'. Also the name of a British sports car manufacturer.

Elvina

English, meaning 'noble friend'. Also an ancient place name.

Elvira
(alt. Elvera)

Spanish, from the ancient city of the same name. Commonly associated with the 1980s film *Elvira, Mistress of the Dark*.

Ember
(alt. Embry)

English, meaning 'spark'. Sometimes used as a shortened version of the name September.

Emerald

English, meaning 'green gemstone'.

Emery
(alt. Emory)

German, meaning 'ruler of work'.

Emiko
(alt. Emuko)

Japanese, meaning 'pretty child'. Popular name for girls in Japan.

Emilia

Latin, meaning 'rival, eager'. British actor Emilia Clarke played lead character Daenerys Targaryen in *Game of Thrones*.

Emily
(alt. Emalee, Emelie, Emely, Emilee, Emili, Emilie, Emlyn)

Latin, meaning 'rival, eager'. Emily Dickinson is one of the most well-known poets of the 19th century. A popular name choice in recent years.

Emma

German, meaning 'embraces everything'. The title character of Jane Austen's novel. Former actor Emma Watson starred as Hermione in the *Harry Potter* films.

Emmanuelle

Feminine form of Emanuel, which is Hebrew for 'God is with us'.

Emmeline

(alt. Emmelina; abbrev. Emmy, Emmie, Emi)

German, meaning 'embraces everything' or 'industrious'. Emmeline Pankhurst was the leader of the Suffragettes, political activists who campaigned in the early 20th century for women's right to vote.

Ena

Shortened form of Georgina, meaning 'farmer'. Ena Sharples was one of the original cast of characters on *Coronation Street*.

Enid

(alt. Eneida)

Welsh, meaning 'life spirit'. Enid Blyton was a hugely popular children's author, known for the *Noddy*, *Famous Five* and *Malory Towers* series, among others.

Enola

Native American, meaning 'solitary'.

Enya

Irish Gaelic, meaning 'fire'. Enya is an Irish singer and songwriter.

Eowyn

Fictional character from J.R.R. Tolkien's *Lord of the Rings* trilogy. Eowyn was a noblewoman who disguised herself as a man in order to fight in a major battle.

Eranthe

Greek, meaning 'delicate like the spring'.

Erica

(alt. Ericka, Erika)

Scandinavian, meaning 'ruler forever'. Also a flowering plant similar to heather.

Erin

(alt. Eryn)

Irish Gaelic, meaning 'from the isle to the west'. Formerly a romanticised name for Ireland. Erin Brockovich is an American housewife turned environmental activist, played by Julia Roberts in the film of the same name.

Eris

Greek, from the mythological goddess. Eris is responsible for chaos, strife and discord.

Erlinda

Hebrew, meaning 'spirited'. Erlinda Cortes was a popular actor after World War II.

Erma

German, meaning 'universal'. Erma Franklin, the sister of soul legend Aretha Franklin, was an American gospel singer.

Ermine

French, meaning 'weasel'. The white winter fur of a stoat is known as ermine.

Erna

English, meaning 'sincere'. Erna was a character in Norse mythology.

Ernestine
(alt. Ernestina)

English, meaning 'sincere'. Ernestine Gilbreth Carey was the co-author of Cheaper by the Dozen, the novel upon which the popular films of the same name were based.

Esme

French, meaning 'esteemed'. Esme Cullen is a key character in the Twilight series.

Esmeralda

Spanish, meaning 'emerald'. Esmeralda is the female protagonist in The Hunchback of Notre Dame.

Esperanza

Spanish, meaning 'hope'. Popular name for girls in Spain.

Estelle
(alt. Estela, Estell, Estella)

French, meaning 'star'. British R&B singer Estelle is known by her first name only.

Esther
(alt. Esta, Ester, Etha, Ethna, Ethne)

Persian, meaning 'star'. Esther is a Jewish and Persian queen mentioned in the Bible.

Eternity

Latin, meaning 'forever'.

Ethel
(alt. Ethyl)

English, meaning 'noble'. Ethel Merman was an enormously popular American actor and singer, and a star of musical theatre.

Etinia
(alt. Eteniah, Etene, Eteniya)

Native American, meaning 'prosperous'.

Etta
(alt. Etter, Ettie)

Shortened form of Henrietta, meaning 'ruler of the house'. Etta James was a blues and soul singer-songwriter.

Eudora

Greek, meaning 'generous gift'.

Eugenia
(alt. Eugenie)

Greek, meaning 'well born'. Also a type of flowering plant. Princess Eugenie is a granddaughter of Queen Elizabeth II.

Eulalia
(alt. Eula, Eulah, Eulalie)

Greek, meaning 'sweet-speaking'. St Eulalia was a Spanish virgin who was martyred for her faith.

Eunice

Greek, meaning 'victorious'. Eunice Kennedy Shriver was John F. Kennedy's sister and the founder of the Special Olympics.

Euphemia

Greek, meaning 'favourable speech'. Great Martyr Euphemia was killed for her Christian faith.

Eva

Hebrew, meaning 'life'. Eva Perón, the First Lady of Argentina from 1946 to 1952, was the inspiration for the musical *Evita*.

Evadne

Greek, meaning 'pleasing one'. Found frequently in Greek mythology.

Evangeline

(alt. Evangelina)

Greek, meaning 'good news'. The very first 'musical comedy' was called *Evangeline*, and it premiered in 1874.

Evanthe

Greek, meaning 'good flower'. Occasionally used as an alternative to the names Eve, Eva and Evelyn.

Eve

(alt. Evie)

Hebrew, meaning 'life'. Found in the Bible.

Evelina

(alt. Evelia)

German, meaning 'hazelnut'. Its popularity was at its peak in the late 18th century, after a novel called *Evelina* by Fanny Burney.

Evelyn

(alt. Evalyn, Evelin, Eveline, Evelyne)

German, meaning 'hazelnut'. Used as a name for girls and boys. Dame Evelyn Glennie is a multi-award-winning Scottish virtuoso percussionist who is profoundly deaf.

Everly

(alt. Everleigh, Everley)

English, meaning 'grazing meadow'.

Evette

French, meaning 'yew wood'. Often used as a spelling variation of Yvette.

Evonne

(alt. Evon)

French, meaning 'yew wood'. Evonne Goolagong was a women's tennis legend in the 1970s.

Girls' names

Fabia
(alt. *Fabiana, Fabienne, Fabiola, Fabriana*)
Latin, meaning 'one who grows beans'.

Fabrizia
Italian, meaning 'works with her hands'.

Fahari
Swahili, meaning 'splendour'. Can also mean 'magnificent'.

Faith
English, meaning 'loyalty'. Faith Hill and Faith Evans are famous singers.

Faiza
Arabic, meaning 'victorious'. The first ever British Muslim superhero to be created by Marvel comics was Faiza Hussain, codenamed Excalibur.

Fallon
Irish Gaelic, meaning 'descended from a ruler'.

Fanny
(alt. *Fannie*)
Latin, meaning 'from France'. Extremely popular name in the 18th and 19th centuries. The protagonist of Jane Austen's *Mansfield Park* was Fanny Price.

Farica
German, meaning 'peaceful ruler'. A feminine form of Frederick.

Farrah
English, meaning 'fair haired', and Arabic, meaning 'joy'. Farrah Fawcett was one of TV's original *Charlie's Angels*.

Fatima
Arabic, meaning 'baby's nurse'. Popular in Muslim communities.

Faustine
Feminine form of Faustinus, which is Latin, meaning 'fortunate'.

Fawn

French, meaning 'young deer'.

Fay

(alt. Fae, Faye)

French, meaning 'fairy'. Bestselling author Fay Weldon has written more than 30 books.

Fayola

(alt. Fayolah, Fayeena)

Swahili, meaning 'walks with honour'. Can also mean 'lucky'.

Felicia

(alt. Felicity, Felecia, Felice, Felicita, Felisha)

Latin, meaning 'lucky and happy'. Actor Felicia Day starred in *Buffy the Vampire Slayer*.

Fenella

(abbrev. Fen)

Irish Gaelic, meaning 'white shoulder'. Actor Fenella Fielding is known for her husky voice and sensual image.

Fenia

Scandinavian, from the mythological giantess of the same name.

Fennel

Latin, name of a herb. Also a boys' name.

Fern

(alt. Fearne, Ferne, Ferrin)

English, from the plant of the same name.

Fernanda

German, meaning 'peace and courage'. A popular name in Brazil and Mexico.

Ffion

(alt. Fion)

Irish Gaelic, meaning 'fair and pale' or 'foxglove'. Popular in Wales.

Fia

Italian, meaning 'flame'. Also used as a nickname for Fiona.

Fifi

Hebrew, meaning 'Jehovah increases'.

Filomena

Greek, meaning 'loved one'. Sometimes used as an alternative spelling to Philomena.

Finlay

(alt. Finley)

Irish Gaelic, meaning 'fair-haired courageous one'. More commonly used as a name for boys.

Finola

(alt. Fionnula)

Irish Gaelic, meaning 'white shoulder'. British actor Finola Hughes appears regularly on American TV, having featured in several soap operas.

Fiona

(alt. Fiora)

Scottish, meaning 'fair and pale'. The name was actually invented by poet James Macpherson in the 18th century. Famous Fionas include TV presenter Fiona Bruce and *Shrek* character Princess Fiona.

Fiorella

Feminine form of Fiorello, which is Italian for 'little flower'.

Flanna
(alt. Flannery)

Irish Gaelic, meaning 'russet hair' or 'red hair'.

Flavia

Latin, meaning 'yellow hair'. Popular name in both ancient and modern literature, but rarely used in the UK. Flavia Cacace was an Italian professional dancer on *Strictly Come Dancing*.

Fleur

French, meaning 'flower'. Fleur Delacour is a character in the *Harry Potter* series.

Flora

Latin, meaning 'flower'. Flora was one of the fairy godmothers (the red one) in Disney's *Sleeping Beauty*.

Florence
(alt. Florencia, Florene, Florine; abbrev. Florrie, Flossie, Floy, Flo)

Latin, meaning 'in bloom'. Also an Italian city.

Florida

Latin, meaning 'flowery'. Also a state in the USA.

Fraisine
(alt. Fraise)

French, meaning 'strawberry'.

Frances
(alt. Francine, Francis; abbrev. Fran, Frankie, Frannie)

Latin, meaning 'from France'. Famous Franceses include actor Frances McDormand, author Frances Trollope and playwright Frances Hodgson Burnett.

Francesca
(alt. Franchesca, Francisca; abbrev. Fran, Frankie, Frannie)

Latin, meaning 'from France'. Francesca Simon is the author of the 'Horrid Henry' children's book series.

Freda
(alt. Freeda, Freida, Frida, Frieda)

German, meaning 'peaceful'. Frida Kahlo was a Mexican artist known for her self-portraits and heavy eyebrows.

Frederica

German, meaning 'peaceful ruler'. A popular name for European princesses, it has been used nearly 20 times since the 17th century.

Freya

Old Nordic, meaning 'lady'.

Fuchsia

German, from the flower of the same name. Fuchsia Dunlop is a renowned British chef who specialises in Chinese food.

Fumiko

Japanese, meaning 'little friend' or 'beautiful child'.

Girls' names

Gabrielle
(alt. Gabriel, Gabriela, Gabriella; abbrev. Gabby, Gabbi)
Hebrew, meaning 'heroine of God'. Gabriella Wilde is a British actor. Gabby Logan is a high-profile female TV sports presenter.

Gadara
Armenian, meaning 'mountain's peak'. The ancient town of Gadara is situated in northern Jordan.

Gaia
(alt. Gaea)
Greek, meaning 'the Earth'. In ancient Greece, Gaia was the Greek Mother Goddess and the most important.

Gail
(alt. Gale, Gayla, Gayle)
Hebrew, meaning 'my father rejoices'. Badminton player Gail Emms represented England at international level for many years.

Gala
French, meaning 'festive merrymaking'. Used more commonly in Spanish-speaking communities.

Galiena
German, meaning 'high one'.

Galina
Russian, meaning 'shining brightly'. Feminine form of Galen.

Garnet
(alt. Garnett)
English, meaning 'red gemstone'.

Gay
(alt. Gaye)
French, meaning 'glad and lighthearted'.

Gaynor
Welsh, meaning 'white and smooth'.

Gemini
Greek, meaning 'twins'. One of the signs of the zodiac.

Gemma

Italian, meaning 'precious stone'. Actor Gemma Arterton was a Bond girl.

Gene

Greek, meaning 'well born'. More commonly used for boys.

Genesis

Greek, meaning 'beginning'.

Geneva
(alt. Genevra)

French, meaning 'juniper tree'. Also the name of the Swiss city.

Genevieve
(abbrev. Genie)

German, meaning 'white wave'. St Genevieve is said to have saved Paris.

Georgette

French, meaning 'farmer'. Georgette Heyer was an author of historical romance novels.

Georgia
(alt. Georgiana, Georgianna, Georgie)

Greek, meaning 'farmer'. Also the name of the European country and a state in the USA.

Georgina
(alt. Georgene, Georgine, Giorgina)

Greek, meaning 'farmer'. The name's popularity was at its peak during the 1980s. Georgina was the spirited character in Enid Blyton's *Famous Five* books, who insisted on being referred to as George.

Geraldine
(abbrev. Geri, Gerri, Gerry)

German, meaning 'spear ruler'. Spice Girls singer Geri Halliwell's full name is Geraldine.

Gerda

Nordic, meaning 'shelter'. Gerda is the female protagonist in Hans Christian Andersen's *Snow Queen*.

Germaine

French, meaning 'from Germany'. Germaine Greer is an Australian author and activist.

Gertrude
(abbrev. Gertie)

German, meaning 'strength of a spear'. Gertrude Stein was an influential 19th-century American author. One of the earliest animated cartoon films was called *Gertie the Dinosaur*, made in 1914.

Ghislaine

French, meaning 'pledge'. Believed to have derived from Giselle.

Gia
(alt. Ghia)

Italian, meaning 'God is gracious'. Often used by itself, or as a shortened form of Gianna.

Gianina
(alt. Giana)

Hebrew, meaning 'God's graciousness'. Sometimes associated with the town of Ioannina in Greece.

Gigi
(alt. Gigel)

Shortened form of Georgina, meaning 'farmer'. Also the name of a successful 1958 musical film.

Gilda

English, meaning 'gilded'. The name of Rigoletto's daughter in Verdi's opera *Rigoletto*.

Gilia

Hebrew, meaning 'joy of the Lord'. Also the name of a genus of flowering plants.

Gillian
(abbrev. Gill, Gilly, Gillie)

Latin, meaning 'youthful'. Famous Gillians include actor Gillian Anderson and children's author Gillian Cross.

Gina
(alt. Geena, Gena)

Shortened form of Regina, meaning 'queen', often used in its own right. Bestselling author Gina Ford has published over 20 parenting books.

Ginger

Latin, from the spicy root of the same name. Ginger Rogers was an Oscar-winning American singer, dancer and actor, best known for dancing with Fred Astaire. Her real first name was Virginia.

Ginny

Shortened form of Virginia, meaning 'virgin'. Made popular by the character of Ginny Weasley in the *Harry Potter* series.

Giovanna

Italian, meaning 'God is gracious'. The English equivalent is Joanna or Jane.

Giselle
(alt. Gisela, Gisele, Giselle, Gisselle)

German, meaning 'pledge'. *Giselle* is the name of a romantic ballet. Gisele Bündchen is a Brazilian supermodel and actor.

Gita
(alt. Geeta)

Sanskrit, meaning 'song'. *Bhagavad Gita* is a 700-verse Hindu scripture.

Giulia
(alt. Giuliana)

Italian, meaning 'youthful'. The Italian form of the name Julia.

Gladys
(alt. Gladyce)

Welsh, meaning 'lame'. Singer Gladys Knight is known as the 'Empress of Soul'.

Glenda

Welsh, meaning 'fair and good'. A variation of Glenna and Glynda. Glenda Jackson is a British actor turned politician.

Glenna
(alt. Glennie)

Irish Gaelic, meaning 'glen'. Feminine form of Glenn.

Gloria
(alt. Glory)

Latin, meaning 'glory'. Famous Glorias including singers Gloria Estefan and Gloria Gaynor.

Glynda
(alt. Glinda)

Welsh, meaning 'fair'. The good witch in the *Wizard of Oz*.

Less common three-syllable names

Cassandra	Jessamy
Dolores	Julia
Gloria	Marilyn
Harriet	Miranda
Imogen	Nigella

Glynis

Welsh, meaning 'small glen'. The first Olympic gold medallist of the heptathlon was Australian athlete Glynis Nunn.

Golda
(alt. Goldia, Goldie)

English, meaning 'gold'. Golda Meir was the prime minister of Israel from 1969 to 1974.

Grace
(alt. Graça, Gracie, Gracin, Grayce)

Latin, meaning 'grace'. Film actor Grace Kelly became Princess Grace of Monaco.

Gráinne
(alt. Grania)

Irish Gaelic, meaning 'love'.

Gratia
(alt. Grasia)

Latin, meaning 'blessing'. Gratia was the ancient Greek goddess of charm, beauty and fertility, among other things.

Greer
(alt. Grier)

Latin, meaning 'alert and watchful'.

Gregoria

Latin, meaning 'alert'. Empress Gregoria was a key figure in the Byzantine empire.

Greta
(alt. Gretel)

Greek, meaning 'pearl'. Gretel is the name of the female protagonist in the fairy tale Hansel and Gretel. Greta also refers to a genus of butterfly.

Gretchen

German, meaning 'pearl'. Actor Gretchen Mol is known for her role in TV series *Boardwalk Empire*.

Griselda
(alt. Griselle; abbrev. Selda, Zelda)

German, meaning 'grey fighting maid'.

Grytha

English, meaning 'fiery'. Denmark's Queen Grytha ruled during the fifth century.

Gudrun

Scandinavian, meaning 'battle'. Key recurring figure in Norse and Germanic literature.

Guinevere

Welsh, meaning 'white and smooth'. The queen in Arthurian legend.

Gwen

Shortened form of Gwenda or Gwendolyn, as well as a name in its own right. Gwen Stefani is a singer-songwriter and member of No Doubt.

Gwenda

Welsh, meaning 'fair and good'. As well as a name in its own right, Gwenda can also be a shortened form of Gwendolyn or Gwyneth.

Gwendolyn

(alt. Gwendolen, Gwenel)

Welsh, meaning 'fair bow'. Gwendolyn Brooks was a Pulitzer Prize-winning poet.

Gwyneth

(alt.. Gwynneth, Gwynyth; abbrev. Gwyn, Gwynn)

Welsh, meaning 'happiness'. Actor and author Gwyneth Paltrow is mum to Apple and Moses.

Gypsy

English, meaning 'of the Roma tribe'.

Girls' names

Habibah
(alt. Habiba)
Arabic, meaning 'beloved'.

Hadassah
Hebrew, meaning 'myrtle tree'. Usually associated with the character of Esther in the Bible, whose Hebrew name is Hadassah.

Hadley
English, meaning 'heather meadow'. Hadley Freeman is an author and journalist.

Hadria
Latin, meaning 'from Hadria'. Also the name of two ancient cities in Italy.

Hala
Arabic, meaning 'halo'. Also the name of a female weather demon in Serbian and Bulgarian mythology.

Halima
(alt. Halimah, Halina)
Arabic, meaning 'gentle'. The prophet Mohammad's foster mother was called Halimah.

Hallie
(alt. Halle, Halley)
German, meaning 'ruler of the home or estate'. Oscar-winning actor Halle Berry was originally given the name Maria Halle.

Hannah
(alt. Haana, Hana, Hanna)
Hebrew, meaning 'grace'. Famous Hannahs include Hannah Cockroft, the wheelchair athlete and world record holder, and American teen sitcom *Hannah Montana*.

Harika
Turkish, meaning 'superior one'. In India, the name is associated with Parvati, the Hindu goddess of power and creation.

Harley
(alt. Harlene)
English, meaning 'the long field'.

Harlow
English, meaning 'army hill'.

Harmony

Latin, meaning 'harmony'.

Harper

English, meaning 'minstrel'. Harper Lee is the author of classic novel *To Kill a Mockingbird*. Harper Seven is the name of David and Victoria Beckham's fourth child.

Harriet

(alt. Harriett, Harriette; abbrev. Hattie)

German, meaning 'ruler of the home or estate'. Famous Harriets include activist Harriet Tubman, author Harriet Beecher Stowe, and politician Harriet Harman.

Haven

English, meaning 'a place of sanctuary'.

Hayden

(alt. Haydn)

Old English, meaning 'hedged valley'. Also ussed as a boys' name.

Hayley

(alt. Haelee, Haely, Hailee, Hailey, Hailie, Haleigh, Haley, Hali, Halie, Haylee, Hayleigh, Haylie)

English, meaning 'hay meadow'.

Hazel

(alt. Hazle)

English, from the tree of the same name. Famous Hazels include children's author Hazel Hutchins, singer Hazel O'Connor and politician Hazel Blears.

Heather

English, from the flower of the same name. Famous Heathers include actors Heather Graham and Heather Locklear, and model Heather Mills.

Heaven

English, meaning 'everlasting bliss'.

Hedda

German, meaning 'warfare'. Also the name of the protagonist in the play *Hedda Gabler*, by Henrik Ibsen.

Hedwig

German, meaning 'warfare and strife'. The name stems from two different St Hedwigs, but is now most associated with Harry Potter's owl!

Heidi

(alt. Heidy)

German, meaning 'nobility'. One of the top-selling children's books of all time is the Swiss novel *Heidi*, by Johanna Spyri.

Helen

(alt. Halen, Helena, Helene, Hellen)

Greek, meaning 'light'. In ancient Greek mythology Helen of Troy was considered to be the most beautiful woman in the world.

Helga

German, meaning 'holy and sacred'. Extemely popular name in Germany and Norway.

Helia

Greek, meaning 'sun'.

Héloïse

French, meaning 'renowned in war'. Héloïse d'Argenteuil was a nun and writer known for having an affair with the theologian Peter Abelard in the 12th century.

Henrietta
(alt. Henriette)

German, meaning 'ruler of the house'. Usually associated with Henrietta Maria of France, who was queen consort to Charles I.

Hephzibah
(alt. Hefzibah)

Hebrew, meaning 'my delight is in her'. Found in the Bible.

Hera

Greek, meaning 'queen'. Hera is the Queen of the Gods, and the goddess of marriage, women and birth in ancient Greek mythology.

Hermia
(alt. Hermina, Hermine, Herminia)

Greek, meaning 'messenger'. Also the name of a character in Shakespeare's play *A Midsummer Night's Dream*.

Hermione

Greek, meaning 'earthly'. Now inseparable from the main female character in the *Harry Potter* series.

Hero

Greek, meaning 'brave one of the people'.

Hertha

English, meaning 'Earth'. Also another name for Nerthus, the goddess of fertility in ancient German mythology.

Hesper
(alt. Hesperia)

Greek, meaning 'evening star'.

Hester
(alt. Hestia)

Greek, meaning 'star'. Also the name of the protagonist in *The Scarlet Letter* by Nathaniel Hawthorne.

Hettie

Shortened form of Hester or Henrietta, also used as a name in its own right.

Hilary
(alt. Hillary)

Greek, meaning 'cheerful and happy'. Also a boys' name. Famous Hilarys include US politician Hillary Rodham Clinton and actor Hilary Swank.

Hilda
(alt. Hildur)

German, meaning 'battle woman'. Famous Hildas include the first female pilot to hold a licence, Hilda Hewlett, and author Hilda Doolittle – known as H.D.

Hildegarde
(alt. Hildegard)

German, meaning 'battle stronghold'.

Hildred

German, meaning 'battle counsellor'. More commonly used as a boys' name.

Hilma

German variant of Wilhelmina, meaning 'helmet'. The feminine form of Hilmar or Hilmer.

Hirkani

Sanskrit, meaning 'like a diamond'.

Hollis

English, meaning 'near the holly bushes'.

Holly
(alt. Holli, Hollie)

English, from the tree of the same name. Famous Hollys include TV presenter Holly Willoughby and actor Holly Hunter.

Honey

English, from the word 'honey'.

Honor
(alt. Honour, Honora, Honoria)

Latin, meaning 'woman of honour'. Actor Honor Blackman played the Bond girl Pussy Galore.

Hope

English, meaning 'desire and expectation'. One of three virtues in most religions: faith, hope and charity. Hope Powell represented England in football for many years before becoming the England Women's coach for more than a decade.

Hortense
(alt. Hortencia, Hortensia)

Latin, meaning 'of the garden'. Also the name of one of Napoleon Bonaparte's stepdaughters, and a character in Charles Dickens's novel *Bleak House*.

Hudson

English, meaning 'adventurous'.

Hulda

German, meaning 'loved one'. Also the name of a prophetess in the Bible.

Hyacinth

Greek, from the flower of the same name. Hyacinth was also a hero in ancient Greek mythology.

I

Girls' names

Ianthe
(alt. Iantha)
Greek, meaning 'purple flower'. Also the name of a character in ancient Greek mythology.

Ichigo
Japanese, meaning 'strawberry'.

Ida
English, meaning 'prosperous'. Also the name of several characters in both ancient Greek mythology and the Hindu religion.

Idella
(alt. Idell)
English, meaning 'prosperous'. Idella Purnell was an academic and author of children's books, best known in the 1930s and '40s.

Idona
Nordic, meaning 'renewal'.

Ignacia
(alt. Iggy)
Latin, meaning 'ardent' or 'burning'. The feminine form of Ignatius.

Ila
French, meaning 'island'. In Hindu mythology Ila is a character able to change sex at will.

Ilana
Hebrew, meaning 'tree'. Ilana Vered is a classical pianist known for her work with dozens of major international orchestras.

Ilaria
Italian, meaning 'cheerful'. The English equivalent is Hilary.

Ilene
American, meaning 'light'. Ilene Woods was a voice actor known for being the voice of Cinderella in the Disney film.

Iliana
(alt. Ileana)

Greek, meaning 'Trojan'. Actor Ileana D'Cruz is a star in Bollywood films.

Ilona

Hungarian, meaning 'light'. Also the name of the Queen of the Fairies in Magyar mythology.

Ilsa

German, meaning 'pledged to God'. Also the name of Ingrid Bergman's character in the film *Casablanca*.

Ima

German, meaning 'embraces everything'. Ima Hogg was an influential philanthropist in the early 20th century.

Iman

Arabic, meaning 'faith'. The Somali supermodel known simply as Iman is also an entrepreneur and was married to David Bowie.

Imara

Hungarian, meaning 'great ruler'. Also the name of a genus of moths.

Imelda

German, meaning 'all-consuming fight'. Famous Imeldas include actor Imelda Staunton, politician Imelda Marcos and actor Anne Crawford, whose real name was Imelda.

Imogen
(alt. Imogene)

Latin, meaning 'last-born'.

Ina

Latin, meaning 'to make feminine'. Famous Inas include author and presenter Ina Garten and childbirth pioneer Ina May Gaskin.

Inaya

Arabic, meaning 'taking care'. Singer Inaya Day's voice features on many dancefloor house music classics.

India
(alt. Indie)

Hindi, from the country of the same name. India Knight is a British journalist and author.

Indiana

Latin, meaning 'from India'. Also the name of a state in the USA.

Indigo

Greek, meaning 'deep blue dye'. Also one of the seven colours of the rainbow.

Indira
(alt. Inira)

Sanskrit, meaning 'beauty'. Indira Gandhi was the first and, to date, only female prime minister of India.

Inez
(alt. Ines)

Spanish, meaning 'pure'. Also a spelling variation of Agnes.

Inga
(alt. Inge, Ingeborg, Inger)

Scandinavian, meaning 'guarded by Ing'. Also the name of a type of tropical shrub and tree.

Ingrid

Scandinavian, meaning 'beautiful'. Actor Ingrid Bergman was known for her roles in *Casablanca*, *Notorious* and *Gaslight*.

Io

(alt. Eyo)

Greek, from the mythological priestess and heroine of the same name in ancient Greek mythology.

Ioanna

Greek, meaning 'grace'. Usually used as a spelling alternative to Joanna.

Iola

(alt. Iole)

Greek, meaning 'cloud of dawn'. The novel *Iola Leroy*, by Frances Harper, was one of the first novels published by a black female author.

Iolanthe

Greek, meaning 'violet flower'. Usually associated with the opera *Iolanthe* by Gilbert and Sullivan.

Iona

Greek, from the island of the same name. Also the name of a small island off the coast of Scotland.

Ione

Greek, meaning 'violet'. Also the name of a type of orchid.

Iorwen

Welsh, meaning 'fair'.

Iphigenia

Greek, meaning 'sacrifice'. Iphigenia was an ancient Greek victim of slaughter whose name became synonymous with strength and being the mother of strong children.

Ira

(alt. Iva)

Hebrew, meaning 'watchful'. More commonly used as a boys' name.

Irene

(alt. Irelyn, Irena, Irina, Irini)

Greek, meaning 'peace'.

Iris

Greek, meaning 'rainbow'. Also from the flower of the same name.

Irma

German, meaning 'universal'. Often associated with Irma Bunt, a Bond villainess.

Isabel

(alt. Isabela, Isabell, Isabella, Isabelle, Isabeth, Isobel, Izabella, Izabelle)

Spanish, meaning 'pledged to God'. Dozens of royals have been called Isabel or Isabella over the centuries, including Queen Isabella I of Spain, who financed Christopher Columbus' voyage to North America.

Isadora

Latin, meaning 'gift of Isis'. Isadora Duncan was a famed dancer at the turn of the 20th century, whose life was made into the film *Isadora*.

Ishana

Sanskrit, meaning 'desire'. One of the names for Shiva in the Hindu faith.

Isis

From the ancient Egyptian goddess of motherhood, magic and fertility.

Isla

(alt. Isa, Isela, Isley)

Scottish Gaelic, meaning 'river'. Actor Isla Fischer was born in Oman to Scottish parents and raised in Australia.

Isolde

Welsh, meaning 'fair lady'. Usually associated with the opera *Tristan und Isolde* by Richard Wagner.

Istas

Native American, meaning 'snow'. In Latin, 'istas' also refers to the feminine form of 'that person'.

Ivana

Slavic, meaning 'Jehovah is gracious'. Model Ivana Trump is known for her former marriage to the 45th US President Donald Trump.

Ivette

Variation of Yvette, meaning 'yew wood'. This spelling is more commonly used in Spanish-speaking communities.

Ivonne

Variation of Yvonne, meaning 'yew wood'. This spelling is more commonly used in Spanish-speaking communities.

Ivory

Latin, meaning 'white as elephant tusks'.

Ivy

English, from the plant of the same name. Famous Ivys include elderly internet sensation Ivy Bean, the first British female lawyer, Ivy Williams, and children's author Ivy Wallace.

Ixia

Afrikaans, from the flower of the same name.

J

Girls' names

Jaamini
Hindi, meaning 'evening'.

Jacinda
(alt. Jacinta)
Spanish, meaning 'hyacinth'. Jacinda Ardern is the Prime Minister of New Zealand. Jacinda Barrett is an Australian-American model turned actor.

Jacqueline
(alt. Jacalyn, Jacklyn, Jaclyn, Jacquelin, Jacquelyn, Jacquline, Jaqlyn, Jaquelin, Jaqueline; abbrev. Jack, Jacky, Jackie, Jacque, Jacqui)
French, meaning 'he who supplants'. Famous Jacquelines include children's author Jacqueline Wilson, actor Jacqueline Bisset and cellist Jacqueline du Pré.

Jade
(alt. Jada, Jaida, Jayda, Jayde)
Spanish, meaning 'green stone'. Famous Jades include athletes Jade Jones and Jade Johnson and designer Jade Jagger.

Jaden
(alt. Jadyn, Jaiden, Jaidyn, Jayden)
Hebrew, meaning 'Jehovah has heard'. More commonly used as a boys' name.

Jael
Hebrew, meaning 'mountain goat'. Found in the Bible.

Jaime
(alt. Jaima, Jaimie, Jami, Jamie)
Spanish, meaning 'he who supplants'. Jamie is a common short form of James, more commonly used for boys.

Jamila
Arabic, meaning 'lovely'. Author Jamila Gavin is known for her children's books, most of which have an Indian influence.

Jan
(alt. Jana, Jann, Janna, Janae)
Hebrew, meaning 'the Lord is gracious'; Arabic, meaning 'dear'; Persian meaning 'life'.

Jane
(alt. Jayne, Janie)
Feminine form of the Hebrew John, meaning 'the Lord is gracious'. A popular name in the 1960s and '70s but less common now. Famous Janes include Tarzan's friend Jane and Henry VIII's third wife, Jane Seymour.

Janelle
(alt. Janel, Janell, Jenelle)
American, meaning 'the Lord is gracious'. A popular name in the 1970s and '80s in both America and Australia but less common now.

Janet
(alt. Janette)
Scottish, meaning 'the Lord is gracious'. Singer Janet Jackson is known for being part of the musical Jackson family, as well as a performer in her own right.

Janice
(alt. Janis)
American, meaning 'the Lord is gracious'. Famous Janices include rower Janice Meek, former supermodel Janice Dickinson and the character of Janice Battersby in *Coronation Street*.

Janine
(alt. Janeen)
English, meaning 'the Lord is gracious'.

Janoah
(alt. Janiya, Janiyah)
Hebrew, meaning 'quiet and calm'. Also used as a spelling alternative for Genoa.

January
Latin, meaning 'the first month'. Actor January Jones is known for her roles in *Mad Men*, *Unknown* and *X-Men: First Class*.

Jarita
Hindi-Sanskrit, meaning 'famous bird'. Usually associated with the bird character in the Hindu *Mahabharata*.

Jasmine
(alt. Jasmin, Jazim, Jazmine)
Persian, meaning 'jasmine flower'.

Jay
Latin, meaning 'jaybird'. Jays are colourful birds from the crow family.

Jayna
Sanskrit, meaning 'bringer of victory'. More commonly used in Indian communitites.

Jean
(alt. Jeane, Jeanne)
Scottish, meaning 'the Lord is gracious'. Famous Jeans include actors Jean Harlow and Jean Marsh and author Jean Auel.

Jeana
(alt. Jeanna)
Latin, meaning 'queen'.

Jeanette
(alt. Jeannette, Janette; abbrev. Jeannie, Jeanie)
French, meaning 'the Lord is gracious'. Jeanette Winterson is a BAFTA-winning British author and journalist. The shortened form is commonly associated with the sitcom *I Dream of Jeannie*.

Jeanine
(alt. Jeannine)
Latin, meaning 'the Lord is gracious'. Jeanine Tesori is known for her musical theatre arrangements and compositions.

Jemima
Hebrew, meaning 'dove'. Jemima Khan is a writer and campaigner.

Jemma
English variant of Gemma, meaning 'precious stone'. Actor Jemma Redgrave is a fourth-generation member of the Redgrave acting dynasty.

Jena
Arabic, meaning 'little bird'. Actor Jena Malone starred in *Donnie Darko*, *Pride and Prejudice* and *The Hunger Games: Catching Fire*.

Jenna
Shortened form of Jennifer, meaning 'white and smooth'. The name was very popular in the 1980s, especially in the USA.

Jennifer
(alt. Jenifer; abbrev. Jenny, Jennie, Jenni)
Cornish alternative to Guinevere, meaning 'white and smooth'. Famous Jennifers include actors Jennifer Lawrence and Jennifer Aniston and singer Jennifer Hudson.

Jerri
(alt. Jeri, Jerrie, Jerrie, Jerry)
German, meaning 'spear ruler'. Famous Jerries include actor Jerri Manthey, model Jerry Hall and pioneering South Pole physician Dr Jerri Nielsen.

Jerusha
Hebrew, meaning 'married'. Jerusha Hess and husband Jared Hess are filmmakers whose films include *Napoleon Dynamite*.

Jeryl
English, meaning 'spear ruler'. Jeryl Prescott is an American actor.

Jessa
Shortened form of Jessica, meaning 'He sees'. Jessa Gamble is an English-Canadian author and scientific researcher.

Jessamy
(alt. Jessame, Jessamine, Jessamyn)
Persian, meaning 'jasmine flower'. Usually associated with the children's book *Jessamy* by Barbara Sleigh.

Jessica
(alt. Jesica, Jesika, Jessika; abbrev. Jess, Jessi, Jessie, Jessye)
Hebrew, meaning 'He sees'. A popular name over several decades. Famous Jessicas include actor Jessica Alba and athlete Jessica Ennis-Hill. Famous Jessies include singer Jessie J.

Jesusa
Spanish, meaning 'mother of the Lord'. Also a shortened form of Jerusalem.

Jethetha
Hebrew, meaning 'princess'.

Jette
(alt. Jetta, Jettie)
Danish, meaning 'black as coal'. Also the name of a town in Belgium.

Jewel
(alt. Jewell)
French, meaning 'delight'. Singer-songwriter, producer and actor Jewel is professionally known just by her first name.

Jezebel
(alt. Jezabel, Jezabelle)
Hebrew, meaning 'pure and virginal'. Conversely, widely used as a term for 'bad women' after the misbehaving wife of a king in the Bible.

Jill
Latin, meaning 'youthful'. Famous Jills include actor Jill Clayburgh, presenter Jill Dando and children's author Jill Murphy.

Jillian
(abbrev. Jill, Jilly)
Latin, meaning 'youthful'. Often used as a spelling alternative to Gillian.

Jimena
Spanish, meaning 'heard'. Jimena Diaz was the ruler of Valencia in the 12th century.

Jo
Shortened form of Joanna, meaning 'the Lord is gracious'. Famous Jos include supernanny Jo Frost, presenter Jo Coburn and athlete Jo Ankier.

Joan
Hebrew, meaning 'the Lord is gracious'. Famous Joans include St Joan of Arc, actor Joan Collins and comedian Joan Rivers.

Joanna
(alt. Joana, Joanie, Joann, Joanne, Johanna, Joni)
Hebrew, meaning 'the Lord is gracious'. Famous Joannas include actors Joanna Lumley and Joanna Page. Author J.K. Rowling's first name is Joanne.

Jocasta
Italian, meaning 'lighthearted'. Jocasta was an influential character in ancient Greek mythology.

Jocelyn
(alt. Jauslyn, Jocelyne, Joscelin, Joslyn)
German, meaning 'cheerful'.

Jody
(alt. Jodee, Jodi, Jodie)

Shortened form of Judith, meaning 'Jewish'. Famous Jodys include actor Jodie Foster and singer Jody Watley.

Joelle
(alt. Joela)

Hebrew, meaning 'Jehovah is the Lord'. Famous Joelles include teen singer Joelle and actor Joelle Carter.

Joie
French, meaning 'joy'.

Jolene
Contraction of Joanna and Darlene, meaning 'gracious darling'. Usually associated with the song 'Jolene' by Dolly Parton.

Jolie
(alt. Joely)

French, meaning 'pretty'.

Jordan
(alt. Jordana, Jordin, Jordyn)

Hebrew, meaning 'down-flowing'. Model and reality television star Katie Price is known by her professional name Jordan. Also used for boys.

Josephine
(alt. Josefina, Josephina; abbrev. Jo, Joss, Josie)

Hebrew, meaning 'Jehovah increases'. Famous Josephines include the first Empress of France, wife of Napoleon, pioneering actor Josephine Baker and mystery author Josephine Bell.

Jovita
(alt. Jovie)

Latin, meaning 'made glad'. St Jovita was a Christian martyr with her brother St Faustinus during the second century.

Joy
Latin, meaning 'joy'. Famous Joys include comedian Joy Behar, actor Joy Lauren and poet Joy Harjo.

Joyce
Latin, meaning 'joyous'. Famous Joyces include author Joyce Carol Oates and actors Joyce Blair and Joyce DeWitt.

Juanita
(alt. Juana)

Spanish, meaning 'the Lord is gracious'.

Jubilee
Hebrew, meaning 'horn of a ram'. Usually associated with the celebration of an anniversary, such as the Queen's Diamond Jubilee.

Judith
(alt. Judit; abbrev. Judi, Judie, Judy)

Hebrew, meaning 'Jewish'. Found in the Bible. Very popular in the 1940s and '50s. Actor Judy Garland was the star of *The Wizard of Oz*.

Jules
French, meaning 'Jove's child'. Sometimes used as a variant of Julie or Julia, but more commonly used as a boys' name.

Julia
(alt. Julie, Juli)

Latin, meaning 'youthful'. Famous Julias include actors Julia Roberts and Julia Sawalha and TV chef Julia Child, while famous Julies include three Golden Globe and BAFTA-winning actors: Julie Andrews, Julie Christie and Julie Walters.

Julianne
(alt. Juliana, Juliann, Julianne)

Latin, meaning 'youthful'. Oscar-nominated British-American actor Julianne Moore has starred in a string of blockbuster films and is also a children's author.

Juliet
(alt. Joliet, Juliette)

Latin, meaning 'youthful'. Usually associated with the heroine of Shakespeare's play *Romeo and Juliet*.

June
(alt. Juna)

Latin, after the month of the same name. Famous Junes include actor June Bland, singer June Carter Cash and presenter June Sarpong.

Juniper

Dutch, from the shrub of the same name, used for distilling the spirit gin.

Juno
(alt. Juneau)

Latin, meaning 'queen of heaven'. Juno was an ancient Roman Queen of the Gods, and the goddess of marriage and Rome.

Justice

English, meaning 'to deliver what is just'.

Justine
(alt. Justina)

Latin, meaning 'fair and righteous'. Famous Justines include singer Justine Frischmann and actors Justine Bateman and Justine Waddell.

Jørgina

Dutch, meaning 'farmer'. More commonly used as a spelling alternative for Georgina.

Girls' names

Kadenza
(alt. Kadence)
Latin, meaning 'with rhythm'. A spelling alternative for Cadenza.

Kadisha
Hebrew, meaning 'religious one'.

Kaitlin
(alt. Kaitlyn)
Greek, meaning 'pure'. Variant of Caitlin that became popular, especially in the USA, after the 1970s. Kaitlin Doubleday is a Hollywood actor.

Kala
(alt. Kaela, Kaiala, Kaila)
Sanskrit, meaning 'black one'. Also known for being the great ape that saved Tarzan as a baby.

Kali
(alt. Kailee, Kailey, Kaleigh, Kaley, Kalie, Kalli, Kally, Kaylee, Kayleigh)
Sanskrit, meaning 'black one'. Also known in Hinduism as the Goddess of Time and Change.

Kalila
Arabic, meaning 'beloved'.

Kalina
Slavic, meaning 'flower'.

Kalliope
(alt. Calliope)
Greek, meaning 'beautiful voice'. From the muse of the same name.

Kama
Sanskrit, meaning 'love'. Known in Hinduism as one of the four goals of life, kama refers to intellectual fulfilment.

Kami
Japanese, meaning 'lord'.

Kamilla
(alt. Kamilah)
Slavic, meaning 'serving girl'. A spelling alternative for Camilla.

Kana

Hawaiian, from the demi-god of the same name. In Hawaiian mythology Kana could take the form of a rope that could stretch from the island of Molokai to Hawaii.

Kanika

Swahili, meaning 'black cloth'. The stage name of Indian actor Divya Venkatasubramaniam.

Kara

Latin, meaning 'dear one'.

Karen

(alt. Karan, Karalyn, Karin, Karina, Karon, Karren; abbrev. Kari, Karrie)

Greek, meaning 'pure'. Very popular during the 1960s and '70s. Famous Karens include comedian Karen Taylor and musician Karen Carpenter. Kari is one of Saturn's moons.

Karimah

Arabic, meaning 'giving'. A spelling variation of Karima.

Karishma

(alt. Karisma)

Sanskrit, meaning 'miracle'. Both Karisma and Karishma are popular names in India.

Karla

German, meaning 'man'. A spelling variation for Carla.

Karly

(alt. Karlee, Karley, Karli)

German, meaning 'free man'. Popular in Scotland especially, from where both Karly Robertson the ice skater and Karly Ashworth from Big Brother hail.

Karma

Hindi, meaning 'destiny'. Known as a principle of Buddhism where good deeds lead to a positive influence on a person's future.

Karol

(alt. Karolina, Karolyn)

Slavic, meaning 'little and womanly'. A spelling variation of Carol.

Kasumi

Japanese, meaning 'of the mist'.

Katarina

(alt. Katarine, Katerina, Katharina)

Greek, meaning 'pure'. Katarina was one of the first companions of Doctor Who.

Kate

(alt. Kat, Katie, Kathi, Kathie, Kathy, Kati, Katy)

Shortened form of Katherine, meaning 'pure'. Famous Kates include actors Kate Winslet and Kate Hudson and the Duchess of Cambridge, Kate Middleton.

Katherine

(alt. Katharine, Katheryn, Kathrine, Kathryn; abbrev. Kathie, Kathy)

Greek, meaning 'pure'. A spelling variation for Catherine.

Kathleen
(alt. Kathlyn)

Greek, meaning 'pure'. Very popular in the 1960s and shared by many actors, politicans and scientists from that generation.

Katrina
(alt. Katina)

Greek, meaning 'pure'. More commonly used as a shortened version of Katherine.

Kaveri

Sanskrit, meaning 'sacred river'. Known for the large river that flows across India.

Kay
(alt. Kaye)

Shortened form of Katherine, meaning 'pure'.

Kaya

Sanskrit, meaning 'nature', or Turkish, meaning 'rock'. Kaya also refers to a sweet coconut jam popular in Asia.

Kayla
(alt. Kaylah)

Greek, meaning 'pure'. Kayla Harrison won a gold medal in judo at the 2012 and 2016 Olympics.

Kayley
(alt. Kayley, Kayli)

American, meaning 'pure'. Also known as one of the main characters in *The Magic Sword: Quest for Camelot*.

Kaylin

American, meaning 'pure'. A spelling variation for Caylin.

Keary

Gaelic, meaning 'black-haired'. Also a boys' name.

Keeley
(alt. Keely)

Irish, meaning 'battle maid'. Actor Keeley Hawes is a popular star of British TV drama.s

Keila

Hebrew, meaning 'citadel'.

Keira

Irish Gaelic, meaning 'dark'. A rise in popularity of the name followed the success of actor Keira Knightley.

Keisha
(alt. Keesha)

Arabic, meaning 'woman'. Keisha Castle-Hughes is an Australian actor.

Kelis

American, meaning 'beautiful'. Award-winning singer Kelis is known widely by her first name only.

Kelly
(alt. Keli, Kelley, Kelli, Kellie)

Irish Gaelic, meaning 'battle maid'. Famous Kellys include singer Kelly Clarkson, TV personality Kelly Osbourne and Olympic athlete Kelly Holmes.

Kelsey
(alt. Kelcee, Kelcie, Kelsea, Kelsi, Kelsie)
Old English, meaning 'victorious ship'. More popular in the USA, where it is the name of several cities and is used for both girls and boys.

Kendall
(alt. Kendal)
English, meaning 'the valley of the River Kent'. Also a place in Cumbria.

Kendra
English, meaning 'knowing'. Name of a character in *Buffy The Vampire Slayer*. Kendra Wilkinson is an American TV personality.

Kenna
Irish Gaelic, meaning 'handsome'.

Kennedy
(alt. Kenadee, Kennedi)
Irish Gaelic, meaning 'helmet head'. Also used as a boys' name.

Kenzie
Shortened form of Mackenzie, meaning 'son of the wise ruler'. Mackenzie is also commonly used as a boys' name.

Kerensa
Cornish, meaning 'love'. Also a variation on the name Karen.

Kerrigan
Irish, meaning 'black haired'.

Kerry
(alt. Keri, Kerri, Kerrie)
Irish, from the county of the same name. Used for both girls and boys.

Khadijah
(alt. Khadejah)
Arabic, meaning 'premature baby'. Khadija bint Khuwaylid was the first wife of Muhammad and is known as the 'Mother of Islam'.

Khaleesi
Dothraki, meaning 'queen'. Royal title from *Game of Thrones*.

Kiana
(alt. Kia, Kianna)
American, meaning 'fibre'. Kiana is an American TV personality known for her physical fitness and physical training videos.

Kiara
It is possible that the name could come from two sources – Irish 'ciar' meaning 'dark' or 'dark haired', or the Latin 'chiara', meaning 'light'.

Kiki
Spanish, meaning 'home ruler'. Also an American slang term for a party centred around gossip and laughter.

Kimana
Native American, meaning 'butterfly'.

Kimberly
(alt. Kimberleigh, Kimberley; abbrev. Kim)
Old English, meaning 'royal forest'. Famous Kimberlys include rapper Kimberly 'Lil' Kim' Denise Jones. Famous Kims include TV personality Kim Kardashian, actor Kim Basinger and singer Kim Wilde.

Kingsley
(alt. Kinsley, Kynslee)
English, meaning 'king's meadow'.
More commonly used for boys.

Kinsey
English, meaning 'king's victory'.

Kira
Greek, meaning 'lady'.

Kiri
Maori, meaning 'tree bark'. Dame
Kiri Te Kanawa is known for her
opera singing career spanning nearly
50 years.

Kirsten
(alt. Kirstin; abbrev. Kirstie, Kirsty)
Scandinavian, meaning 'Christian'.
Kirsten Dunst is a German-American
actor, singer and model. Famous
Kirsties include TV presenters Kirsty
Young and Kirstie Allsopp and
American actor Kirstie Alley.

Kitty
(alt. Kittie)
Shortened form of Katherine, meaning
'pure'. Can be used in its own right.

Kizzy
Hebrew, meaning the plant 'cassia'.
Singer Kizzy Crawford sings in both
English and Welsh.

Klara
Hungarian, meaning 'bright'.
Commonly used in German-speaking
communities.

Komal
Hindi, meaning 'soft and tender'.
Most commonly used for boys.

Konstantina
Latin, meaning 'steadfast'. Feminine
form of Constantine.

Kora
(alt. Kori)
Greek, meaning 'maiden'. A spelling
variation for Cora.

Kristen
*(alt. Kristan, Kristin, Kristine, Krysten;
abbrev. Kris, Krista, Kristie, Kristy)*
Greek, meaning 'Christian'. Actor
Kristen Stewart is known for her roles
in the *Twilight* films.

Kwanza
(alt. Kwanzaa)
Swahili, meaning 'beginning'. Also
known for the week-long celebration
of African–American culture near
Christmas time.

Kyla
(alt. Kya, Kylah, Kyle)
Scottish, meaning 'narrow spit of land'.

Kylie
(alt. Kiley, Kylee)
Irish Gaelic, meaning 'graceful'.
The rise in popularity of this name
is linked to actor and singer Kylie
Minogue.

Kyoko
Japanese, meaning 'girl who sees her
own true image'.

Girls' names

Lacey
(alt. Laci, Lacie, Lacy)

French, from a nobleman's surname. Most popular in North America, but Lacey Turner is an English actor and *EastEnders* star.

Ladonna
Italian, meaning 'lady'. Also a spelling alternative to Madonna.

Lady
English, meaning 'bread kneader'. Also an aristocratic title.

Laidh
Scottish meaning 'a ship's course'. Also a spelling alternative to Lady.

Laila
(alt. Laelia, Layla, Leila, Lejla, Lela, Lelah, Lelia)

Arabic, meaning 'night'. Famous Lailas include boxer Laila Ali and the song 'Layla' by Eric Clapton. Has become popular in recent years.

Lainey
(alt. Laine, Laney, Lany)

French, meaning 'bright light'. In Poland, the most common spelling is Lany, whereas in other countries it can be Lainey or Laney.

Lakeisha
(alt. Lakeshia)

American, meaning 'woman'. Its origins seem to be a combination of La and Keisha.

Lakshmi
(alt. Laxmi)

Sanskrit, meaning 'good omen'. Also the Hindu goddess of wealth.

Lana
Greek, meaning 'light'. Famous Lanas include singer Lana Del Rey, actor Lana Turner and the language-communication chimpanzee Lana.

Lani
(alt. Lanie)

Hawaiian, meaning 'heaven and sky'.

Lara

Latin, meaning 'famous'. Famous Laras include actor Lara Flynn Boyle, *Tomb Raider* protagonist Lara Croft, and the ancient Roman nymph of the same name.

Larissa

(alt. Larisa)

Greek, meaning 'lighthearted'. Larissa was a nymph in ancient Greek mythology.

Lark

(alt. Larkin)

English, meaning 'playful songbird'.

Larsen

(alt. Larsen)

Scandinavian, meaning 'son of Lars'.

Latifa

(alt. Latifah)

Arabic, meaning 'gentle and pleasant'. Queen Latifah is the stage name of the singer and pioneer of female hip hop.

Latika

(alt. Lotika)

Hindi, meaning 'a plant'. Usually associated with the character of Latika from *Slumdog Millionaire*.

Latisha

Latin, meaning 'happiness'. More commonly used in the USA.

Latona

(alt. Latonia)

Roman, from the ancient Roman mythological heroine of the same name who had twin sons with the god Zeus.

Latoya

Spanish, meaning 'victorious one'. Singer LaToya Jackson is known for being a member of the musical Jackson family.

Latrice

(alt. Latricia)

Latin, meaning 'noble'. More commonly used in the USA.

Laura

(alt. Lora)

Latin, meaning 'laurel'. Famous Lauras include designer Laura Ashley, author Laura Ingalls Wilder and actor Laura Dern.

Laurel

Latin, meaning 'laurel tree'. A Laurel is also a term used for young women in the Mormon Church.

Lauren

(alt. Lauran, Loren)

Latin, meaning 'laurel'. Famous Laurens include actors Lauren Bacall and Lauren Crace and DJ Lauren Laverne.

Laveda

(alt. Lavada)

Latin, meaning 'cleansed'.

Lavender

Latin, from the flowering plant of the same name.

Laverne

(alt. Lavern, Laverna)

Latin, from the goddess of the same name. Famous Lavernes include the Andrews Sisters member Laverne Andrews, and US sitcom *Laverne & Shirley*.

Lavinia

(alt. Lavina)

Latin, meaning 'woman of Rome'. Lavinia was an ancient Roman character whose hair caught fire during sacrifices to the gods.

Lavita

American, meaning 'charming'. The original 'la vita' means 'life' in Latin.

Lavonne

(alt. Lavon)

French, meaning 'yew wood'. More commonly used in the USA.

Leah

(alt. Lea, Leia)

Hebrew, meaning 'weary'.

Leandra

Greek, meaning 'lion man'. In the novel *Don Quixote* by Miguel de Cervantes, Leandra is a beautiful woman whose many suitors withdraw to the mountains to write about how beautiful she is.

Leanne

(alt. Leann, Leanna, Leeann, Lee Ann)

Contraction of Lee and Ann, meaning 'meadow grace'. Famous Leannes include singers LeAnn Rimes and Lee Ann Womack and actor Leanne Wilson.

Leda

Greek, meaning 'gladness'. Leda was an ancient Greek character seduced by the god Zeus in the form of a white swan, and whose children included Helen of Troy.

Lee

(alt. Leigh)

English, meaning 'pasture' or 'meadow'. Used equally for girls and boys.

Leilani

Hawaiian, meaning 'flower from heaven'. Actor Leilani Jones is known for her roles in *Little Shop of Horrors* and various voice acting roles.

Leith

Scottish Gaelic, meaning 'broad river'.

Lena

(alt. Leena, Lina)

Latin, meaning 'light'. Famous Lenas include actors Lena Dunham, Lena Headey and Lena Ashwell.

Lenna

(alt. Lennie)

German, meaning 'lion's strength'.

Lenore
(alt. Lenora, Leonora, Leonor, Leonore)

Greek, meaning 'light'. Usually associated with the poem *Lenore* by Edgar Allan Poe.

Léonie
(alt. Leona, Leone)

Latin, meaning 'lioness'. Poet Leonie Adams wrote during the mid-20th century.

Leora
(alt. Liora)

Hebrew, meaning 'light'. The masculine form of Leora is Leor.

Lerola

Latin, meaning 'like a blackbird'.

Lesley
(alt. Leslee, Lesli)

Scottish Gaelic, from the name of the prominent clan. Also meaning 'holly garden'. The boys' variation is usually spelt Leslie.

Leta

Latin, meaning 'glad and joyful'. Leta Hollingworth was an influential child psychologist in the 20th century.

Letha

Greek, meaning 'forgetfulness'. Also the name of a type of butterfly.

Letitia
(alt. Leticia, Lettice, Lettie)

Latin, meaning 'joy and gladness'. St Leticia was a Spanish virgin martyr.

Lexia
(alt. Lexi, Lexie)

Greek, meaning 'defender of mankind'. Also the name of a type of butterfly.

Lia

Italian, meaning 'bringer of the gospel'. Actor Lia Williams is known for her roles in both theatre and film.

Liana

French, meaning 'to twine around'. Also the name of a type of vine.

Libby
(alt. Libbie)

Shortened form of Elizabeth, meaning 'consecrated to God'. Famous Libbys include journalist Libby Purves and singer Libby Holman.

Liberty

English, meaning 'freedom'.

Lida

Slavic, meaning 'loved by the people'.

Liese
(alt. Liesel, Liesl)

German, meaning 'pledged to God'. Also used as a shortened form of Elizabeth.

Lila
(alt. Lilah)

Arabic, meaning 'night'. In the Hindu faith, Lila refers to playtime or pastimes.

Lilac

Latin, from the flower of the same name. Also associated with the pale purple colour.

Lilia
(alt. Lilias)

Scottish, meaning 'lily'. More commonly used in Russian and Ukrainian communities.

Lilith

Arabic, meaning 'ghost'. Also the name of a female demon in Hebrew mythology.

Lillian
(alt. Lilian, Liliana, Lilla, Lillianna)

Latin, meaning 'lily'. Famous Lillians include actor Lillian Gish, playwright Lillian Hellman and pioneering nurse Lillian Wald.

Lily
(alt. Lili, Lillie, Lilly)

Latin, from the flower of the same name. Famous Lilys include singer Lily Allen, actor Lily Collins and model Lily Cole.

Linda
(alt. Lynda)

Spanish, meaning 'pretty'. Famous Lindas include presenter Linda Barker, actor Linda Blair and singer Linda Ronstadt.

Linden
(alt. Lindie, Lindy)

From the tree of the same name. Used more commonly for boys.

Lindsay
(alt. Lindsey, Linsey)

English, meaning 'island of linden trees'. Famous Lindsays include actors Lindsay Lohan, Lindsay Sloane and Lindsay Wagner.

Linnea
(alt. Linnae, Linny)

Scandinavian, meaning 'lime or linden tree'.

Lirit

Hebrew, meaning 'musically talented'.

Lisa
(alt. Leesa, Lise, Liza)

Hebrew, meaning 'pledged to God'. Famous Lisas include singer Lisa Bonet, *Friends* actor Lisa Kudrow and *The Simpsons* character Lisa Simpson.

Lissa

Greek, meaning 'bee'. Also used as a shortened form of Melissa.

Lissandra
(alt. Lisandra)

Greek, meaning 'man's defender'.

Liv

Nordic, meaning 'defence'. Actor Liv Tyler appeared in the *Lord of the Rings* trilogy.

Livia

Latin, meaning 'olive'. Livia Drusilla was a prominent ancient Roman woman, wife of the Emperor Augustus.

Liz
(alt. Lizzie, Lizzy)

Shortened form of Elizabeth, meaning 'consecrated to God'. Many Elizabeths go by Liz, including actor Liz Taylor.

Logan

Irish Gaelic, meaning 'small hollow'. More commonly used as a name for boys.

Lois

German, meaning 'renowned in battle'. Usually associated with the character of Lois Lane from the Superman comic series.

Lola

Spanish, meaning 'sorrows'. Also used as a shortened form of Delores.

Lolita
(alt. Lollie)

Spanish, meaning 'sorrows'. Usually associated with the character of Lolita in Vladimir Nabokov's novel *Lolita*.

Lona

Latin, meaning 'lion'. Lona is a moon deity in Hawaiian mythology.

Lora

Latin, meaning 'laurel'. Sometimes used as a spelling alternative to Laura.

Lorelei
(alt. Loralai, Loralie)

German, meaning 'dangerous rock'. Ancient German mythology tells of a maiden who lives on the Lorelei Rock in the river Rhine and lures sailors to their deaths.

Lorenza

Latin, meaning 'from Laurentium'.

Loretta
(alt. Loreto)

Latin, meaning 'laurel'. Mostly used in the USA, where actors with this name include Loretta Devine and Loretta Swit.

Lori
(alt. Laurie, Lorie, Lorri)

Latin, meaning 'laurel'. Actor Lori Petty is known for her roles in *Point Break*, *A League of Their Own* and *Tank Girl*.

Lorna

Scottish, from the town of Lorne. Usually associated with the protagonist in R.D. Blackmore's novel *Lorna Doone*.

Lorraine
(alt. Laraine, Loraine)

French, meaning 'from Lorraine'. TV presenter Lorraine Kelly is best known for breakfast TV and chat show work.

Lottie
(alt. Lotta, Lotte)

French, meaning 'little and womanly'. Usually used as a shortened form of Charlotte.

Lotus

Greek, meaning 'lotus flower'.

Louise
(alt. Louisa, Luisa; abbrev. Lou, Louie)

German, meaning 'renowned in battle'.

Lourdes

French, from the town of the same name. Madonna famously chose this name for her daughter in 1996.

Love

English, from the word 'love'.

Lowri

Welsh, meaning 'crowned with laurels'. Lowri Turner is a TV presenter.

Luanne
(alt. Luann, Luanna)

German, meaning 'renowned in battle'. In Hawaiian, the name also means 'enjoyment'.

Luba

Hebrew, meaning 'dearly loved'.

Lucia
(alt. Luciana)

Italian, meaning 'light'. Feminine form of the ancient Roman name Lucius.

Lucille
(alt. Lucile, Lucilla)

French, meaning 'light'. American Lucille Ball was the star of *I Love Lucy*.

Lucinda

English, meaning 'light'. Lucinda Green (Lucinda Prior-Palmer) was a world champion equestrian who won Badminton six times.

Lucretia
(alt. Lucrece)

Spanish, meaning 'light'. Also an important character in ancient Roman mythology.

Lucy
(alt. Lucie)

Latin, meaning 'light'. St Lucy was a martyr in the fourth century.

Ludmilla

Slavic, meaning 'beloved of the people'.

Luella
(alt. Lue)

English, meaning 'renowned in battle'. Designer Luella Bartley is known for her fashion brands and journalism for various fashion magazines.

Lulu
(alt. Lula)

German, meaning 'renowned in battle'. Singer Lulu became a star in the 1960s and is still successful today.

Luna

Latin, meaning 'moon'. Luna was the personification of the moon in ancient Roman mythology.

Lupita

Spanish, short form of Guadelupe. Actor Lupita Nyong'o is known for her role in *12 Years a Slave*.

Luz

Spanish, meaning 'light'. Also the name of an ancient city in the Bible.

Lydia
(alt. Lidia)

Greek, meaning 'from Lydia'. Famous Lydias include activist Lydia Becker, ballerina Lydia Lopokova and the character of Lydia Bennet in *Pride and Prejudice*.

Lyla

Hebrew, meaning 'night'.

Lynette
(alt. Linette)

Welsh, meaning 'idol'.

Lynn
(alt. Lyn, Lynne)

Spanish, meaning 'pretty'; English, meaning 'waterfall'. Actor Lynn Redgrave is part of the Redgrave acting dynasty.

Lynton

English, meaning 'town of lime trees'. Also the name of a town in Devon. Most commonly used for boys.

Lyra

Latin, meaning 'lyre'. The central character in Philip Pullman's *His Dark Materials* trilogy.

Girls' names

Mab

Irish Gaelic, meaning 'joy'. Queen Mab is a character in Shakespeare's play *Romeo and Juliet*.

Mabel
(alt. Mabelle, Mable)

Latin, meaning 'loveable'. Although the name Mabel is very old and dates from the fifth century, it did not become popular until the 19th century, when the novel *The Heir of Redclyffe* was published.

Macaria

Spanish, meaning 'blessed'.

Machiko

Japanese, meaning 'knowledgeable child'. Machiko Kawana is a Japanese voice artist.

Macy
(alt. Macey, Maci, Macie)

French, meaning 'weapon'. Macy Gray is the stage name of the award winning R&B singer-songwriter and actor Natalie McIntyre.

Mada

English, meaning 'from Magdala'. In Hindu mythology, Mada also refers to an enormous monster who is able to swallow the entire universe.

Madaio

Hawaiian, meaning 'gift from God'.

Madden
(alt. Maddyn)

Irish, meaning 'little dog'.

Madeline
(alt. Madaline, Madalyn, Madeleine, Madelyn, Madelynn, Madilyn; abbrev. Maddy, Maddi, Maddie, Madie)

Greek, meaning 'from Magdala'. Madeleine Albright was the first female Secretary of State in the US. Maddy Prior is one of the best-known English folk singers.

Madge

Greek, meaning 'pearl'. Also a shortened form of several names including Margaret, Madeline and Marjorie. Madge was especially common around 1880–1900, being the name of several actors of that time. More recently, it's the nickname of pop icon Madonna.

Madhuri

Hindi, meaning 'sweet girl'. Madhuri Dixit is one of Bollywood's most well-known and popular actors, appearing in dozens of Hindi films.

Madison
(alt. Maddison, Madisen, Madisyn, Madyson)

English, meaning 'son of the mighty warrior'. The increase in the popularity of Madison can be traced back to the mermaid character of Madison in the film *Splash*, played by Daryl Hannah.

Madonna

Latin, meaning 'my lady'. Usually associated with the pop legend Madonna, or as one of the Virgin Mary's many names.

Maeve

Irish Gaelic, meaning 'intoxicating'. Famous Maeves include Queen Maeve from Irish mythology, author Maeve Binchy and writer Maeve Brennan.

Mafalda

Spanish, meaning 'battle-mighty'. Mafalda is a popular Argentine comic strip.

Magali

Greek, meaning 'pearl'. More commonly used in French- or Portuguese-speaking communities.

Magdalene
(alt. Magdalen, Magdalena)

Greek, meaning 'from Magdala'. Mary Magdalene was one of Jesus's disciples in the Bible.

Magnolia

Latin, from the flowering plant of the same name.

Mahala
(alt. Mahalia)

Hebrew, meaning 'tender affection'.

Maia
(alt. Maja, Maya)

Greek, meaning 'mother'. Also an important character in ancient Greek mythology.

Maida

English, meaning 'maiden'.

Maisie
(alt. Maisey, Maisy, Maizie, Masie, Mazie)

Greek, meaning 'pearl'. Famous Maisies include children's book character Maisey Mouse and Maisie Williams, star of *Game of Thrones*.

Malin

Hebrew and English, meaning 'of Magdala'. Malin is most common in Sweden.

Maliya
(alt. Malia, Maliyah)

Hawaiian, meaning 'beloved'. Malia Obama is the daughter of the 44th President of the USA, Barack Obama.

Malka

Hebrew, meaning 'queen'.

Mallory
(alt. Malorie)

French, meaning 'unhappy'. Author Malorie Blackman is known for her children's literature.

Malvina

Gaelic, meaning 'smooth brow'. The name was invented by poet James Macpherson in the 18th century.

Mamie
(alt. Maimie, Mammie)

Shortened form of Margaret, meaning 'pearl'. Famous Mamies include former US first lady Mamie Eisenhower, wife of President Dwight Eisenhower.

Mandy
(alt. Mandie)

Shortened form of Amanda, meaning 'much loved'. Famous Mandys include actor Mandy Moore and the song *Mandy* by Barry Manilow.

Manisha

Sanskrit, meaning 'desire'. Manisha is the goddess of wisdom in the Hindu faith.

Mansi

Hopi, meaning 'plucked flower'. Also the name of an indigenous group of people in Russia.

Manuela

Spanish, meaning 'the Lord is among us'. More commonly used in German-speaking communities.

Mara

Hebrew, meaning 'bitter'. Famous Maras include actor Mara Wilson and children's author Mara Bergman.

Marcela
(alt. Marceline, Marcella, Marcelle)

Latin, meaning 'war-like'.

Marcia
(alt. Marcy, Marci, Marcie)

Latin, meaning 'war-like'. Famous Marcias include legendary British leader Queen Marcia, actor Marcia Cross and voice actor Marcia Wallace.

Margaret
(alt. Margarete, Margaretta, Margarette, Margret; abbrev. Maggie)

Greek, meaning 'pearl'. Famous Margarets include former prime minister Margaret Thatcher, author Margaret Atwood and actor Margaret Rutherford. Famous Maggies include actors Maggie Gyllenhaal and Maggie Grace, and the song 'Maggie May' by Rod Stewart.

Margery
(alt. Marge, Margie, Margit, Margy, Marjorie)

French, meaning 'pearl'. Author Margery Kempe wrote the first English-language autobiography, *The Book of Margery Kempe*, in the 15th century. Marjorie Bruce was daughter of Robert the Bruce of Scotland.

Margot
(alt. Margo)

French, meaning 'pearl'. Famous Margots include ballerina Margot Fonteyn, actor Margot Robbie and the sister of Anne Frank, Margot Frank.

Marguerite
(alt. Margarita)

French, meaning 'pearl'. Marguerite de Valois was Queen of France during the 16th century.

Maria
(alt. Mariah)

Latin, meaning 'bitter'. Famous Marias include tennis pro Maria Sharapova, performer Maria von Trapp and the character of Maria from the musical *West Side Story*.

Marian
(alt. Mariam, Mariana, Mariann, Marianne, Maryann, Maryanne, Marion)

French, meaning 'bitter grace'. Usually associated with the character of Maid Marian from the legend of Robin Hood. Marianne Faithfull is an English singer-songwriter.

Maribel

Hebrew, meaning 'bitter'. Also used as a contraction of Maria and Isabel.

Marie

French, meaning 'bitter'. Famous Maries include French Queen Marie Antoinette, physicist Marie Curie, and singer Marie Osmond.

Mariel
(alt. Mariela, Mariella)

Dutch, meaning 'bitter'. Also the name of a city in Cuba.

Marietta
(alt. Marieta)

French, meaning 'bitter'. Activist Marietta Stow was an influential campaigner for women's suffrage during the 19th century.

Marigold

English, from the flowering plant of the same name.

Marika

Dutch, meaning 'bitter'. More commonly used in Greek-speaking communities.

Marilyn
(alt. Marilee, Marilene, Marilynn)

English, meaning 'bitter'. Marilyn Monroe starred in films such as *Gentlemen Prefer Blondes*, *The Seven Year Itch* and *Some Like It Hot*.

Marina
(alt. Marine)

Latin, meaning 'from the sea'. Marina is a truly global name, with famous Marinas of many nationalities and backgrounds. Journalist Marine Hyde is… is one of few Brits with the name.

Mariposa

Spanish, meaning 'butterfly'. Also the name of a group of lilies.

Marisa
(alt. Maris, Marissa)

Latin, meaning 'of the sea'.
Famous Marisas include actor Marisa
Tomei and the notorious Yahoo!
business executive Marissa Mayer.

Marisol

Spanish, meaning 'bitter sun'. Also a
contraction of Maria de la Soledad,
which is another title for the Virgin
Mary in Spain.

Marjolaine

French, meaning 'marjoram'.

Marlene
(alt. Marlen, Marlena; abbrev. Marla)

Hebrew, meaning 'bitter'. Actor
Marlene Dietrich was German born
but became an American in 1939
and was a front-line entertainer for
the troops during World War II. The
character of Marla Singer in the film
Fight Club, was played by Helena
Bonham Carter.

Marley
(alt. Marlee)

American, meaning 'bitter'.

Marlo
(alt. Marlowe)

American, meaning 'bitter'. More
commonly used as a boys' name.

Marnie
(alt. Marney)

Scottish, meaning 'from the sea'.
Famous Marnies include the character
of Marnie from *Girls* and the film
Marnie by Alfred Hitchcock. It was
also the birth name of ballerina Dame
Darcey Bussell.

Marseille

French, from the city of the same
name in France.

Marsha

English, meaning 'war-like'. Famous
Marshas include actor Marsha
Thomason, singer Marsha Hunt and
playwright Marsha Norman.

Martha
(alt. Marta)

Aramaic, meaning 'lady'. Found in
the Bible. Martha Lane Fox was a
leading dotcom entrepreneur in the
2000s, later becoming the youngest
female member of the House of
Lords.

Martina

Latin, meaning 'war-like'. Famous
Martinas include tennis pros Martina
Hingis and Martina Navratilova and
Martina, Empress of the Byzantine
empire.

Marvel

French, meaning 'something to
marvel at'. Usually associated with
the comic book brand.

Mary

Hebrew, meaning 'bitter'. Famous Marys include the Virgin Mary, author Mary Shelley and morality campaigner Mary Whitehouse.

Masada

Hebrew, meaning 'foundation'. Also the name of an ancient Jewish fortification in Israel.

Matilda
(alt. Mathilda, Mathilde, Matilde)

German, meaning 'battle-mighty'. Famous Matildas include the lead character from the novel *Matilda* by Roald Dahl, Queen consort of England Matilda of Flanders, and 12th-century Queen Matilda of England.

Mattea

Hebrew, meaning 'gift of God'.

Maude
(alt. Maud)

German, meaning 'battle-mighty'. Usually associated with the character of Maude Flanders from *The Simpsons* or the film *Harold and Maude*.

Maura

Irish, meaning 'bitter'. Also the name of a French saint of the fourth century.

Maureen
(alt. Maurine)

Irish, meaning 'bitter'. Famous Maureens include actors Maureen Lipman, Maureen McCormick and Maureen O'Hara.

Mavis

French, meaning 'thrush'. The name originated in the 19th century after the publication of the novel *The Sorrows of Satan*.

Maxine
(alt. Maxie)

Latin, meaning 'greatest'. Famous Maxines include the Andrews Sisters member Maxine Andrews, and actors Maxine Audley and Maxine Peake.

May
(alt. Mae, Maye)

Hebrew, meaning 'gift of God'. Also the name of the fifth month.

Maya
(alt. Mya, Myah)

Greek, meaning 'mother'. Famous Mayas include author Maya Angelou, comedian Maya Rudolph and the Mayan people of Central America.

Mckenna
(alt. Mackenna)

Irish Gaelic, meaning 'son of the handsome one'.

Mckenzie
(alt. Mackenzie, Mckenzy, Mikenzi)

Irish Gaelic, meaning 'son of the wise ruler'. More commonly used as a boys' name.

Meara

Gaelic, meaning 'filled with happiness'.

Medea
(alt. Meda)

Greek, meaning 'ruling'. Also the name of a prominent figure in ancient Greek mythology.

Meg

Shortened form of Margaret, meaning 'pearl'. Famous Megs include actor Meg Ryan and the character of Meg from Disney's *Hercules*.

Megan
(alt. Meagan, Meghan, Meghann)

Welsh, meaning 'pearl'. Famous Megans include actors Megan Fox and Megan Mullally and Duchess of Sussex, Meghan Markle.

Mehri

Persian, meaning 'kind'. Also the name of a group of people and a language spoken in southern Arabia.

Meiwei

Chinese, meaning 'forever enchanting'.

Melanie
(alt. Melania, Melany, Melonie; abbrev. Mel)

Greek, meaning 'dark-skinned'. Famous Melanies include singers Melanie Brown and Melanie Chisholm of the Spice Girls. Melania Trump is the current First Lady of the USA.

Melba

Australian, meaning 'from Melbourne'.

Melia
(alt. Meliah)

German, meaning 'industrious'.

Melina

Greek, meaning 'honey'. Actor Melina Kanakaredes has appeared in several US-based crime dramas, including *CSI:NY*.

Melinda

Latin, meaning 'honey'. Famous Melindas include TV presenter and model Melinda Messenger, philanthropist Melinda Gates and actor Melinda Clarke.

Melisande

French, meaning 'bee'. Melisandre is a character from George R.R. Martin's *A Song of Ice and Fire* series.

Melissa
(alt. Melisa, Mellissa)

Greek, meaning 'bee'. Famous Melissas include singer Melissa Etheridge and actors Melissa Joan Hart and Melissa George.

Melody
(alt. Melodie)

Greek, meaning 'song'. Aptly, there are a number of Melodys who have gone on to be singers as well as actors. Melody is also a character in Disney's *The Little Mermaid*.

Melvina

Celtic, meaning 'chieftain'.

Menora
(alt. Menorah)
Hebrew, meaning 'candlestick'.

Mercedes
Spanish, meaning 'mercies'. Usually associated with the luxury car manufacturer Mercedes-Benz.

Mercy
English, meaning 'mercy'.

Meredith
(alt. Meridith)
Welsh, meaning 'great ruler'.

Merle
French, meaning 'blackbird'. Used equally for girls and boys, though not a common name anywhere.

Merritt
English, from the word 'merit'. Can be used for both boys and girls.

Merry
English, meaning 'light-hearted'.

Meryl
(alt. Merrill)
Irish Gaelic, meaning 'sea-bright'. Actor Meryl Streep is Hollywood royalty, having starred in a string of hugely successful films.

Meta
German, meaning 'pearl'. Also a Greek term for 'after or beyond'.

Mia
Italian, meaning 'mine'. Famous Mias include actors Mia Wasikowska and Mia Farrow and singer M.I.A.

Michaela
(alt. Makaela, Makaila, Micaela, Mikaila, Mikayla)
Hebrew, meaning 'resembles God'. Famous Michaelas include presenter Michaela Strachan, actor Michaela Conlin, and gymnast McKayla Maroney.

Michelle
(alt. Machelle, Mechelle, Michaele, Michal, Michele, Michen; abbrev. Mickey, Mickie)
French, meaning 'resembles God'. Famous Michelles include actor Michelle Rodriguez and the former First Lady of the USA, Michelle Obama.

Mieko
(alt. Meiko)
Japanese, meaning 'born into wealth'.

Migdalia
Greek, meaning 'from Magdala'.

Mignon
French, meaning 'sweet'.

Mika
(alt. Micah)
Hebrew, meaning 'resembles God'.

Milada
Czech, meaning 'my love'. More commonly used in Slavic and Czech communities.

Milagros

Spanish, meaning 'miracles'. Also a term used for folk charms with healing properties in Mexico.

Milan

Italian, from the city of the same name in Italy.

Mildred

English, meaning 'gentle strength'. Famous Mildreds include the character of Mildred Hubble from the *Worst Witch* series, author Mildred B. Davies and actor Mildred Dunnock.

Milena

Czech, meaning 'love and warmth'.

Miley

American, meaning 'smiley'. Made popular by singer and actor Miley Cyrus.

Millicent

(alt. Milicent; abbrev. Millie, Milly)

German, meaning 'high-born power'. Famous Millicents include suffragist Millicent Fawcett and British spy Milicent Bagot.

Mimi

Italian, meaning 'bitter'. Also the name of the female protagonist in the opera *La bohème*, by Giacomo Puccini.

Mina

(alt. Mena)

German, meaning 'love'; Persian, meaning 'coloured glass'.

Mindy

(alt. Mindi)

Latin, meaning 'honey'. Used as a shortened form of Melinda as well as a name in its own right. Mindy Kaling is an American-Indian actor and comedian.

Minerva

Latin, from the goddess of the same name. Minerva was the goddess of wisdom, the arts and defence, in ancient Roman mythology.

Ming

Chinese, meaning 'bright'. Usually associated with the Ming Dynasty, which ruled China from the 14th to the 17th century.

Minnie

(alt. Minna)

German, meaning 'helmet'. Usually associated with the Disney character Minnie Mouse and actor Minnie Driver.

Mira

(alt. Meera)

Latin, meaning 'admirable'. Also the name of a giant red star.

Mirabel

(alt. Mirabella, Mirabelle)

Latin, meaning 'wonderful'. Also the name of a type of plum.

Miranda

(alt. Meranda; abbrev. Randi, Randy)

Latin, meaning 'admirable'. Famous Mirandas include actors Miranda Richardson and Miranda Hart and model Miranda Kerr.

Mirella
(alt. Mireille, Mirela)
Latin, meaning 'admirable'. Opera singer Mirella Freni is known in Italy as being one of the finest in her art.

Miriam
Hebrew, meaning 'bitter'. Also the name of a prophetess in the Bible. Miriam Margolyes is a popular British BAFTA-winning character actor.

Mirta
Spanish, meaning 'crown of thorns'.

Missy
Shortened form of Melissa, meaning 'bee'. Famous Missys include musician Missy Elliot, singer Missy Higgins, and performer Missy Malone.

Misty
(alt. Misti)
English, meaning 'mist'. Misty Copeland was the first black ballerina to become a principal dancer with a national ballet company.

Mitzi
German, meaning 'bitter'. Actor Mitzi Gaynor appeared in *South Pacific*.

Miu
Japanese, meaning 'beautiful feather'. Also the name of an endangered language spoken in Papua New Guinea.

Moana
Maori, meaning 'ocean'. Made famous by the Disney animation of the same name.

Moira
(alt. Maira)
Irish, meaning 'bitter'. Famous Moiras include actor Moira Brooker, ballet dancer Moira Shearer and news presenter Moira Stuart.

Molly
(alt. Mollie)
American, meaning 'bitter'. Famous Mollys include actors Molly Ringwald and Molly Sims.

Mona
Irish Gaelic, meaning 'aristocratic'. A character from the children's television programme *Mona the Vampire*.

Monica
(alt. Monika, Monique)
Latin, meaning 'adviser'. Famous Monicas include singer Monica, infamous White House intern Monica Lewinsky and tennis pro Monica Seles.

Monroe
Gaelic, meaning 'mouth of the river Rotha'. Usually associated with Marilyn Monroe.

Montserrat
(alt. Monserrate)

Spanish, from the town of the same name. Opera singer Montserrat Caballe is known for her work in the bel canto technique, and for the song 'Barcelona' with Freddie Mercury.

Morag

Scottish, meaning 'star of the sea'. Also the pet name of a monster that supposedly inhabits Loch Morar in Scotland.

Morgan
(alt. Morgann)

Welsh, meaning 'great and bright'. Used for both girls and boys.

Moriah

Hebrew, meaning 'the Lord is my teacher'. Also the name of a mountain mentioned in the Bible.

Morwenna
(alt. Modwenna)

Welsh, meaning 'maiden'. Morwenna Banks is a British comedy actor, writer and producer. She is known to toddlers everywhere as the voice of Mummy Pig in *Peppa Pig*.

Moselle
(alt. Mozell, Mozella, Mozelle)

Hebrew, meaning 'saviour'. Also the name of a river and a German wine.

Mulan

Chinese, meaning 'wood orchid'. Usually associated with the protagonist from the Disney film *Mulan*.

Munin

Scandinavian, meaning 'good memory'.

Muriel

Irish Gaelic, meaning 'sea-bright'. Author Muriel Spark was known for her novel *The Prime of Miss Jean Brodie*.

Myfanwy

Welsh, meaning 'my little lovely one'. The name originally appeared in a song called 'Myfanwy' by Joseph Parry.

Myleene

English, from the Latin Melaine meaning 'dark as night'. Associated with musician and presenter Myleene Klass.

Myra

Latin, meaning 'scented oil'. Famous Myras include pioneering lawyer Myra Bradwell and pianist Myra Hess, and also Moors murderer Myra Hindley.

Myrna
(alt. Mirna)

Irish Gaelic, meaning 'tender and beloved'. Actor Myrna Fahey appeared in Walt Disney's *Zorro*.

Myrtle

Irish, from the flowering shrub of the same name. Usually associated with the character of Myrtle Wilson from F. Scott Fitzgerald's novel *The Great Gatsby*.

Girls' names

Nadia
(alt. Nadya)
Russian, meaning 'hope'. Romanian Nadia Elena Comăneci was the first female Olympic gymnast to be awarded a perfect score of 10, and has three gold medals. Nadia Petrova is a tennis pro and Nadia Sawalha is a TV presenter and actor.

Nadine
French, meaning 'hope'. Also the title of a Chuck Berry song. Nadine Gordimer is a South African writer and activist who won the Nobel Prize for literature.

Nahara
Aramaic, meaning 'light'.

Nahla
(alt. Nala, Nalo)
Arabic, meaning 'first drink of water', and Sanskrit meaning 'hollow reed'. Made popular by the character from Disney's *The Lion King*.

Naima
Arabic, meaning 'water nymph'. Naima Belkhiata is a singer with the group Honeyz.

Nakia
Egyptian, meaning 'pure'.

Nalani
Hawaiian, meaning 'serenity of the skies'.

Nan
(alt. Nanna, Nannie)
Hebrew, meaning 'grace'. A character in Louisa May Alcott's *Little Women*.

Nancy
(alt. Nanci, Nancie)
Hebrew, meaning 'grace'. Nancy Reagan was a First Lady of the USA and anti-drug advocate who began her career as a film actor.

Nanette
(alt. Nannette)

French, meaning 'grace'. *No, No Nanette* is a musical comedy from the 1920s. Nanette Lepor is an American fashion designer and Nanette Newman is a British actor.

Naomi
(alt. Naoma, Noemi)

Hebrew, meaning 'pleasant'. Found in the Bible. Naomi Campbell is one of the original five supermodels.

Narcissa

Greek, meaning 'daffodil'. Narcissa Whitman, a missionary, became one of the most famous women of the early American West.

Nastasia

Greek, meaning 'resurrection'. Can also mean 'born on Christmas Day'.

Natalie
(alt. Natalee, Natalia, Natalya, Nathalie)

Latin, meaning 'birth day'. From the Latin name Natalia, meaning 'Christmas Day'. Its popularity increased in the USA after the 1940s due to actor Natalie Wood, who was the daughter of Russian immigrants.

Natasha
(alt. Natasa)

Russian, meaning 'birth day'. A character in Leo Tolstoy's *War and Peace*. Used in the English-speaking world only since the 20th century.

Natividad

Spanish, meaning 'Christmas'.

Neda

English, meaning 'wealthy'. Neda was also an Arcadian nymph who nursed the infant Zeus.

Nedra

English, meaning 'underground'.

Neema

Swahili, meaning 'born of prosperity'.

Neka

Native American, meaning 'goose'.

Nell
(alt. Nelda, Nell, Nella, Nellie, Nelly)

Shortened form of Eleanor, meaning 'light'. May have roots in old German *nelle*, meaning 'crown of the head', perhaps suggesting an obstinate person.

Nemi

Italian, from the lake of the same name.

Neoma

Greek, meaning 'new moon'.

Nereida

Spanish, meaning 'sea nymph'. A mermaid in Greek mythology.

Nerissa

Greek, meaning 'sea nymph'. The name of Portia's waiting woman in Shakespeare's *The Merchant of Venice*.

Nettie
(alt. Neta)
Shortened form of Henrietta, meaning 'ruler of the house'.

Neva
Spanish, meaning 'snowy'.

Nevaeh
American, meaning 'heaven'. The name Nevaeh is the word 'Heaven' spelled backwards. May also be linked with Neva, Spanish for 'snowy'.

Neytiri
Na'vi, meaning 'princess'. From the *Avatar* film series.

Nhung
Vietnamese, meaning 'velvet'.

Niamh
(alt. Neave, Neve)
Gaelic, meaning 'brightness'. In Irish mythology, Niamh was a goddess, the daughter of the god of the sea and a queen of the land of eternal youth.

Nicola
(alt. Nichola, Nichole, Nicole, Nicolette, Nicolle, Nikole; abbrev. Nicky, Nicki, Nikki)
Greek, meaning 'victory of the people'. Nicola is a boys' name in Italy, but became widely used in England and Germany as a girls' name, perhaps due to the -a ending of the name. Nicole Kidman is an Oscar-winning Australian actor. Nicole Farhi is a French fashion designer and sculptor.

Nidia
Spanish, meaning 'graceful'.

Nigella
Irish Gaelic, meaning 'champion'. Nigella Lawson is a TV chef and author, famous for her sensual style of cookery.

Nikita
Greek, meaning 'unconquered'. Popular in Russia. Also the one-word title of a song by Elton John, a film and a US TV series.

Nila
Egyptian, meaning 'Nile'.

Nilda
German, meaning 'battle woman'.

Nimra
Arabic, meaning 'number'. Also a name of Punjabi origin, meaning 'humble'.

Nina
Spanish, meaning 'girl'. One of the three ships used by Christopher Columbus on his first voyage. Nina Conti is a comedian and ventriloquist and Nina Simone was a jazz singing legend and civil rights campaigner.

Nissa
Hebrew, meaning 'sign'.

Nita
Spanish, meaning 'gracious'.

Nixie
German, meaning 'water sprite'.

Noel
(alt. Noelle)

French, meaning 'Christmas'. Noel is used most commonly for boys; Noelle is the feminine variant.

Nola

Irish Gaelic, meaning 'white shoulder'. Also a city and area in Italy.

Nona

Latin, meaning 'ninth'.

Nora
(alt. Norah)

Shortened form of Eleanor, meaning 'light', used in its own right. Nora Roberts is an American author who has written over 200 romance novels, some under pseudonyms.

Noreen
(alt. Norine)

Irish, meaning 'light'. Professor Noreen Murray was a highly regarded molecular geneticist who helped develop a vaccine against hepatitis B.

Norma

Latin, meaning 'pattern'. In Bellini's tragic opera of the same name, Norma is a druidess at the time of the Roman occupation of England. Norma Jeane was the real name of Marilyn Monroe.

Normandie
(alt. Normandy)

French, from the province of the same name.

Novia

Latin, meaning 'new'.

Nuala

Irish Gaelic, meaning 'white shoulder'. A popular name in Ireland.

Nydia

Latin, meaning 'nest'.

Nyimbo

Swahili, meaning 'song'.

Nyoko

Swahili, meaning 'snake'. Made popular by the 'Nyoka the Jungle Girl' comic book series.

Nysa
(alt. Nyssa)

Greek, meaning 'ambition'. A mountainous district in Greek mythology.

Girls' names

Oceana
(alt. Ocean, Océane, Ocie)
Greek, meaning 'ocean'.

Octavia
Latin, meaning 'eighth'. Sister
to Caesar and wife to Antony in
Shakespeare's *Antony and Cleopatra*.

Oda
(alt. Odie)
Shortened form of Odessa, meaning
'long voyage'. Also Germanic,
meaning 'wealth' or 'inheritance'.

Odele
(alt. Odell)
English, meaning 'woad hill'. Woad is
a plant used as a natural blue dye.

Odelia
Hebrew, meaning 'I will praise the
Lord'. Also an eighth-century French
saint.

Odessa
(alt. Odyssey)
Greek, meaning 'long voyage'. A
place in the Ukraine, known as the
pearl of the Black Sea.

Odette
(alt. Odetta)
French, meaning 'wealthy'. In the
famous ballet *Swan Lake*, Odette is
the good swan.

Odile
(alt. Odilia)
French, meaning 'prospers in battle'.
The evil black swan in the famous
ballet *Swan Lake*.

Odina
Feminine form of Odin, from the
Nordic god of the same name,
meaning 'creative inspiration'.

Oksana

Russian, meaning 'praise to God'. Famous Oksanas include Oksana Baiul, a Ukrainian Olympic figure-skater; Oksana Grigorieva, a Russian pianist; and a character in the hit TV series *Killing Eve*.

Ola

(alt. Olie)

Greek, meaning 'man's defender'.

Olena

(alt. Olene)

Russian, meaning 'light'.

Olga

Russian, meaning 'holy'. The first Russian female ruler, later canonised as the first Russian saint of the Orthodox Church.

Oliana

American, meaning 'the Lord has answered'.

Olivia

(alt. Olive, Olivev, Oliviana, Olivié; abbrev. Ollie)

Latin, meaning 'olive'. Has featured in the Top 10 names for girls in England for several years now, including at number one.

Olwen

Welsh, meaning 'white footprint'. Olwen Hufton is a British historian of early modern Europe, women's history and social history.

Olympia

(alt. Olimpia)

Greek, meaning 'from Mount Olympus'. A sanctuary of ancient Greece, known as the site of the Olympic Games in classical times.

Oma

(alt. Omie)

Arabic, meaning 'leader'. In German, oma often refers to 'grandmother'.

Omyra

Latin, meaning 'scented oil'.

Ondine

French, meaning 'wave of water'. Also the name of a French play.

Oneida

(abbrev. Ona, Onnie)

Native American, meaning 'long awaited'. The Oneida Indians were believed to have emerged as a tribe in the 14th century.

Onyx

Latin, meaning 'veined gem'. A precious stone.

Oona

(alt. Oonagh)

Irish, meaning 'unity'.

Opal

Sanskrit, meaning 'gem'. A gemstone made of this mineral, noted for its rich iridescence.

Ophelia
(alt. Ofelia, Ophélie)
Greek, meaning 'help'. Lead character from Shakespeare's play *Hamlet*.

Oprah
Hebrew, meaning 'young deer'. Most often associated with Oprah Winfrey.

Orabela
(abbrev. Ora)
Latin, meaning 'prayer'.

Oralie
(alt. Oralia)
French, meaning 'golden'. Oralia Dominguez is a Mexican opera singer.

Orane
French, meaning 'rising'.

Orchid
Greek, from the flower of the same name.

Oriana
(alt. Oriane)
Latin, meaning 'dawning'. Oriana was the nickname for Queen Elizabeth I.

Orla
(alt. Orlaith, Orly)
Irish Gaelic, meaning 'golden lady'. Orla Kiely is an Irish fashion designer.

Orlean
French, meaning 'plum'. Orleans is a city in France.

Ornelia
Italian, meaning 'flowering ash tree'.

Orsa
(alt. Osia, Ossie)
Latin, meaning 'bear'.

Otthid
Greek, meaning 'prospers in battle'.

Ottilie
(alt. Ottie)
French, meaning 'prospers in battle'. Ottilie Metzger was a German opera singer well known in the early 1900s.

Ouida
French, meaning 'renowned in battle'. Pseudonym of the English novelist Maria Louise Ramé, known for her extravagant melodramatic romances.

Oyintsa
Native American, meaning 'white duck'.

Ozette
Native American, from the village of the same name.

P

Girls' names

Pacifica
(alt. Pacifika)

Spanish, meaning 'peaceful'. Pacifica Fernández was once Costa Rica's first lady; she also designed the Costa Rican flag.

Padma

Sanskrit, meaning 'lotus'. A major Buddhist symbol. Padma Lakshmi is an Indian-born American chef, cookbook author, model and TV presenter.

Paige
(alt. Page)

French, meaning 'serving boy'.

Paisley

Scottish, from the town of the same name.

Palma
(alt. Palmira)

Latin, meaning 'palm tree'.

Paloma

Spanish, meaning 'dove'. Paloma Picasso is the youngest daughter of artist Pablo Picasso. Singer Paloma Faith is known for her eccentric style.

Pamela
(alt. Pamala, Pamella, Pamla; abbrev. Pam)

Greek, meaning 'all honey'. Pamela Stephenson is an actor and comedian turned clinical psychologist and author. Pamela (P.L.) Travers is the author of Mary Poppins.

Pandora

Greek, meaning 'all gifted'. Also from the Greek myth, Pandora was given a box containing all the evils of the world, not to be opened. Now also commonly associated with the jewellery company.

Pangiota

Greek, meaning 'all is holy'. Comes from a Greek epithet widely used in reference to the Virgin Mary.

Paniz
Persian, meaning 'candy'.

Pansy
French, from the flower of the same name. Pansy Potter is a strong girl character in comic *The Beano* and Pansy Parkinson appears in the *Harry Potter* series.

Paprika
English, meaning 'spice'.

Paradisa
(alt. Paradis)
Greek, meaning 'garden orchard'.

Paris
(alt. Parisa)
Greek, from the mythological hero of the same name. Also from the city. Paris Hilton is the hotel heiress and socialite.

Parker
English, meaning 'park keeper'.

Parthenia
Greek, meaning 'virginal'.

Parthenope
Greek, from the mythological Siren of the same name. Parthenope Nightingale was the elder sister of Florence Nightingale.

Parvati
Sanskrit, meaning 'daughter of the mountain'. The Hindu goddess of love and devotion.

Pascale
French, meaning 'Easter'.

Patience
French, meaning 'the state of being patient'. A Shakespearean name. Patience Wheatcroft was a respected journalist, and is now in the House of Lords.

Patricia
(alt. Patrice; abbrev. Pat, Patsy, Patti, Pattie, Patty)
Latin, meaning 'noble'. Patricia Routledge and Patricia Hodge are English actors. Patricia Neal was an American actor whose birth name was Patsy Louise Neal.

Paula
Latin, meaning 'small'. Paula Radcliffe is a British long-distance runner, and current world record holder for the marathon.

Pauline
(alt. Paulette, Paulina)
Latin, meaning 'small'. The name of a British opera.

Paxton
Latin, meaning 'town of peace'.

Paz
Spanish, meaning 'peace'.

Pazia
Hebrew, meaning 'golden'.

Peace
English, meaning 'peace'.

Peaches

English, from the fruit of the same name. Rarely used. Peaches Geldof was the most famous bearer of the name.

Pearl
(alt. Pearle, Pearlie, Perla)

Latin, meaning 'pale gemstone'. Pearl Buck was an American author.

Peggy
(alt. Peggie)

Greek, meaning 'pearl'. Peggy Parish was the author of the children's story series Amelia Bedelia.

Pelia

Hebrew, meaning 'marvel of God'.

Penelope
(abbrev. Penny, Penni, Pennie)

Greek, meaning 'bobbin worker'. In Homer's *Odyssey*, Penelope is the faithful wife of Odysseus.

Peony

Greek, from the flower of the same name.

Perdita

Latin, meaning 'lost'. Perdita is one of the heroines of William Shakespeare's play *The Winter's Tale*.

Peri
(alt. Perri)

Hebrew, meaning 'outcome'. In Persian mythology, the Peri are spirits who have been denied paradise until they have done penance.

Perry
(alt. Perrie)

French, meaning 'pear tree'. Also an English alcoholic drink made from pears. Perrie Edwards is part of the pop group Little Mix.

Persephone

Greek, meaning 'bringer of destruction'. In Greek mythology, Queen of the Underworld.

Petra
(alt. Petrina)

Greek, meaning 'rock'. City in Jordan dating back to the time of Jesus and the Apostles.

Petula

Latin, meaning 'to seek'. Petula Clark is an English singer, actor and composer.

Petunia

Greek, from the flower of the same name.

Phaedra

Greek, meaning 'bright'.

Philippa
(abbrev. Pippa, Pippie)

Greek, meaning 'lover of horses'. Philippa Foot was a 20th-century philosopher and pioneer in the field of modern ethics.

Philomena
(alt. Philoma)

Greek, meaning 'loved one'. Also a Catholic saint.

Phoebe

Greek, meaning 'shining and brilliant'. In Greek mythology, Phoebe was one of the original Titans and is associated with the moon.

Phoenix

Greek, meaning 'dark red'. In ancient Greek mythology, a phoenix is a bird that has the power to regenerate itself from its ashes.

Phyllida

Greek, meaning 'leafy bough'. Phyllida Lloyd is a British director, best known for her work in theatre and as the director of *Mamma Mia!* and *The Iron Lady*.

Phyllis
(alt. Phillia, Phylis)
Greek, meaning 'leafy bough'.

Pia

Latin, meaning 'pious'.

Piera

Italian, meaning 'rock'.

Pilar

Spanish, meaning 'pillar'. In Latin America, Nuestra Señora del Pilar (Our Lady of the Pillar), the name given to the Blessed Virgin Mary.

Piper

English, meaning 'pipe player'. Piper Laurie, an American actor, was born Rosetta Jacobs. Piper Kerman is the real-life inspiration behond the character Piper Chapman in hit TV series *Orange is the New Black*.

Plum

Latin, from the fruit of the same name.

Polly

Hebrew, meaning 'bitter'. A nickname for 'Mary'. Polly Dunbar is a British author-illustrator.

Pomona

Latin, meaning 'apple'. Pomona was a goddess of fruitful abundance in ancient Roman religion and myth.

Poppy

Latin, from the flower of the same name. Poppy Delevingne is a British socialite and model.

Portia
(alt. Porsha)
Latin, meaning 'from the Portia clan'. The heroine in Shakespeare's *The Merchant of Venice*.

Posy

English, meaning 'small flower'. Posy Hawthorne is a character in *The Hunger Games* series.

Precious

Latin, meaning 'of great worth'.

Priela

Hebrew, meaning 'fruit of God'.

Primavera

Italian, meaning 'springtime'. Also the name of a painting by Botticelli.

Primrose

English, meaning 'first rose'.

Princess

English, meaning 'daughter of the monarch'.

Priscilla

(alt. Prisca, Priscila)

Latin, meaning 'ancient'. Priscilla Wakefield was an 18th-century Quaker educational writer and philanthropist. Priscilla Presley is an actor, businesswoman and was the wife of Elvis Presley.

Priya

Hindi, meaning 'loved one'.

Prudence

(abbrev. Pru, Prue, Prudie)

Latin, meaning 'caution'. Known as the mother of all virtues.

Prunella

Latin, meaning 'small plum'. Prunella Clough was a prominent British artist and Prunella Scales is an actor best known for playing Sybil in *Fawlty Towers*.

Psyche

Greek, meaning 'breath'. In Greek mythology, the wife of Eros. Also the name of an opera.

Girls' names

Qiana
(alt. Qianah, Qiania, Qyana, Qianne)
American, meaning 'gracious'. Qiana
Chase is an American model.

Qiturah
Arabic, meaning 'incense'.

Queen
(alt. Queenie)
English, meaning 'queen'.

Quiana
American, meaning 'silky'. Quiana
Grant is an American model.

Quincy
(alt. Quincey)
French, meaning 'estate of the fifth
son'. Also used as a boys' name.

Quinn
Irish Gaelic, meaning 'counsel'.
Quinn Fabray is a character from the
American musical comedy-drama
series *Glee*.

Quintessa
Latin, meaning 'creative'.

Girls' names

Rachel
(alt. Rachael, Rachelle)
Hebrew, meaning 'ewe'. Rachel is a figure in the Bible. Famous Rachels include actors Rachel Weisz and Rachel Bilson, and the character of Rachel Green from *Friends*.

Radhika
(alt. Raadhika)
Sanskrit, meaning 'prosperous'. Raadhika Sarathkumar is one of Bollywood's most prolific actors and producers.

Rae
(alt. Ray)
Shortened form of Rachel, meaning 'ewe'. Rae Armantrout is known for her poetry and academic writing.

Rafferty
Irish, meaning 'abundance'. More commonly found as a surname.

Rahima
Arabic, meaning 'compassionate'.

Raina
(alt. Rain, Raine, Rainey, Rayne)
Latin, meaning 'queen'.

Raisa
(alt. Raissa)
Yiddish, meaning 'rose'. Extremely popular name in Russia, particularly as Mikhail Gorbachev's wife was called Raisa.

Raleigh
(alt. Rayleigh)
Old English, meaning 'deer's meadow'.

Rama
(alt. Ramey, Ramya)
Hebrew, meaning 'exalted'. Also one of the god Vishnu's avatars in the Hindu faith.

Ramona
(alt. Romona)

Spanish, meaning 'wise guardian'. Also the *Ramona* children's novels and the film *Ramona and Beezus*, by Beverly Cleary.

Ramsey
(alt. Ramsay)

Old English, meaning 'wild garlic island'. Can be used for girls and boys.

Rana
(alt. Rania, Rayna)

Arabic, meaning 'beautiful thing'.

Rani

Sanskrit, meaning 'queen'. Also a character from *Doctor Who*.

Raphaela
(alt. Rafaela, Raffaella)

Spanish, meaning 'God has healed'. Feminine form of Raphael, name of the painter and artist.

Raquel
(alt. Racquel)

Hebrew, meaning 'ewe'. Famous Raquels include actor Racquel Welch and the character in *Only Fools and Horses*.

Rashida

Turkish, meaning 'righteous'. Rashida Jones is an actor.

Raven
(alt. Ravyn)

English, from the black bird of the same name. Raven-Symoné is an actor often known as just Raven.

Razia

Arabic, meaning 'contented'. Razia Sultan was the only female ruler of the Sultanate Delhi and of the Mughal period of Indian history, during the 13th century.

Reagan
(alt. Reagen, Regan)

Irish Gaelic, meaning 'descendant of Riagán'.

Reba

Shortened form of Rebecca, meaning 'joined'. Reba McEntire is an American country singer.

Rebecca
(alt. Rebekah; abbrev. Becca, Becky, Becs, Beka, Bex, Reb)

Hebrew, meaning 'joined'. Rebecca is a figure in the Bible. Also a classic novel by Daphne Du Maurier. An enduringly popular name.

Reese

Welsh, meaning 'fiery and zealous'. Actor Reese Witherspoon starred in *Legally Blonde* and *Walk the Line*.

Regina

Latin, meaning 'queen'. Famous Reginas include actors Regina King and Regina Hall and the character of Regina George in the film *Mean Girls*.

Reiko

Japanese, meaning 'thankful one'.

Reina
(alt. Rey, Reyna, Rheyna)

Spanish, meaning 'queen'.

Rena
(alt. Reena)

Hebrew, meaning 'serene'.

Renata

Latin, meaning 'reborn'. Renata Tebaldi was one of the best-loved post-war opera singers.

Rene

Greek, meaning 'peace'. Actor Rene Russo appeared in *Get Shorty*, *The Thomas Crown Affair* and the *Thor* series.

Renée
(alt. Renae, Renee)

French, meaning 'reborn'. Famous Renées include actors Renée Zellweger and Renee Roberts, and one half of the singing duo Renée and Renato.

Renira

A rare name with no clear agreed origin. Used, but rarely, in a range of countries including England and Scotland, the USA, Germany, Brazil and Hungary.

Renita

Latin, meaning 'resistant'. Most commonly used in the USA.

Reshma
(alt. Resha)

Sanskrit, meaning 'silk'.

Reta
(alt. Retha, Retta)

Shortened form of Margaret, meaning 'pearl'. In Portuguese the name also means 'straight'.

Rhea

Greek, meaning 'Earth'. Also the name of the mother of the gods in ancient Greek mythology.

Rheta

Greek, meaning 'eloquent speaker'.

Rhiannon
(alt. Reanna, Reanne, Rhian, Rhianna)

Welsh, meaning 'witch'. Also the name of the mother of Pryderi, King of Dyfed, in Welsh mythology.

Rhoda

Greek, meaning 'rose'. Found in the Bible.

Rhona

Nordic, meaning 'rough island'. Popular in Scotland. Rhona Martin represented Britain in curling at the 2002 Salt Lake City Olympics. Rhona Cameron is a comedian.

Rhonda
(alt. Ronda)

Welsh, meaning 'noisy'.

Ría
(alt. Rie, Riya)

Shortened form of Victoria, meaning 'victor'.

Ricki
(alt. Rieko, Rika, Rikki)

Shortened form of Frederica, meaning 'peaceful ruler'. Actor and presenter Ricki Lake hosted a talk show bearing her name for a decade.

Riley

Irish Gaelic, meaning 'courageous'. Used equally for both boys and girls.

Rilla

German, meaning 'small brook'.

Rima

Arabic, meaning 'antelope'. Rima the Jungle Girl is the fictional heroine of novel *Green Mansions* and was briefly a comic book character also.

Riona

Irish Gaelic, meaning 'like a queen'. Sometimes used as a spelling alternative to Fiona.

Ripley

English, meaning 'shouting man's meadow'.

Risa

Latin, meaning 'laughter'. More commonly used in Japanese- and Spanish-speaking cultures.

Rita

Shortened form of Margaret, meaning 'pearl'. Famous Ritas include actors Rita Hayworth and Rita Moreno and singer Rita Coolidge.

River
(alt. Riviera)

English, from 'river'. Used as both a boys' and a girls' name, sometimes in the plural.

Roberta
(abbrev. Robbie, Robi, Roby, Bobby, Bobbie)

English, meaning 'bright fame'. Singer Roberta Flack is best known for the songs 'The First Time Ever I Saw Your Face' and 'Killing Me Softly with His Song'.

Robin
(alt. Robbin, Robyn)

English, meaning 'bright fame'. Used slightly more often for boys than for girls. Famous Robins include actor Robin Wright Penn and singer Robyn.

Rochelle
(alt. Richelle, Rochel)

French, meaning 'little rock'. Singer and presenter Rochelle Humes featured in S Club 8 and The Saturdays.

Rogue

French, meaning 'beggar'. A character from the *X-Men* comic series.

Rohina
(alt. Rohini)

Sanskrit, meaning 'sandalwood'.

Roisin

Irish Gaelic, meaning 'little rose'. Singer Roisin Murphy was one half of group Moloko before going solo.

Roja

Spanish, meaning 'red-haired lady'. The name also means 'rose' in Tamil.

Rolanda

German, meaning 'renowned land'.

Roma

Italian, meaning 'Rome'. Also the name of an ancient Roman deity, and of a group of nomadic European people.

Romaine
(alt. Romina)

French, meaning 'from Rome'.

Romola
(alt. Romilda, Romily)

Latin, meaning 'Roman woman'. Actor Romola Garai appeared in films including *Atonement* and *Emma*.

Romy

Shortened form of Rosemary, meaning 'dew of the sea', and often the German variation. Actor Romy Rosemont is known for her TV roles in *Prison Break*, *Grey's Anatomy* and *Glee*.

Rona
(alt. Ronia, Ronja, Ronna)

Nordic, meaning 'rough island'. Also the name of two Scottish islands, North Rona and South Rona.

Ronnie
(alt. Roni, Ronni)

English, meaning 'strong counsel'. Impressionist and actor Ronni Ancona has also appeared on TV panel shows.

Roro

Indonesian, meaning 'nobility'. Sometimes used as a nickname for Ro- names (Rosa, Rosalind, etc).

Rosa

Italian, meaning 'rose'. Activist Rosa Parks is credited with being the 'First Lady of American civil rights' after she refused to give up her seat to a white passenger on a bus in 1955.

Rosabel
(alt. Rosabella)

Contraction of Rose and Belle, meaning 'beautiful rose'. Most commonly used in the USA.

Rosalie
(alt. Rosale, Rosalia, Rosalina)

French, meaning 'rose garden'. Actor Andie MacDowell's birth name is Rosalie.

Rosalind
(alt. Rosalinda)

Spanish, meaning 'pretty rose'. A character in Shakespeare's *As You Like It*.

Rosalyn
(alt. Rosaleen, Rosaline, Roselyn)

Contraction of Rose and Lynn, meaning 'pretty rose'. Also a song by The Pretty Things, which was later recorded by David Bowie.

Rosamund
(alt. Rosamond)

German, meaning 'renowned protector'. Famous Rosamunds include actor Rosamund Pike, author Rosamunde Pilcher and the long-time mistress of Henry II, Rosamund Clifford.

Rose

Latin, from the flower of the same name. Famous Roses include actors Rose Byrne and Rose McGowan and the character of Rose DeWitt Bukater from the film *Titanic*.

Roseanne

(alt. Rosana, Rosann, Rosanna, Rosanne, Roseann, Roseanna)

Combination of Rose and Anne, meaning 'graceful rose'.

Rosemary

(alt. Rosemarie; abbrev. Ros, Rosy, Rosie, Romy)

Latin, meaning 'dew of the sea'. Rosemary is the title of several songs. Famous Rosies include actors Rosie O'Donnell and Rosie Perez, and supermodel Rosie Huntington-Whiteley.

Rosita

Spanish, meaning 'rose'. A character in *Sesame Street*.

Rowena

(alt. Rowan)

Welsh, meaning 'slender and fair'. In ancient British mythology, Rowena was a powerful and beautiful seductress.

Roxanne

(alt. Roxana, Roxane, Roxanna; abbrev. Roxie, Roxey, Roxy)

Persian, meaning 'dawn'. A song by The Police. Famous Roxies include the character of Roxie Hart from the musical *Chicago*, inventor Roxey Ann Caplin, and the band Roxy Music.

Rubina

(alt. Rubena)

Hebrew, meaning 'behold, a son'. Also a tropical plant.

Ruby

(alt. Rubi, Rubie)

English, meaning 'red gemstone'. Associated with the comedian Ruby Wax, or the songs 'Ruby Tuesday' by The Rolling Stones and 'Ruby' by Kaiser Chiefs.

Rusty

American, meaning 'red-headed'. Used for girls and, more commonly, boys.

Ruth

(alt. Ruthe, Ruthie)

Hebrew, meaning 'friend and companion'. A prominent figure in the Bible.

Girls' names

Saba
(alt. Sabah)

Greek, meaning 'from Sheba'. Also the name of a small Caribbean island.

Sabina
(alt. Sabine)

Latin, meaning 'from the Sabine tribe'. Sabina was also the name given to certain women of political standing in ancient Rome.

Sabrina

Latin, meaning 'the River Severn'. Also a film starring Audrey Hepburn, and the title character of the sitcom *Sabrina, the Teenage Witch*.

Sadella

American, meaning 'fairytale princess'. More commonly used in the USA.

Sadie
(alt. Sade, Sadye)

Hebrew, meaning 'princess'. Famous Sadies include actor and businesswoman Sadie Frost, actor Sadie Miller and academic pioneer Sadie Tanner Mossell Alexander.

Saffron
(alt. Saffie)

English, from the reddish-yellow spice of the same name. Saffie is a character from ther TV series and films *Absolutely Fabulous*.

Safiyya
(alt. Safiya)

Arabic, meaning 'sincere friend'. Also the name of one of Muhammad's wives.

Sage
(alt. Saga, Saige)

Latin, meaning 'wise and healthy'. Also the name of a herb.

Sahara
Arabic, meaning 'desert'.

Sakura
Japanese, meaning 'cherry blossom'.

Sally
(alt. Sallie)

Hebrew, meaning 'princess'. Famous Sallys include actors Sally Field and Sally Whittaker and athlete Sally Gunnell.

Salma
Arabic, meaning 'peaceful'; Persian, meaning 'sweetheart'. Mexican-American actor Salma Hayek is a star of both film and TV.

Salome
(alt. Salma)

Hebrew, meaning 'peace'. Also found in the Bible.

Samantha
(abbrev. Sam, Sammie, Sammy)

Hebrew, meaning 'told by God'. Famous Samanthas include actors Samantha Morton and Samantha Bond.

Samara
(alt. Samaria, Samira)

Hebrew, meaning 'under God's rule'. Also the name of several places in Russia.

Sanaa
Arabic, meaning 'brilliance'. Also the capital of Yemen.

Sandra
(alt. Saundra; abbrev. Sandi, Sandy)

Shortened form of Alexandra, meaning 'defender of mankind'. Famous Sandras include actor Sandra Bullock, and Sandy is the main female character in the film Grease.

Sangeetha
Hindi, meaning 'musical'. Actor Sangeetha Arvind Krish is known in Bollywood simply as Sangeetha.

Sanna
(alt. Saniya, Sanne, Sanni)

Hebrew, meaning 'lily'. Also sometimes used as a shortened version of Susanna.

Santana
(alt. Santina)

Spanish, meaning 'holy'. Usually associated with the (male) guitar legend Carlos Santana.

Saoirse
Irish, meaning 'freedom'. Pronounced 'Ser-sha', Irish-American actor Saoirse Ronan has been nominated for numerous awards.

Sapphire
(alt. Saphira)

Hebrew, meaning 'blue gemstone'. Usually associated with the blue gem popular in jewellery.

Sarah
(alt. Sara, Sarai, Sariah)

Hebrew, meaning 'princess'. Found in the Bible. A particularly popular name in the 1960s.

Sasha
(alt. Sacha, Sascha)

Russian, meaning 'defender of mankind'. Used for both girls and boys. Sasha is one of Barack Obama's daughters.

Saskia
(alt. Saskie)

Dutch, meaning 'the Saxon people'. In Danish the name also means 'valley of light'.

Savannah
(alt. Savanah, Savanna, Savina)

Spanish, meaning 'treeless'. Also one of Queen Elizabeth II's great-grandchildren, Savannah Phillips.

Scarlett
(alt. Scarlet)

English, meaning 'scarlet'. Usually associated with the character of Scarlett O'Hara, from the novel and film Gone with the Wind, or actor Scarlett Johansson.

Scout

French, meaning 'to listen'. The main female character from the classic novel To Kill a Mockingbird, by Harper Lee.

Sedona
(alt. Sedna)

Spanish, from the city of the same name. Also the name of a city in Arizona, USA.

Selah
(alt. Sela)

Hebrew, meaning 'cliff'. Also a phrase used in the Hebrew Bible meaning 'stop and listen'.

Selby

English, meaning 'manor village'.

Selena
(alt. Salena, Salima, Salina, Selene, Selina)

Greek, meaning 'moon goddess'. Famous Selenas include singers Selena Gomez and Selena Quintanilla-Perez (known simply as Selena) and actor Selena Royle.

Selma

German, meaning 'Godly helmet'. Versatile actor Selma Blair has starred in a range of film genres as well as Hollywood hits.

Seneca

Native American, meaning 'from the Seneca tribe'. Also the name of a prominent ancient Roman philosopher, Seneca the Younger.

Sephora

Hebrew, meaning 'bird'; Greek, meaning 'beauty'.

September

Latin, meaning 'seventh month'.

Seraphina
(alt. Serafina, Seraphia, Seraphine)
Hebrew, meaning 'ardent'.
St Serafina was an Italian woman whose illness and suffering contributed to her strong faith.

Seren
Welsh, meaning 'star'.

Serena
(alt. Sarina, Sereana)
Latin, meaning 'tranquil'. Serena Williams has dominated women's tennis in the 21st century.

Serenity
Latin, meaning 'serene'. Also a sci-fi film.

Shania
(alt. Shaina, Shana, Shaniya)
Hebrew, meaning 'beautiful'. Shania Twain is the Canadian country/pop singer-songwriter whose real first name is Eilleen.

Shanice
American, meaning 'from Africa'. Singer Shanice is known for songs including 'I Love Your Smile'.

Shaniqua
(alt. Shanika)
English, adapted from the Swahili word Shanika, meaning 'God is gracious'. More commonly used in the USA.

Shanna
English, meaning 'old'. There is a comic book character called *Shanna the She-Devil* and Shanna Zolman is a professional basketball player.

Shannon
(alt. Shannan, Shanon)
Irish Gaelic, meaning 'old and ancient'. The name is believed to be a reference to Sionna, who was a goddess in ancient Irish mythology.

Shantal
(alt. Shantel, Shantell)
French, meaning 'stone'. Often used as a spelling alternative to Chantal.

Shanti
(alt. Shantih)
Hindi, meaning 'peaceful'. Also mentioned in T.S. Eliot's poem *The Waste Land*.

Sharlene
German, meaning 'man'. Often used as a spelling alternative to Charlene.

Sharon
(alt. Sharen, Sharona, Sharron, Sharyn)
Hebrew, meaning 'a plain'. Famous Sharons include swimmer Sharon Davies, presenter Sharon Osbourne and actor Sharon Stone.

Shasta
American, from the mountain of the same name. Also the name of a Native American tribe.

Shauna
(alt. Shawna)

Irish, meaning 'the Lord is gracious'. More commonly used in the USA.

Shayla
(alt. Shaylie, Shayna, Sheyla)

Irish, meaning 'blind'. Shayla Worley is an American gymnast.

Shea

Irish Gaelic, meaning 'from the fairy fort'. Usually associated with the tree and the nut that goes into creating shea butter.

Sheena

Irish, meaning 'the Lord is gracious'. Singer Sheena Easton rocketed to fame when she featured in an early British reality TV show, *The Big Time*, in the late 1970s.

Sheila
(alt. Shelia)

Irish, meaning 'blind'. Actor Sheila Hancock has had a long and varied career on stage, screen and radio.

Shelby
(alt. Shelba, Shelbie)

Norse, meaning 'willow'. Can also be used as a boys' name.

Shelley
(alt. Shelli, Shellie, Shelly)

English, meaning 'meadow on the ledge'. Famous Shelleys include skeleton athlete Shelley Rudman and actor Shelley Winters.

Shenandoah

Iroquoian (Native American), meaning 'deer'. A river in the state of Virginia, USA.

Sheridan

Irish Gaelic, meaning 'wild man'. Actor Sheridan Smith appeared in *Gavin and Stacey*.

Sherry
(alt. Sheree, Sheri, Sherie, Sherri, Sherrie)

Shortened form of Cheryl or Sheryl, meaning 'man'. Also an alcoholic drink.

Sheryl
(alt. Sherryl)

German, meaning 'man'. Famous Sheryls include singer Sheryl Crow, presenter Sheryl Gascoigne and Sheryl Sandberg, and businesswoman Sheryl Sandberg.

Shiloh

Hebrew, meaning 'his gift'. From the biblical place of the same name, made popular by Angelina Jolie and Brad Pitt's daughter.

Shirley
(alt. Shirlee)

English, meaning 'bright meadow'. Famous Shirleys include singer Dame Shirley Bassey, actor Shirley MacLaine and child star Shirley Temple.

Shivani

Sanskrit, meaning 'wife of Shiva'.

Shola

Arabic, meaning 'energetic'. More commonly a boys' name.

Shona

Irish Gaelic, meaning 'God is gracious'. Also associated with the Shona people of southern Africa.

Shoshana
(alt. Shoshanna)

Hebrew, meaning 'lily'. Made popular by the character of Shoshanna Shapiro in *Girls*.

Shura

Russian, meaning 'man's defender'. In Arabic it also means 'consultation'.

Sian
(alt. Siân, Sianna)

Welsh, meaning 'the Lord is gracious'. Famous Sians include presenters Sian Lloyd and Sian Williams, and actors Sian Phillips and Sian Clifford of *Fleabag*.

Sibyl
(alt. Sybil)

Greek, meaning 'seer and oracle'. Sibyl was a prophetess in ancient Greek mythology.

Sidney
(alt. Sydney)

English, meaning 'wide meadow'. Used for both boys and girls.

Sidonie
(alt. Sidonia, Sidony)

Latin, meaning 'from Sidonia'. Also the name of a French-German princess of the 15th century.

Sienna
(alt. Siena)

Latin, from the city of the same name. Also the name of a type of yellowy-red earth pigment. Sienna Miller is an English model, BAFTA-nominated actor and fashion designer.

Sierra

Spanish, meaning 'saw'.

Siffhi

Hindi, meaning 'spiritual powers'.

Signa
(alt. Signe)

Scandinavian, meaning 'victory'. Also the name of a town in the province of Florence, Italy.

Sigrid

Nordic, meaning 'fair victory'. Sigrid the Haughty was said to have been the wife of Eric the Victorious in ancient Norse mythology.

Siksika

First Nation, meaning 'silken foot'. The Siksika Nation is a tribe in Canada whose name comes from 'silk' and 'foot'.

Silja

Scandinavian, meaning 'blind'.

Simcha

Hebrew, meaning 'joy'.

Simone
(alt. Simona)

Hebrew, meaning 'to hear'. Feminine form of Simon, except in Italy, where Simone is the masculine form of Simon and the female form is Simona. Famous Simones include philosopher Simone de Beauvoir and first female scuba diver, Simone Melchior.

Sinéad

Irish, meaning 'the Lord is gracious'. Used with and without the accent on the 'e'. Famous Sineads include singer Sinéad O'Connor, actor Sinéad Cusack and ice-dancing skater Sinead Kerr.

Siobhan

Irish, meaning 'the Lord is gracious'. Actor Siobhan McKenna is credited with reviving the name in the 20th century.

Siren
(alt. Sirena)

Greek, meaning 'entangler'. Sirens were beautiful and deadly creatures who lured men to their deaths at sea in ancient Greek mythology.

Siria

Spanish, meaning 'glowing'. Often used as a spelling alternative to Syria.

Skye
(alt. Sky, Skylyn)

Scottish, from the large island of the same name in Scotland.

Skyler
(alt. Skyla, Skylar)

Dutch, meaning 'giving shelter'. The name Skyler saw a jump in popularity after the success of the drama series Breaking Bad, which featured a main character called Skyler White.

Sloane
(alt. Sloan)

Irish Gaelic, meaning 'man of arms'. Usually associated with Sloane Square in London, after which the Sloane Rangers are named.

Socorro

Spanish, meaning 'to aid'.

Sojourner

English, meaning 'temporary stay'. In the 19th century, civil rights and women's activist Sojourner Truth was known for her phrase 'And ain't I a woman?'

Solana

Spanish, meaning 'sunlight'. The solana is the Spanish word for the side of a mountain or valley where the sun hits.

Solange

French, meaning 'with dignity'. A Christian saint from the ninth century. American singer and actor Solange Knowles is unusual among famous Solanges in that she's not from a French-speaking country.

Soledad

Spanish, meaning 'solitude'.

Soleil
French, meaning 'sun'.

Solveig
Scandinavian, meaning 'woman of the house'.

Sona
Arabic, meaning 'golden one'. Sona MacDonald is an actor of stage and screen.

Sonia
(alt. Sonja, Sonya)

Greek, meaning 'wisdom'. Sonia Rykiel is a French fashion designer. Sonia O'Sullivan was a world-class Irish long-distance runner who won medals at World Championships and Olympics.

Sophia
(alt. Sofia, Sofie, Sophie)

Greek, meaning 'wisdom'. Sophia Loren was actually named Sofia. Italy's most famous actor, she won an Oscar, BAFTA and Golden Globes. Other famous Sophias include film director Sofia Coppola and actors Sofia Vergara and Sophia Myles.

Sophronia
Greek, meaning 'sensible'. Usually associated with the character of Sophronia from the epic poem *Jerusalem Delivered*, by Torquato Tasso.

Soraya
Persian, meaning 'princess'. Queen Soraya Tarzi was the wife of King Amanullah of Afghanistan (reigned 1919–1929).

Sorcha
Irish and Scottish Gaelic, meaning 'bright and shining'. Irish actor Sorcha Cusack has appeared in *Coronation Street* and *Casualty*.

Sorrel
English, from the edible herb of the same name.

Stacey
(alt. Stacie, Stacy)

Greek, meaning 'resurrection'. Famous Staceys include actors Stacey Keibler and Stacey Dash, and presenter Stacey Dooley.

Star
(alt. Starla, Starr)

English, meaning 'star'.

Stella
Latin, meaning 'star'. Leading fashion designer Stella McCartney is known for her ethics and creativity.

Stephanie
(alt. Stefanie, Steffanie, Stephani, Stephania, Stephany, Stephenie)

Greek, meaning 'crowned'. Famous Stephanies include actor Stephanie Beacham, tennis pro Stefanie 'Steffi' Graf and author Stephenie Meyer.

Sue
(alt. Susie, Suzy)

Shortened form of Susan, meaning 'lily'. Famous Sues include comedian Sue Perkins and tennis pro turned TV presenter Sue Barker.

Sukey
(alt. Sukey, Sukie)

Shortened form of Susan, meaning 'lily'. Usually associated with the character of Sukey from the nursery rhyme 'Polly Put the Kettle On'.

Summer

English, from the season of the same name. Famous Summers include opera singer Summer Watson and actor Summer Glau.

Sunday

English, meaning 'the first day'.

Sunny
(alt. Sun)

English, meaning 'of a pleasant temperament'.

Suri

Persian, meaning 'red rose'. Suri Cruise is the daughter of Katie Holmes and Tom Cruise.

Surya

Hindi, from the god of the sun.

Susan
(alt. Susann, Suzan, Suzanne; abbrev. Sue, Susie, Suzy)

Hebrew, meaning 'lily'. Famous Susans include actor Susan Sarandon, singer Susan Boyle and suffragette Susan B. Anthony.

Susannah
(alt. Susana, Susanna, Susanne, Suzanna, Suzanne)

Hebrew, meaning 'lily'. Famous Susannahs include artist Susannah Fiennes and actors Susannah York and Susannah Doyle.

Svea

Swedish, meaning 'of the motherland'.

Svetlana

Russian, meaning 'star'. A popular name in Slavic countries, now starting to spread west. Svetlana Stalin was the daughter of Soviet dictator Josef Stalin.

Swanhild

Saxon, meaning 'battle swan'.

Sylvia
(alt. Silvia, Sylvie)

Latin, meaning 'from the forest'. Famous Sylvias include poet Sylvia Plath, suffragette Sylvia Pankhurst and singer Sylvia Robinson.

T

Girls' names

Tabitha
(alt. Tabatha, Tabetha)
Aramaic, meaning 'gazelle'. A woman raised from the dead by St Peter in the Bible. A very popular name in the USA in the 1970s and '80s, after Tabitha the child witch TV character.

Tahira
Arabic, meaning 'virginal'.

Tai
Chinese, meaning 'big'.

Taima
(alt. Taina, Tayma)
Native American, meaning 'peal of thunder'. Also the name of an oasis in Saudi Arabia.

Tajsa
Polish, meaning 'princess'.

Talia
(alt. Tali)
Hebrew, meaning 'heaven's dew'. Famous Talias include actors Talia Shire and Talia Balsam.

Taliesin
Welsh, meaning 'shining brow'. Usually associated with the Welsh poet Taliesin.

Talise
(alt. Talyse)
Native American, meaning 'lovely water'.

Talitha
Aramaic, meaning 'young girl'. The name is mentioned in the Bible when Jesus raises a child from the dead.

Tallulah
(alt. Taliyah)
Native American, meaning 'leaping water'. Famous Tallulahs include actors Tallulah Bankhead and Tallulah Riley, and the character of club singer Tallulah in the film Bugsy Malone.

Tamara
(alt. Tamera)

Hebrew, meaning 'palm tree'.
Famous Tamaras include socialite
Tamara Ecclestone and actors Tamera
Mowry and Tamara Taylor.

Tamatha
(alt. Tametha)

American, meaning 'dear Tammy'.
Sometimes used as a spelling
alternative to Samantha.

Tamika
(alt. Tameka)

American, meaning 'people'.

Tammy
(alt. Tami, Tammie)

Shortened form of Tamsin, meaning
'twin'. Country singer Tammy
Wynette's best-known song is 'Stand
by Your Man'.

Tamsin

Hebrew, meaning 'twin'. Sometimes
used as a shortened form of
Thomasina.

Tanis

Spanish, meaning 'to make famous'.

Tanya
(alt. Tania, Tanya, Tonya)

Shortened form of Tatiana, meaning
'from the Tatius clan'. Dr Tanya Byron
is a child psychologist, author and TV
presenter on parenting issues.

Tao

Chinese, meaning 'like a peach'. Tao
is also the notion of a route or path in
Chinese cultures.

Tara
(alt. Tahra, Tarah, Tera)

Irish Gaelic, meaning 'rocky hill'.
Famous Taras include actors Tara
Fitzgerald and Tara Reid.

Tasha
(alt. Taisha, Tarsha)

Shortened form of Natasha, meaning
'birth day'. Famous Tashas include
athlete Tasha Danvers, singer Tasha
Thomas and author and illustrator
Tasha Tudor.

Tatiana
(alt. Tatyana)

Russian, meaning 'from the Tatius
clan'. Famous Tatianas include
actor Tatyana Ali, author Tatiana de
Rosna and the character of Tatiana
Romanova from the James Bond film
From Russia With Love.

Tatum

English, meaning 'light hearted'.
Tatum O'Neal was the youngest
person to win a competitive Oscar,
picking up the award for Paper
Moon.

Tawny
(alt. Tawanaa, Tawnee, Tawnya)

English, meaning 'golden brown'.
Usually associated with the colour
tawny, as used in the descriptive
name of the tawny owl.

Taya

Greek, meaning 'poor one'. In
several languages the name also
means 'princess' or 'goddess'.

Taylor
(alt. Tayler)

English, meaning 'tailor'. Can be used for boys as well as girls. Famous Taylors include singer Taylor Swift and actor Taylor Schilling.

Tea

Greek, meaning 'goddess'. Actor Tea Leoni is known by her middle name, rather than her first name of Elizabeth.

Teagan
(alt. Teague, Tegan)

Irish Gaelic, meaning 'poet'.

Teal

English, from the bird of the same name. Often associated with the bluish-green colour.

Tecla

Greek, meaning 'fame of God'.

Tehile

Hebrew, meaning 'song of praise'.

Temperance

English, meaning 'virtue'.

Tempest

French, meaning 'storm'. Also the title of a Shakespearean play.

Teresa
(alt. Terese, Tereza, Theresa, Therese; abbrev. Terri, Teri, Terrie, Terry)

Greek, meaning 'harvest'. Famous Teresas include nun Mother Teresa, former Prime Minister Theresa May and actor Teresa Graves.

Tessa
(alt. Tess, Tessie)

Shortened form of Teresa, meaning 'harvest'. Tessa Virtue is a Canadian ice dance champion, and javelin thrower Tessa Sanderson represented Great Britain at every Olympics from 1976 to 1996.

Thais

Greek, from the mythological ancient Greek concubine of the same name.

Thalia

Greek, meaning 'blooming'. There are several ancient Greek muses, nymphs and graces who share the name Thalia.

Thandie
(alt. Thana, Thandi)

Arabic, meaning 'thanksgiving'. Thandie Newton is a British film and TV actor.

Names with positive meanings

Allegra – cheerful

Augusta – magnificent

Felicia – lucky

Hilary – cheerful

Lucy – light

Phoebe – radiant

Thalia – flourishing

Yoko – positive

Thea

Greek, meaning 'goddess'. Also a shortened form of Theodora or Dorothea.

Theda

German, meaning 'people'. Theda Bara was one of the silent film era's most prolific and popular actors, appearing in over 40 films.

Thelma

Greek, meaning 'will'. Famous Thelmas include the actor Thelma Barlow, singer Thelma Houston and the film *Thelma and Louise*.

Theodora
(alt. Theodosia)

Greek, meaning 'gift of God'. There are many ancient Roman empresses and other figures named Theodora.

Thisbe

Greek, from the mythological heroine of the same name in the ancient Roman poem *Metamorphoses* by Ovid.

Thomasina
(alt. Thomasin, Thomasine, Thomasyn)

Greek, meaning 'twin'. Singer Tammi Terrell, who was known for her Motown duets with singer Marvin Gaye, was born Thomasina Montgomery.

Thora

Scandinavian, meaning 'Thor's struggle'. Famous Thoras include actors Thora Hird and Thora Birch and the figure of Thora Bogarhjort of ancient Norse mythology.

Tia
(alt. Tiana)

Spanish, meaning 'aunt'. Famous Tias include actor Tia Mowry and the goddess Tia from Native American Haida tribal mythology.

Tiara

Latin, meaning 'jewelled headband'.

Tien

Vietnamese, meaning 'fairy child'.

Tierney

Irish Gaelic, meaning 'Lord'.

Tierra
(alt. Tiera)

Spanish, meaning 'land'. Used most commonly in the USA.

Tiffany
(alt. Tiffani, Tiffanie)

Greek, meaning 'God's appearance'. Famous Tiffanys include the singer Tiffany, socialite Tiffany Trump and the book/film/song *Breakfast at Tiffany's*.

Tiggy
(alt. Tigris)

Irish Gaelic, meaning 'tiger'. Tiggy Legge-Bourke (whose birth name is Alexandra) is known for being a royal nanny to Princes William and Harry.

Tilda

Shortened form of Matilda, meaning 'battle-mighty'. Oscar-winning actor Tilda Swinton's full name is Katherine Matilda.

Tilly
(alt. Tillie)

Shortened form of Matilda, meaning 'battle-mighty'. Has seen a rise in popularity in recent years.

Timothea

Greek, meaning 'honouring God'.

Tina
(alt. Teena, Tena)

Shortened form of Christina, meaning 'anointed Christian'. Famous Tinas include singer Tina Turner, comedian Tina Fey and actor Tina Louise.

Tirion

Welsh, meaning 'kind and gentle'.

Tirzah

Hebrew, meaning 'pleasantness'. Found in the Bible.

Titania

Greek, meaning 'giant'. Also the Fairy Queen in Shakespeare's *A Midsummer Night's Dream*.

Toby
(alt. Tobi)

Hebrew, meaning 'God is good'. More commonly used as a boys' name.

Tomoko

Japanese, meaning 'intelligent'.

Toni
(alt. Tony)

Latin, meaning 'invaluable'. Also a shortened form of Antoinette. Famous Tonis include author Toni Morrison, singer Toni Braxton and choreographer Toni Basil.

Tonia
(alt. Tonja, Tonya)

Russian, meaning 'praiseworthy'.

Topaz

Latin, meaning 'golden gemstone'.

Tori
(alt. Tora, Toria)

Shortened form of Victoria, meaning 'victory'. Singer Tori Amos was born Myra Ellen Amos.

Tova
(alt. Tovah, Tove)

Hebrew, meaning 'good'.

Tracy
(alt. Tracey, Tracie)

Greek, meaning 'harvest'. Famous Tracys include singer Tracy Chapman, artist Tracey Emin and actor Tracey Ullman.

Treva

Welsh, meaning 'homestead'.

Trilby

English, meaning 'vocal trills'.

Trina
(alt. Trena)

Greek, meaning 'pure'. Usually a shortened form of Katrina.

Trinity

Latin, meaning 'triad'. Usually associated with the Christian Holy Trinity. Also the impossibly cool lead female character in *The Matrix*.

Trisha
(alt. Tricia)

Shortened form of Patricia, meaning 'noble'.

Trista

Latin, meaning 'sad'. More commonly used in the USA.

Trixie

Shortened form of Beatrix, meaning 'blessed' or 'voyager'. Also a name used frequently in children's television and film, such as the characters of Trixie the Triceratops in *Toy Story 3* and Trixie the Troublemaker in *LazyTown*.

Trudie
(alt. Trudy, Truye; abbrev. Tru)

Shortened form of Gertrude, meaning 'strength of a spear'. Famous Trudies include actor Trudie Goodwin and producer and actor Trudie Styler.

Tullia

Latin, meaning 'bound for glory'.

Tunder

Hungarian, meaning 'fairy'.

Twyla
(alt. Twila)

American, meaning 'star'.

Tyler
(alt. Tyla)

English, meaning 'tile maker'. More commonly used as a boys' name.

Tyra

Scandinavian, meaning 'Thor's struggle'. Supermodel Tyra Banks is known for her extensive modelling career and is presenter of *America's Got Talent*.

Tzipporah

Hebrew, meaning 'bird'. Used as a spelling alternative to Zipporah.

Girls' names

Udaya
Sanskrit, meaning 'dawn'.

Ula
(alt. Ulla)
Celtic, meaning 'gem of the sea'. Also the name of a Manchu tribe from China.

Ulrika
(alt. Urica)
German, meaning 'power of the wolf'. Swedish Ulrika Jonsson made a TV career in Britain.

Uma
Sanskrit, meaning 'flax'. Actor Uma Thurman is known for her roles in *Pulp Fiction*, *Gattaca* and the *Kill Bill* series.

Una
Latin, meaning 'one'. Famous Unas include enduring British actor Una Stubbs and Irish singer Una Healy of The Saturdays.

Undine
Latin, meaning 'little wave'. Also the name of a water element in alchemy.

Unice
Greek, meaning 'victorious'. A spelling alternative to Eunice.

Unique
Latin, meaning 'only one'.

Unity
English, meaning 'oneness'.

Uriela
(alt. Uriella)
Hebrew, meaning 'angel of light'. Found particularly in German-speaking communities.

Urja
(alt. Urjitha)
Sanskrit, meaning 'energy'.

Ursula
Latin, meaning 'little female bear'. A character in Disney's film *The Little Mermaid*.

Uta
German, meaning 'prospers in battle'.

Girls' names

Vada
German, meaning 'famous ruler'.

Valdis
(alt. Valdiss, Valdys, Valdyss)
Norse, meaning 'goddess of the dead', based on the mythological goddess of the same name.

Valencia
(alt. Valancy, Valarece; abbrev. Vale)
Latin, meaning 'strong and healthy'. Also one of the largest cities in Spain.

Valentina
(alt. Valentine)
Latin, meaning 'strong and healthy'. Valentina Cortese is an Italian actor. Russian Valentina Tereshkova was the first female astronaut, in 1963.

Valerie
(alt. Valarie, Valery, Valorie, Valeria; abbrev. Valia)
Latin, meaning 'to be healthy and strong'. Also a song by The Zutons, which was famously covered by Amy Winehouse. Valia Venitshaya was an actor in the silent film era.

Vandana
Sanskrit, meaning 'worship'. Also the name of a genus of moths.

Vanessa
(alt. Vanesa)
English, from the *Gulliver's Travels* character of the same name. Famous Vanessas include TV presenter Vanessa Feltz and American actor Vanessa Hudgens.

Vanetta
(alt. Vanettah, Vaneta, Vanete, Vanity)
Greek, alternative of Vanessa, meaning 'like a butterfly'.

Vanity
Latin, meaning 'self-obsessed'.

Vashti
Persian, meaning 'beauty'. Also the name of a Persian queen in the Hebrew Bible.

Veda

Sanskrit, meaning 'knowledge and wisdom'. The Vedas are an important set of texts from ancient India.

Vega

Arabic, meaning 'falling vulture'. Also the name of a bright star in the night sky.

Velda

German, meaning 'ruler'. Also the name of a common ancestor named in *The Seven Daughters of Eve*.

Vella

American, meaning 'beautiful'. Also the name of a genus of leafy plants.

Velma

English, meaning 'determined protector'. A character in the *Scooby-Doo* series.

Venice
(alt. Venetia, Venita)

Latin, meaning 'city of canals'. From the city of the same name in Italy.

Venus

Latin, from the ancient Roman goddess of sexuality and fertility. Also the name of the planet.

Vera
(alt. Verla, Verlie)

Slavic, meaning 'faith'. Famous Veras include actor Vera Farmiga, singer Vera Lynn and fashion designer Vera Wang.

Verda
(alt. Verdie)

Latin, meaning 'spring-like'.

Verena

Latin, meaning 'true'. St Verena was a third-century Roman saint who healed the sick.

Verity

Latin, meaning 'truth'.

Verna
(alt. Vernie)

Latin, meaning 'spring green'. Actor Verna Felton was a voice actor for Disney films and productions.

Verona

Latin, shortened form of Veronica. From the city of the same name in Italy.

Veronica
(alt. Verica, Veronique)

Latin, meaning 'true image'. Famous Veronicas include actors Veronica Lake and Veronica Carlson and the protagonist of the *Veronica Mars* series and film.

Veruca

Latin, meaning 'wart'. Usually associated with the character of Veruca Salt from the children's novel *Charlie and the Chocolate Factory*, by Roald Dahl.

Vesta

Latin, from the ancient Roman goddess of the same name, said to be in charge of the hearth, home and family.

Vevina

Scottish, meaning 'pleasant lady'. More commonly used in the USA.

Vicenta

Latin, meaning 'prevailing'. More commonly used in Italian-speaking communities.

Victoria

(abbrev. Vicky, Vicki, Vickie, Vikki, Vix)

Latin, meaning 'victory'. The name became popular during and after the reign of Queen Victoria in the 19th century, and has remained pretty steadfastly popular ever since.

Vida

Spanish, meaning 'life'.

Vidya

Sanskrit, meaning 'knowledge'. Often used in the Hindu faith to refer to learning and knowledge.

Vienna

Latin, from the city of the same name in Austria.

Vigdis

Scandinavian, meaning 'war goddess'. Most commonly used in Icelandic communities.

Vina

(alt. Vena)

Spanish, meaning 'vineyard'.

Viola

Latin, meaning 'violet'. Also a musical instrument like a large violin.

Violet

(alt. Violetta)

Latin, meaning 'purple'. Also a small purple flower of the same name.

Virginia

(alt. Virginie; abbrev. Virgie, Ginny)

Latin, meaning 'maiden'. Famous Virginias include author Virginia Woolf and tennis player Virginia Wade.

Visara

Sanskrit, meaning 'celestial'.

Vita

Latin, meaning 'life'. Often used to refer to the life story of a saint, or their biography.

Vittoria

Variation of Victoria, meaning 'victory'. More commonly used in Italian-speaking communities.

Viva

Latin, meaning 'alive'. Actor Viva was one of Andy Warhol's muses during the 1960s.

Viveca

(alt. Vivica)

Scandinavian, meaning 'war fortress'. Actor Vivica A. Fox is known for her roles in Independence Day, Kill Bill and Soul Food.

Vivian

(alt. Vivien, Vivienne)

Latin, meaning 'lively'. Famous Vivians include actor Vivien Leigh and designer Vivienne Westwood.

Vonda

Czech, meaning 'from the tribe of Vandals'. Singer Vonda Shepard was known for her soft-pop songs and appearances on Ally McBeal.

Girls' names

Waleska

Polish, meaning 'beautiful'. Most commonly used in German-speaking communities.

Wallis

English, meaning 'from Wales'. Famous Wallises include Wallis Simpson, the late Duchess of Windsor, and the singer Wallis Bird.

Walta

Swahili, meaning 'like a shield'. Also feminine form of Walter.

Wanda

(alt. Waneta, Wanita)

Slavic, meaning 'tribe of the vandals'. Princess Wanda was a queen of Poland in the eighth century.

Waneta

(alt. Wanita)

Variation of Wanda, meaning 'tribe of the vandals'. Also the name of an infamous Yanktonai Dakota Native American tribal chief during the 18th and 19th centuries.

Wava

English, meaning 'way'. More commonly used in the USA.

Waveney

Old English, from the river of the same name.

Waverly

Old English, meaning 'meadow of aspens'. Can be used as a girls' name or, more commonly, a boys' name.

Wendy

English, meaning 'friend'. Famous Wendys include actors Wendy Richard and Wendy Hiller and the character of Wendy Darling in Peter Pan.

Wharton

English, meaning 'from the river'.

Whisper

English, meaning 'whisper'.

Whitley

Old English, meaning 'white meadow'.

Whitney

Old English, meaning 'white island'. Singer Whitney Houston was a pop sensation of the 1980s and appeared in the film *The Bodyguard* with Kevin Costner.

Wilda

German, meaning 'willow tree'. More commonly used in Polish-speaking communities.

Wilfreda

English, meaning 'to will peace'. Feminine form of Wilfred.

Wilhelmina

Old German, meaning 'strong-willed warrior'. Many members of the German royal family have been named Wilhelmina.

Willa
(alt. Willene, Willia)

German, meaning 'helmet'. American Willa Cather was a Pulitzer Prize-winning author.

Willow

English, from the tree of the same name. Celebrity children named Willow include Willow Smith (Will Smith's daughter) and Willow Hart (Pink's daughter).

Wilma
(alt. Wilmer)

German, meaning 'protection'. A character from the cartoon *The Flintstones*.

Winifred
(abbrev. Winnie)

Old English, meaning 'holy and blessed'. Famous Winifreds include Winifred Atwell, prison breaker Winifred Herbert, author Winifred Mary Letts and South African activist Winnie Madikizela-Mandela.

Winona
(alt. Wynona)

Sioux Indian, meaning 'first-born daughter'. Actor Winona Ryder is named after the town where she was born, Winona in Minnesota, USA.

Winslow

English, meaning 'friend's hill'.

Winter

English, meaning 'winter'.

Wisteria

English, meaning 'flower'.

Wren

Old English, meaning 'tiny bird'. Often associated with the species of small birds found throughout the world.

Wynda

Scottish, meaning 'of the narrow passage'.

Wynne
(alt. Wynn)

Welsh, meaning 'very blessed'.

Girls' names

Xanadu

A city in Mongolia. Xanadu was the summer capital of Kubla Khan's empire and the inspiration of Samuel Taylor Coleridge's poem *Kubla Khan*. Also a 1980 film starring Olivia Newton-John.

Xanthe

Greek, meaning 'blonde'. Also the name of several characters in ancient Greek mythology.

Xanthippe

Greek, meaning 'nagging'. Also the name of an influential figure in ancient Greek mythology.

Xaverie
(alt. Xaviera)

Spanish, meaning 'the new house'. Feminine form of Xavier.

Xena
(alt. Xenia)

Greek, meaning 'foreigner'. The popularity of this name rose after the success of *Xena: Warrior Princess*.

Ximena

Spanish, meaning 'to hear'. More commonly used in Mexico.

Xiomara

Spanish, meaning 'battle-ready'.

Xiu

Chinese, meaning 'elegant'.

Xochitl

Nahuatl, meaning 'flower'. Queen Xochitl was a legendary queen of the Toltec culture.

Xoey

Variant of Zoe, meaning 'life'. Often used as a spelling variation for Zoe or Zoey.

Xristina

Variation of Christina, meaning 'follower of Christ'. Usually associated with singer Christina Aguilera, who often spells her name Xtina.

Xylia
(alt. Xylina, Xyloma)

Greek, meaning 'from the woods'.

Girls' names

Yadira
Arabic, meaning 'worthy'. More commonly used in Spanish- and Portuguese-speaking communities.

Yael
Hebrew, meaning 'mountain goat'. Found in the Bible.

Yaffa
(alt. Yahaira, Yajaira)
Hebrew, meaning 'lovely'.

Yamilet
Arabic, meaning 'beautiful'. More commonly used in Spanish-speaking communities.

Yana
Hebrew, meaning 'the Lord is gracious'. Also the name of a spiritual practice in Buddhism.

Yanha
Arabic, meaning 'dove-like'.

Yanira
Hawaiian, meaning 'pretty'. Also the name of a character in ancient Greek mythology.

Yareli
Latin, meaning 'golden'. More commonly used in Spanish-speaking communities.

Yaretzi
(alt. Yaritza)
Aztec, meaning 'forever beloved'. More commonly used in the USA.

Yasmin
(alt. Yasmeen, Yasmina)
Persian, meaning 'jasmine flower'. Famous Yasmins include actor Yasmin Paige, model Yasmin le Bon and DJ Yasmin.

Yelena
Greek, meaning 'bright and chosen'. Extremely popular name in Russia and Ukraine.

Yeraldina

Spanish, meaning 'ruled with a spear'.

Yesenia

Arabic, meaning 'flower'. Used as a name in the 1970s for a Spanish-language television production.

Yetta

English, from Henrietta, meaning 'ruler of the house'. Also used in Yiddish-speaking communities.

Yeva

Hebrew variant of Eve, meaning 'life'.

Ylva

Old Norse, meaning 'she wolf'. The name originated in Sweden in the 13th century.

Yoki
(alt. Yoko)

Native American, meaning 'rain'. In Japanese the name also means 'happiness' and 'life force'.

Yolanda
(alt. Yolonda)

Spanish, meaning 'violet flower'. There have been several monarchs of Europe known as Yolanda.

Yoselin

English, meaning 'lovely'. Can also be used as a spelling alternative to Jocelyn.

Yoshiko

Japanese, meaning 'good child'. Princess Yoshiko was the Empress of Japan during the 18th and 19th centuries.

Yovela

Hebrew, meaning 'jubilee'.

Ysabel

English, meaning 'God's promise'. Often used as a spelling alternative to Isabel.

Ysanne

Contraction of Isabel and Anne, meaning 'pledged to God' and 'grace'.

Yuki

Japanese, meaning 'lucky'. Also the name of a popular Japanese singer and songwriter.

Yuliana

Latin, meaning 'youthful'. Often used as a spelling alternative to Giuliana.

Yuridia

Russian, meaning 'farmer'. Singer Yuridia is one of the most popular pop stars in Mexico.

Yusia

Arabic, meaning 'success'.

Yvette
(alt. Yvonne)

French, meaning 'yew'. Famous Yvettes include presenter Yvette Fielding, actor Yvette Nicole Brown and politician Yvette Cooper.

Girls' names

Zafira

Arabic, meaning 'successful'.

Zahara

(*alt. Zahava, Zahra, Zayah*)

Arabic, meaning 'flowering and shining'. The most famous Zahara is the daughter of Angelina Jolie and Brad Pitt.

Zaida

(*alt. Zaide*)

Arabic, meaning 'prosperous'. Also a familiar term for grandfather in Yiddish.

Zalika

Swahili, meaning 'well born'. More commonly used in Egypt.

Zaltana

Arabic, meaning 'high mountain'.

Zamia

Greek, meaning 'pine cone'. Also the name of a plant.

Zaneta

(*alt. Zanceta, Zanetah, Zanett, Zanetta*)

Hebrew, meaning 'a gracious present from God'. More commonly used in Polish and Latvian communities.

Zaniyah

Arabic, meaning 'lily'. Most commonly used in the USA.

Zara

(*alt. Zaria, Zariah, Zora*)

Arabic, meaning 'radiance'. Famous Zaras include Queen Elizabeth II's granddaughter Zara Tindall, actor Zara Cully and fashion brand Zara.

Zelda

German, meaning 'dark battle'. Usually associated with the Nintendo video game series *The Legend of Zelda* or American novelist Zelda Fitzgerald.

Zelia
(alt. Zella)
Scandinavian, meaning 'sunshine'.

Zelma
German, meaning 'helmet'. Sometimes used as a spelling alternative to Thelma.

Zemira
(alt. Zemirah)
Hebrew, meaning 'joyous melody'. An opera by Francesco Bianchi.

Zena
(alt. Zenia, Zina)
Greek, meaning 'hospitable'. Usually used as a spelling alternative to Xena.

Zenaida
Greek, meaning 'the life of Zeus'. St Zenaida is recognised as one of the first Christian physicians, during the second century.

Zenobia
Latin, meaning 'the life of Zeus'. Queen Zenobia was the leader of the Palmyrene empire in Syria during the third century.

Zephyr
Greek, meaning 'the west wind'.

Zetta
Latin, meaning 'seven'. In modern maths, zetta means 10^{21} (that's number 1 followed by 21 zeros).

Zia
Arabic, meaning 'light and splendour'. Musician Zia McCabe is known for being a founding member of the band the Dandy Warhols.

Zinaida
Greek, meaning 'belonging to Zeus'. More commonly used in Russian-speaking communities.

Zinnia
Latin, meaning 'flower'. Also the name of a flowering perennial plant.

Zipporah
Hebrew, meaning 'bird'. Zipporah was one of the wives of Moses in the Bible.

Zita
(alt. Ziva)
Spanish, meaning 'little girl'. St Zita is an Italian patron saint of maids and domestic servants.

Zoë
(alt. Zoe, Zoi, Zoie, Zoey, Zoeya, Zoila, Zooey)
Greek, meaning 'life'. Famous Zoes include TV and radio presenter Zoë Ball and actors including Zoë Wanamaker, Zoe Saldana and Zooey Deschanel.

Zoraida
Spanish, meaning 'captivating woman'.

Zorina
Slavic, meaning 'golden'.

Zosia
(alt. Zosima)

Greek, meaning 'wisdom'. Actor Zosia Mamet is known for her roles in *Mad Men*, *Parenthood* and *Girls*.

Zoya

Greek, meaning 'life'. Zoya Kosmodemyanskaya is one of the former Soviet Union's most revered heroines, after fighting for the Russian rebellion during World War II.

Zula

Swahili, meaning 'brilliant'.

Zuleika

Arabic, meaning 'fair and intelligent'. Also the name of Potiphar's wife in the Bible.

Zulma

Arabic, meaning 'peace'.

Zuzana

Hebrew, meaning 'lily'. More commonly used in the Czech and Slovak republics.

Zuzu

Czech, meaning 'flower'. The nickname for one of George Bailey's children in the film *It's A Wonderful Life*.

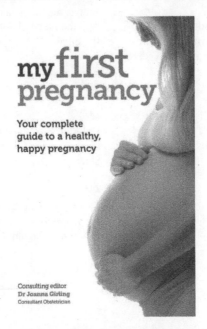

my first pregnancy

Your complete
guide to a healthy,
happy pregnancy

Consulting editor
Dr Joanna Girling
Consultant Obstetrician

Finding out you are expecting for the first time is a magical experience. It can also be pretty daunting and nerve-wracking. We bet you're bursting with questions! *My First Pregnancy* is here to guide you through all stages of your pregnancy journey, from finding out the good news to preparing for labour, giving birth and meeting your baby. Inside you'll find:

· What to expect at antenatal appointments and how to decipher your notes
· Detailed information on scans and what tests are available to you
· How your baby is growing week by week
· Tried and tested advice on relieving the inevitable aches and pains
· Looking after yourself at work and how to plan maternity leave
· Preparing for labour and giving birth

YOUR BABY SKIN TO SKIN

LEARN TO TRUST
YOUR BABY'S
INSTINCTS IN THE
FIRST YEAR

Rachel Fitz-Desorgher
MIDWIFE

New baby? Here's the reassuring news: your baby is a highly evolved being, pre-set instinctively to survive and thrive. A baby's instincts are not learned and can never be wrong. Why, then, do we feel the need to work against our newborns – and try to teach them how to be a baby? Sounds crazy, doesn't it?

Your Baby Skin to Skin helps you understand your baby and teaches you to stop fighting against their inbuilt reflexes and instinctive cues. From your baby's first days, through feeding and sleeping issues to realistic routines and weaning advice, your questions are answered with a calm, practical reassurance:

· Why does my baby cry every time I put her down?
· How do I breastfeed without it hurting?
· Can I co-sleep or will this create bad habits?
· My baby is unsettled and cries all evening. What can I do?